Project Management and Project Network Techniques

Sixth edition of
Critical Path Analysis and Other Project Network Techniques

Keith Lockyer BSc

Emeritus Professor of Operations Management,
University of Bradford

James Gordon PhD, MSc, DLC, CEng, FIEE, FAPM, FRSA

Project Management Consultant,
Chairman BSI Committee on Project Management,
Convener ISO Working Group on 'Guidelines to Quality in Project Management.'

FINANCIAL TIMES
Prentice Hall

An imprint of Pearson Education

Harlow, England · London · New York · Reading, Massachusetts · San Francisco · Toronto · Don Mills, Ontario · Sydney
Tokyo · Singapore · Hong Kong · Seoul · Taipei · Cape Town · Madrid · Mexico City · Amsterdam · Munich · Paris · Milan

Pearson Education Limited
Edinburgh Gate, Harlow
Essex CM20 2JE, England
and Associated Companies throughout the world

Visit us on the World Wide Web at:
http://www.pearsoneduc.com

First published in Great Britain in 1964
Sixth edition 1996

© Keith Lockyer and James Gordon 1996

The right of Professor Keith Lockyer and Dr James Gordon to be identified
as Authors of this Work has been asserted by them in accordance
with the Copyright, Designs and Patents Act 1988.

ISBN 0 273 61454 1

British Library Cataloguing in Publication Data
A CIP catalogue record for this book can be obtained from the British Library.

10 9 8 7 6
04 03 02 01 00

Typeset by Pantek Arts, Maidstone, Kent
Printed and bound in Great Britain by Bell and Bain Ltd., Glasgow

To Doris and to Antoinette

CONTENTS

The following are particular to:
   Activity-on-arrow (AoA) systems : Chapters 11, 13.
   Activity-on-node (AoN) systems : Chapters 12, 14, 15.

PREFACE

The present text is intended for all those entering, or intending to enter, the fascinating and challenging field of project management. The authors have tried to produce text which is of immediate use to the reader. It is believed that it will be of value to the increasing number of students, both post- and undergraduate, who seek to know something of project management. Let it be clear, neither this book, nor any other book, can *create* a successful project manager. Such an animal requires to have an inborn personality and resilience which will enable him or her to lead a team of individualists through times which often appear traumatic. The hope is that it will shed some light on areas which may not have been previously considered.

The text is broadly divided into two parts. The first deals with the managerial aspects of project management, the second, which is a condensation of the previous text *Critical Path Analysis and other Project Network Techniques*, with project management techniques. Both may be read separately, and indeed the whole book is intended to be suitable for selective reading if this is what is required. A chapter on 'some practical considerations' which was much appreciated in the previous edition has been enlarged and restructured to take in the problems of managing a project. Two questions which both authors have been asked countless times, and have been unable to answer, are treated in a brief appendix. There are, however, a set of questions, some dealing with management aspects and some with project network techniques (PNT), for which answers to the numerical questions will be found in the *Instructor's Manual*. The answers to the essay questions are embedded in the main text.

It is interesting to realise that although projects have been carried out as long as man and woman have existed, it is only within the last few decades that it has been thought necessary to define a project. Even more recently has come the need to recognise that there is a significant difference between managing a project and any other form of management. This realisation has come about for two reasons: first, the emergence of a new toolkit, project network techniques, which enable a project to be planned with some considerable confidence. Second, the development of the cheap, high capacity microcomputer which puts into the hands of the project manager the means whereby the tool-kit can be used whenever required.

Younger readers will not be able to realise the problems early (that is to say 1960s!) project managers had when, having planned a project using, say, CPA, the only computer in the company (if there was one at all) was the vastly expensive mainframe which always seemed to be occupied by the payroll, the monthly financial statements, or the chairman's statement for the AGM when the computer was used as a 'big typewriter'. The chance of getting a rerun with modifications to the original network was often minimal. A 'what-if' run was never heard of. The only analysis was provided by a printout on huge concertina sheets of paper. The vision of the project manager with piles of these printouts remains vividly in both authors' minds today. It is the cheap dedicated micro which has allowed the consideration of the study of the art and science of project management.

As far as possible, nomenclature agrees with BS 4335:1987, a standard which now has wide international acceptance. Where words are used which do not appear in that glossary, every attempt has been made to conform to that which is in general use in the UK. The only exception to this is the use of the word 'log' in place of 'diary' in 'project log'. The importance of a comprehensive record of the project cannot be overstated, and the authors feel that the word 'log' carries with it a weight, a feeling of importance, which may be lacking in 'diary'. The definition in the Concise Oxford Dictionary underlines the point: 'Logbook: a permanent record made daily of all events occurring in the ship's voyage including rate of progress ...'.

As previously, any mistakes in the present text are the responsibility of the other author.

K.G. Lockyer
J.H. Gordon

CHAPTER 1

Introduction

DEFINITION OF A PROJECT

No definition of a 'project' will suit every situation, but one appearing in ISO documents appears to be acceptable to a wide range of users. ISO 8402 states:

Project – unique process, consisting of a set of co-ordinated and controlled activities with start and finish dates, undertaken to achieve an objective conforming to specific requirements including constraints of time, cost and resources.

To this definition ISO documents can add notes to amplify the use of the term 'project' within the document. ISO 10006 – *Guideline to Quality in Project Management* will add the following notes:

Notes
1. **The organisation is temporary and established for the life of the project**
2. **In many cases a project forms part of a larger project structure.**
3. **The project objectives and product characteristics may be defined and achieved progressively during the course of the project.**
4. **The result of a project may be the creation of one or several units of a product.**
5. **The interrelation between project activities may be complex.**

Project management is thus principally concerned with the introduction and management of change. All projects are unique in some respect or other and may differ from the usual business for which the parent company exists. The project organisation, often referred to as the project team – though this is but a small part of the total project organisation – is set up to achieve a particular objective: the project product. Teams which remain together at the conclusion of a project and take over the next project are common in some industries but less so in others, particularly manufacturing.

COMMON ELEMENTS OF A PROJECT

The project product can take many forms, from the wholly physical – the creation of a new town or the building of a new locomotive, to the virtually abstract – a procedure for dealing with a possible emergency. Between these two extremes there is a diversity of products each with its own particular requirements, which in turn require variations in the management of the project. This diversity, spread over companies and industries, has impeded the recognition that there are common elements to all projects. However, they all have a:

- specification for the product;
- project plan;
- time frame;
- budget;
- cost plan;
- statement of quality required;
- identification of any areas of uncertainty;
- evaluation of possible risks and the appropriate responses.

Systems must be set up to collect, *in real time*, the data concerning progress and costs. Facilities must be available to analyse the data and distribute the results of that analysis as rapidly as possible. These elements are common to all projects, but their implementation will depend on the product, the size of the project and the industry in which it is being carried out. To impose a multi-thousand activity project system on a project with a few hundred only would be absurd, losing clarity, increasing cost and wasting time.

REVENUE AND CAPITAL PROJECTS

Projects come in many sizes, from the very small to the very large. They may be simple or complex, although size and complexity are not necessarily related. It is, however, convenient to divide them into two categories:

- *Revenue projects* are those which are carried out within the normal organisational structure and normally within a single accounting period.
- *Capital projects* are those which are not carried out within the normal organisational structure and which may extend over a number of accounting periods.

Clearly, in practice, many projects fall between these two broad categories, and the acid test is the need to set up a special organisation to deal with the project. It is *also* true that capital projects *always* require considerable capital investment, though this may sometimes be true of revenue projects. Thus, the two main characteristics of capital projects are:

- they usually occupy considerable time
- they always employ considerable capital

As a consequence, they do not fit readily into a conventional organisational structure but cut across functional and time boundaries and thus require an organisation particular to themselves. It is with this organisation, its structure and behaviour that this present text is mainly concerned. For the sake of simplicity, the term 'project' will be henceforth used to stand for 'capital project'. Equally, the term 'product' will be used to describe the output of a project irrespective of whether it is hardware, software, a service, a system or any other kind of output.

A project may arise from not just one company but from several (a consortium). This can raise serious problems if there is not full and free communication on all matters between the various partners. Poor or limited communications can lead to distrust between partners and thus to partners taking unilateral action.

The main characteristics of a project which differentiate it from conventional operations are:

- its uniqueness
- its defined start and finish

Even with these characteristics it is sometimes difficult to decide whether a group of activities is a project or not. For example, the design, launch and initial production of a new product is a project, while the subsequent bulk production of the product is not.

HOW IS A PROJECT DIFFERENT FROM OTHER OPERATIONS?

Operations which proceed under conventional line management are involved in what is normally a substantially stable situation. Such changes which do take place are generally under the control of the line manager and the rate of change is likely to be slow. Project management, on the other hand, is concerned wholly with the introduction and management of change. Such change is likely to cross conventional functional boundaries and may well be concerned with activities outside those usually found within the organisation, though this last is not true of a project-centred organisation.

FOUR PHASES OF A PROJECT

All projects pass through at least four identifiable phases (*see* Fig. 1.1).

1 Conception

In many ways this is the most crucial phase of a project's life in that all that follows is determined by decisions and commitments made in this phase. An idea for a new product will be presented to the organisation, which may come internally from an employee, or externally from a potential client asking if the product can be provided. Assuming that the product is within the capability and ethos of the organisation, then, before any decision is made on the possible desirability of accepting the project, a comprehensive feasibility study must take place. This should involve, if organisationally possible, the probable project manager, as well as all the functions which will be involved within the organisation and any external suppliers of items or services. Where the project is for a consortium, the way in which the work is to be divided between the various members must be resolved. This division must be accepted by the members before any work on the project is undertaken.

At the conclusion of the study, the following are the factors which should have been determined as a minimum:

- the capability of the organisation to provide the product in the time required
- the final price for the product
- the costs involved
- the budget required for the project
- the outline specification of the product, including the quality and reliability requirements
- the ability of the organisation to support the capital outlay
- the availability of any items or services to be procured from outside the organisation
- the acceptability of any geographical requirements on procurement or ecology which are specified in the project enquiry
- the acceptability of any contract conditions which are specified in the enquiry

At the conclusion of the conception phase the product purpose and its design parameters must be documented in clear and unambiguous terms and agreed with the customer.

2 Development

Assuming that the proposed new product is acceptable to the organisation, the product has to be designed or specified in such detail as is necessary to allow it to be created within the limits set in the conception phase. Since the organisation is now committed to the project, its manager should be appointed and he or she will work closely with the customer in this and subsequent phases. Consideration should also be given to assembling at least the senior members of the project team. A detailed project plan, as the major element in the developing documentation for the project, must be drawn up under the direction of the project manager.

3 Realisation

Once designed or specified, the project team has to turn the development into reality. An appropriate reporting system has to be provided as part of the project plan to keep the team, top management and the customer informed on:

● project progress
● expenditure
● costs
● foreseen possible adverse events.

As part of the reporting system, a comprehensive project log is maintained with details of any problems which have been met and the way in which they have been resolved.

Note: The authors prefer the term 'log' to 'diary' since a log is something which *must* be kept whereas a diary implies a degree of judgement in its upkeep.

4 Termination

An analysis of the project reports will provide invaluable information which can be helpful in other projects. This will include:

● success of methods used
● performance of team members
● reliability of suppliers.

In addition to the above analyses, many projects will be completed with a residue of capital equipment which is then surplus to the organisation's needs. This has to be disposed of as rapidly and as profitably as possible.

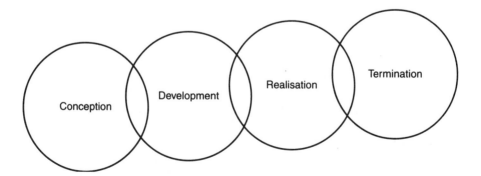

Fig. 1.1 The four phases of a project.

Each of these phases could form a project in its own right. It is normal for there to be an interval between the initial conception phase and the later phases, whilst in most cases the others overlap in time and merge into one another. This is particularly likely if the project request is an internal one with a vigorous project champion. Equally, although there is usually one project manager, if the phases are discrete, there may be a different project manager for each phase.

WHY PROJECT MANAGEMENT?

When a company which has been operating in a conventional functionally based manner finds that the number of projects which it has to deal with becomes uncomfortably great and large enough to require frequent board consultation and approval, consideration must be made at board level of the need to amend the organisational structure. It is often not realised that the timescale implicit in such a change can be substantial. Observation by one of the authors suggests that in a company of any size, three to five years are necessary for the new organisation to settle down and people to become comfortable with it. Questions will be asked, objections to apparent loss of status will be made, political moves worked out, and the informal structures which ease so much of working life developed. Initially, each new project will not only be seen as a new problem to be solved but also as something to be resisted.

Change is something which takes place in all organisations. While it takes place within the control of the functional manager, it will generally be considered as quite normal and requiring no special steps to be taken. However, once the rate of change increases to the extent that resources become overstretched, and/or the change involves other functions, difficulties arise. It is at this stage that the need to change to some form of 'project management' is recognised, even if it is not explicitly identified as such, and a 'project manager' is appointed. The interaction of resource requirements between the 'normal' work and the 'project' is usually, and uncomfortably, complex and requests for resources to be devoted to the 'project' are met with the 'We'll do it when we can fit it in' response. This, almost always, is too late for the needs of the 'project'. Furthermore, functional managers may well believe that their authority is being threatened by the introduction of this new-fangled project manager. This is often resented, a resentment which is often expressed in a generally unhelpful attitude, if not in downright covert obstruction, an attitude which is extremely difficult to identify.

Many organisations try out 'project management' on a small scale, often under the eye of top management. The interest which this generates will usually add such weight to the project and its management that the trial is a resounding success. Project management then becomes instituted as the normal practice for anything identified as a project. Sadly, unless the implications have been properly digested, and the effect of top management interest realised, the extension will be far from successful. A further pressing need for some form of management which differs from normal functional management is created by the fact that many projects are physically separated from the host organisation and, therefore, have no ability to call upon the functional specialists.

Making the change to project management itself is, of course, in itself a project and should be treated as such. It has to be planned, implemented and monitored as carefully as any other project. After all, the future prosperity of the organisation probably depends on its successful completion. In any but the very largest organisations it is unlikely that the personnel skills to carry through such a change will be available and external assistance may be required. One thing is certain, the change must be actively supported by the board and a board member should become project champion for the change itself. One problem which is found in strongly hierarchical organisations is that the functional heads will see that projects require resources – previously totally under their own control – to be shared. In turn this will be seen as a loss of status and security, and defensive mechanisms will be set up. Careful handling and lengthy explanation are required to change such an attitude, a change which may never happen in some cases.

CHAPTER 2

Projects and company organisational structures

Any group which comes together to make a product, be it hardware or software or to provide a service, must form itself into an organisation with a structure. This structure will affect the way the organisation can respond to change and the introduction of projects.

THE HIERARCHICAL FUNCTIONAL STRUCTURE

The majority of industrial organisations which have been set up to manufacture products develop a common form of organisation, the conventional hierarchical functional structure as shown in Fig. 2.1.

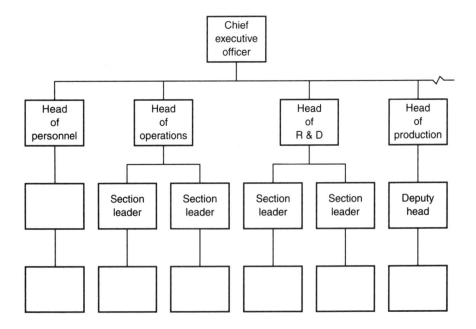

Fig. 2.1 Hierarchical functional organisation.

In this form of organisation the heads of the various specialist functions report directly to the chief executive who is responsible to the board for co-ordinating the work of the specialist functions to meet the objectives of the organisation. The functional heads in turn have the section heads within their function reporting to them and they, in turn, have their own subordinates who report to them. This form of organisational structure has existed for a long time in industry because of its advantages, which include the way in which the structure:

- maintains tight control at the top
- logically represents the functions
- maintains the power and prestige of the functions
- reduces any duplication of functional effort
- allows for concentration of functional skills
- has very simple reporting relationships
- can achieve extremely high plant/capital utilisation.

As discussed in Chapter 1, there are no problems with this structure so long as the rate of change, which occurs in all organisations, does not over-stretch the functional resources or cross functional boundaries. When that happens, the disadvantages of the structure become apparent. These include that it may:

- cause over-specialisation
- cause parochialism of key personnel
- weaken co-ordination between functions
- stifle the development of generalist (project) managers
- limit the ability to respond in periods of fast change and diversification in the market
- impose an increasing burden on the chief executive as the rate of change increases
- require extremely detailed pre-production planning.

The situation may arise when a new job is obviously going to require greater resources than any one function can provide while continuing its normal work, or is going to cut across a number of functional boundaries without belonging to any one in particular. The chief executive, who will have responsibility for the job in addition to his/her other duties, may well then decide to appoint a 'project manager' reporting directly to him/her. This manager will, of course, require staff as support in managing the 'project' which may initially be of the form shown in Fig. 2.2 (but should eventually be of the form shown in Fig. 3.1 for a full team).

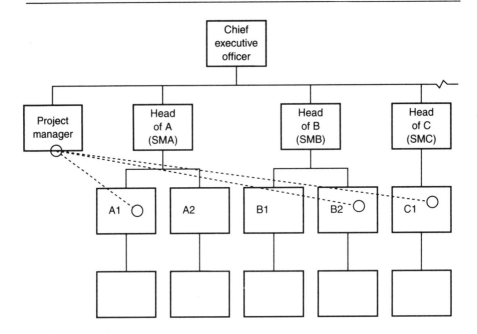

Fig. 2.2 Hierarchical functional organisation with a single project.

Even with a full team, specialist assistance will still need to be drawn from the functional groups for various aspects of the project. For instance, in a hardware project, engineering design work will be carried out in the appropriate functional groups but the co-ordination and timing of the work will be the responsibility of the project team in conjunction with the functional head to whom the design staff report for their professional competence.

THE MATRIX STRUCTURE

These problems will continue to exist while there is only one project at a time within the organisation and, although they may be recognised by the chief executive, it will not be worth changing the functional structure just to accommodate one project which is known to have a limited life. However, once it is clear that projects are continuing to be carried out within the organisation, and that there may be several running simultaneously, a different situation arises and a change of organisational structure becomes essential; it becomes necessary to set up a project management function group with its own functional staff of project specialists. Furthermore, if many of the projects require it, it may also be necessary to obtain dedicated functional specialists as part of the group either by withdrawing them from the existing functional groups or by external recruit-ment. If they are obtained internally – which if at all possible they should be – then they *must be organisationally disengaged from their previous positions*. Ideally, the project group should also be physically separated and located within their own area. This will have the benefit of freeing and speeding up the communication system and increasing the feeling of com-mitment to the project. The functional specialists will still be able to refer to the functional supervisors, but *only for functional technical problems*.

This type of organisational form is shown in Fig. 2.3.

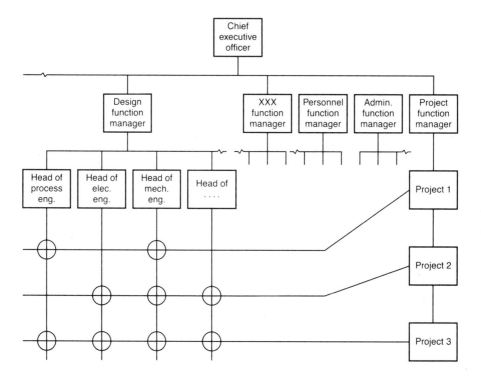

Fig. 2.3 Matrix organisation.

Such a structure is an inevitable consequence of a multi-project situation, and whilst it may solve some problems, some remain and some new ones are created. However firmly a functional specialist is nominally disengaged from his/her previous supervisor, some latent responsibility and loyalty will always remain. In many cases, even if there is a geographical separation, the functional supervisor can still affect the functional specialist's career. This can lead to a dual reporting situation (one official, one unofficial) which can be confusing and possibly malign. For example, specialist A1 may have a technical disagreement with project manager PM1 which is not resolved to the satisfaction of A1. In the hope of overturning the decision, A1 may appeal to the functional supervisor SMA who, while having no authority over the project, has direct access to the chief executive who does have that authority.

THE PROBLEM OF DUAL REPORTING

A more unpleasant situation can arise if A1 believes that the project manager is somehow at fault. A 'word' may be passed by A1 to the functional supervisor SMA which can seriously affect the behaviour of many in senior management. It is essential that the reports emanating from the project are the regular planned progress reports from the project manager prepared with the *help and agreement* of the project team and directed to the chief executive. It cannot be stressed too strongly that functional specialists, and others, within the team should not be permitted to submit their own separate specialist reports as this will, at best, confuse the lines of communication and, at worst, cause the project team to fall apart with serious consequences for the project. In a study of matrix organisations (Barllett, C.A. and Ghosal, S. (1990) 'Matrix organisations, a state of mind', *Harvard Business Review*, Vol. 68 pp 138–142) its authors stated that they had found that '... dual reporting leads to conflict and confusion'.

THE NEED FOR A CORPORATE CULTURE

The changes in managerial behaviour which are required by the adoption of a matrix organisational structure are far reaching, stretching to the board itself. To ensure that different project teams react the same way to similar circumstances and that both project managers and functional supervisors have the same view on the priority of objectives, a powerful corporate culture must be developed. This is neither an easy nor a rapid goal to achieve, probably consuming several years, but without its achievement there may be inconsistent behaviour between teams and functions which could prove embarrassing to the whole organisation. It must also be remembered that project teams may be physically distant from the parent company and each other, and that communication between them, on those non-programmable problems which are only dealt with by the use of the personal skills, experience, judgement and enterprise of the senior staff, will be difficult.

The matrix organisational structure has, of course, a number of advantages in an environment of change. It allows:

- a more rapid response to changes in demand
- a better balance to be achieved between time, cost and resources than in the pure functional form
- the preparation of independent policies and budgets for projects, although they must not conflict with established policies and procedures
- a clear definition of the responsibility and authority of the project manager
- the creation of a strong base of technical expertise which is built up through experience in a range of projects
- project costs to be properly identified.

The disadvantages are that, in addition to the time required to reach maturity, it will require, on the part of top management, considerable effort to:

- define policies, procedures, responsibilities and authorities *throughout the whole organisation*
- monitor and control the balance of power between the project and functional supervisors
- ensure that the project and functional supervisors have the same views on company objectives.

A difficulty with this form of structure, and one reason why it is often resisted, is that the *cost of management* is clearly revealed, probably for the first time for many companies since it is normally hidden in the overheads. Another possible difficulty is that, in organisations which are not completely project centred, when a project is completed there may not be another for the project team to pick up. As a result they may be dispersed either back to their original function – which may prove difficult if their place has been filled – or to some other part of the organisation, possibly to assist on another project. This can result in some confusion of loyalties, and beliefs that career prospects are jeopardised, unless clear policies are set down and understood by the staff concerned.

THE PURE PROJECT STRUCTURE

These problems tend to disappear as the organisation becomes more project centred, carrying out nothing else but projects. While this is relatively rare outside organisations providing a service or consultancy, it does exist with advantage in companies in jobbing production or those with a very limited product range, for example, oil rig maintenance. Such an organisation is likely to have a structure such as that shown in Fig. 2.4.

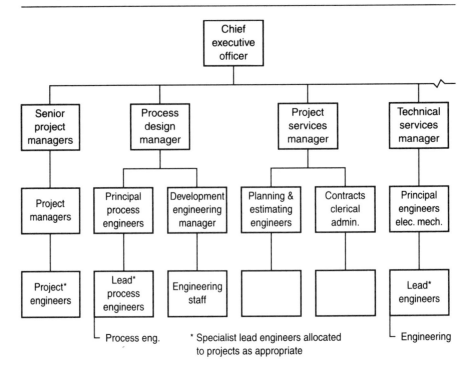

Fig. 2.4 Project organisation.

Here the separate functions have virtually disappeared, the functional ability being concentrated in the project teams with some reserve held as a central pool under a manager, which is available to provide extra resources to the projects when required. Unlike the other organisational forms, the project team is seldom dispersed but remains as a unit ready to pick up the next project which the marketing executive will, hopefully, provide. The 'top' of the organisation has also virtually disappeared.

While this form of organisation does not assist in the development of functional supervisors it has the following advantages over the other forms of functional and matrix organisation:

- the lines of project responsibility and authority are clearly identified;
- project budgets can be clearly defined and controlled;
- communications between the projects and top management are improved;
- managers who *can* manage change are developed;
- strong team understanding and loyalties are developed;
- the costs of management are clearly identified.

Figure 2.5 shows schematically how the authority structure changes as an organisation moves from being purely functional through a matrix to a pure project structure.

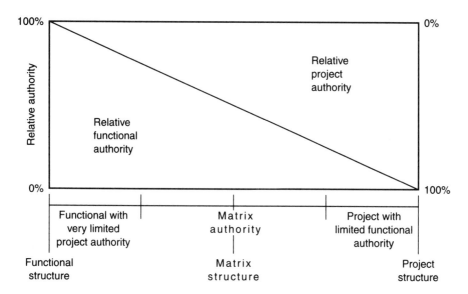

Fig. 2.5 Authority relationships in organisational structures

CHAPTER 3

Project organisation

The variety of products produced by projects is immense, the connecting threads being their uniqueness, the fact that each has a defined start and finish and the need for each to be planned. This diversity means that it is not possible to lay down the 'best way' in which a project should be organised, and no text can hope to cover all the possible variations of the project team organisation. However, one important difference between the organisation of hardware and information technology teams does seem to have emerged. This difference is concerned with the authority, responsibility and accountability of the project manager. In hardware and most service provision projects there is invariably one person, the project manager, who has executive authority, within defined terms of reference, for all aspects of the project. It appears that in IT and software projects the person appointed as project manager reports to an executive committee who make the executive decisions.

As discussed earlier, the size and detailed structure of a project team will depend on the technology, size and cost of a project, but even at its smallest there must always be a project manager.

THE PROJECT MANAGER

The project manager for any project should be appointed as early as possible in the life of the project, ideally in the conception phase. This is not always possible, so that the project manager, when appointed, may find he/she is committed to decisions with which he/she is not in agreement. This always creates problems and the manager must formally record the problem as early as possible with a view to possible modification of the decisions. The early commitments which have to be made in many projects will also have significant effects and the project manager, on appointment, should carry out an audit and assessment of the project for reassurance that it is feasible within the given terms of reference.

Project management is essentially team management. Where the project is a consortium project, team members may come from different cultures and speak different languages so that the acceptance of the team as the driving force, rather than the functional and/or national interests, by all its members is particularly important. Optimising one part will almost inevitably result in suboptimising the whole.

Project managers, to be successful, must possess capabilities which cannot be learnt. They must be *leaders*, and those who are being led must respect their honesty, integrity and vision. They will need to demonstrate drive, enthusiasm, dedication and humour, and a willingness to back their staff, to whom they have delegated responsibility, when things go wrong. It has been said that:

> **To win a battle it is essential to inspire the army with confidence in itself and its general.**

Additionally the project manager *must* be an eternal optimist!

DESIRABLE SKILLS

The desirable skills of a good project manager are:

1 **Technological understanding.** Since the project manager will have to evaluate technical proposals and recommendations, including an assessment of any risks involved in the use of new or untried technologies, possibly without recourse to assistance from the parent company, an adequate technological understanding of the project is vital. Since, by their very nature, projects tend to be multi-disciplinary some of this understanding will probably come from the project manager's basic discipline and training; the rest may have to be learned very rapidly. It is, however, undesirable for the project manager to be a specialist in the project technology, as he/she may tend to get involved in the technology to the detriment of the management of the project.

2 **An understanding of project economics.** This will require a thorough understanding of the customer's total view of the project and its subsequent operation or use. It will require financial skills applied to the project and the use of such techniques as life-cycle costing.

3 **A knowledge of man management techniques.** This will include a knowledge of and the ability to use:
   - payment and bonus systems;
   - interviewing techniques;
   - team building and motivation;
   - industrial relations legislation and its application in the project environment;
   - the health and safety at work regulations and their application to the project.

4 **A competence in systems design and maintenance.** This includes knowledge of, and the ability to implement, appropriate office and technological systems for both the project team and the project.

5 **A competence in planning and control.** A sound knowledge of all the techniques for planning and controlling projects, with the ability to decide which is the most appropriate to use as circumstances arise.

6 **Financial competence.** The ability to read and understand company accounts, together with an understanding of the various financial accounting techniques including:
- setting and controlling budgets;
- cost control;
- variance analysis;
- cash flow statements;
- discounted cash flow methods (DCF);
- net present value (NPV);
- credit control;
- loan and interest repayment systems;
- risk analysis (financial);
- lifecycle costing.

7 **A competence in procurement.** This will include knowledge of:
- contract law;
- techniques for the procurement of goods and services;
- costs of holding stock;
- expediting;
- materials control.

8 **Good personal communication abilities.** The project manager will often be called upon to address meetings, both business and public, on a variety of matters concerning the project. Additionally, there will be the need to teach project and customer's staff on the use of techniques and methods and to assess training needs and courses.

These issues are summarised in Table 3.1

Table 3.1 Desirable skills of the project manager

- Technological understanding
- Understanding of project economics
- Knowledge of man management
- Competence in systems design and maintenance
- A competence in planning and control
- Financial competence
- Competence in procurement
- Good personal communication skills

THE PROJECT TEAM

The size of the project team will naturally be related to the size of the project so that in a small project it may only have one full-time member, the project manager, who draws on others for specialist assistance when required (*see* Fig. 2.2). As the size of the project grows so does the team until a complete team structure emerges. For larger projects still it is the numbers in the team that change, not the structure of the team. A full project team will be made up as in Fig. 3.1.

As discussed earlier, even with a full project team, assistance from the functional specialists may be required for many aspects of the project. These specialists then have a dual responsibility which is at the heart of many of the problems of project management in functional industry. Staff who are seconded to a project have in effect two supervisors:

1 the head of the function who is their normal supervisor and is the one to whom they look for salary, promotion and career prospects; and

2 the project manager to whom they are responsible for their work in the project and who will report on that work, and their general conduct, to their functional head.

This inevitably leads to divided loyalties and problems as a result, particularly when staff are seconded full-time to the project and may be physically absent from the function office at the time of annual reviews and similar occasions and so feel that they do not receive the recognition that their work on the project deserves. Oddly enough, this problem appears to be at its worst if the physical separation is so slight that communications appear to be easy and no formal structure is set up. A distant location forces the set-

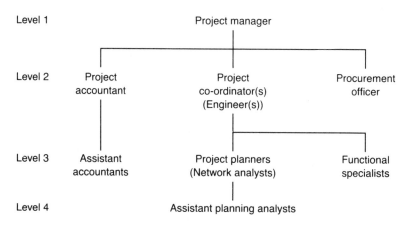

Fig. 3.1 Structure of a full project team.

ting up of formal communications channels. Equally, when a problem, not necessarily technical, arises concerning some aspect of the project to whom do staff turn? They are in an invidious dual reporting situation, and to whomever reference is made, the other 'supervisor' will feel aggrieved.

As a project of any size progresses the project team membership will change as functional specialists enter and leave the team in response to the changing technical demands of the project. Some people will stay with the project throughout its life; others will be concerned only with a particular phase and on its completion will return to their functional group in the parent company or transfer to another project. It is a major part of the project manager's job to ensure the smooth integration of these people into the project team to progress the work as harmoniously as possible.

As with the project manager, in addition to their technical skills, the personal skills of the members of the project team are of considerable importance. Projects can become very demanding and lack of harmony in the team can be disastrous. For this, if for no other reason, the project manager must be involved in the selection and appointment of, at the very least, the two top levels of the team.

The project manager should aim to build a team in which people will:

- behave innovatively, if necessary, and generally adopt a problem-solving approach
- openly discuss ideas before they are adopted
- communicate freely between functions
- sell the ideas and work of the team
- obtain co-operation from people outside the team
- ensure that work is progressed at an acceptable level
- assess their own and other people's work pragmatically
- remain cohesive as a group even when things go wrong.

The team must be aware of the need for good communications both within the group and with others. Communication is a two-way process – the project not only requires information, it must also supply it. The formal reporting systems and regular meetings are only one aspect of the communication network. The customer and other stakeholders, suppliers of goods and services, and others who have only transitory links with the project should be encouraged to raise problems and concerns as early as they become aware of them. Discussions and, when necessary, actions can then be taken to resolve the difficulties. Commercial and Official Secrecy requirements must, of course, be respected and, as discussed earlier, the dangers of dual reporting well understood and avoided.

CHAPTER 4

Planning the project

Any endeavour should be planned and, the larger or more complex or uncertain it is, the more essential a plan becomes. This is particularly true of projects because of their uniqueness and, except for very small projects, the planning activity needs to be formalised. Even small projects can be complex and require careful planning to resolve the interactions between the various jobs or activities which make up the work in the project.

OUTLINE OF PLANNING CONCEPTS

Present decisions affect both present and *future* actions and, if immediate, short-term decisions are not made within the framework of long-term plans, then the short-term decisions may effectively impose some long-term actions which are undesirable but inescapable. Military writers categorise these long- and short-term plans as:

- *strategic plans* – which are those made to 'serve the needs of generalship'
- *tactical plans* – which are those made 'when in contact with the enemy'.

Ideally, of course, strategic plans are made before the start of an operation and, by following them, the operation is successfully concluded. Inevitably, however, tactical decisions will have to be made and these can only be successful if they are made within the context of the strategic plan.

To permit effective tactical decision making, it is necessary for the strategy to be expressed in a form that is:

- explicit
- intelligible
- capable of accepting change
- capable of being monitored.

It must be realised that there is no absolute definition of strategy and tactics: at any one level in a hierarchy a tactical plan should be made to fit the needs of the strategy received from a higher level and this tactical plan then becomes the strategy for a lower level. Freedom to make appropriate decisions must be given to those who will be held responsible for performance and, if these decisions are to be meaningful in a larger context, then it is imperative that this larger context be known. Freedom 'within the law' is as important a concept in management as in the community. Too often tactical decisions are taken to meet the needs of immediate expediency, and the results may well be disastrous in the long term.

OPPORTUNITY COSTS

In planning, as indeed in project control, a valuable concept for the project manager is that of *opportunity cost*:

> **Opportunity cost – that which is sacrificed by choosing or failing to adopt a different course of action to that which is currently planned to be taken.**

Probably the simplest example to illustrate the concept is to consider a person with £1000 in cash. For safety this is put in a box hidden under the bed. At the end of a year the £1000 is unchanged. However, it could have been placed in an equally safe investment with an annual return of 10 per cent. What has been lost – sacrificed – is £100, so the opportunity cost of the 'box under the bed' policy is therefore £100.

This concept can be widely applied. Thus, for example, at a project milestone it is forecast that the project will overrun by one week and the penalty clause states that for each week of overrun a penalty of £1000 will be levied. The opportunity cost of not taking any corrective action to pull the project back by one week is £1000, and this will give an idea of the extra cost which can be economically incurred to avoid the overrun.

A second example concerns procurement. Suppose a piece of capital equipment is to be hired for use on the project at a weekly rate of £1000. It is brought onto site three weeks before it is needed. The opportunity cost of this early hiring is £3000 plus any financing charges and the weekly cost of storage and insurance. Equally, material which is over-ordered or delivered early will attract an opportunity cost which is often alarmingly high.

It should be noted that opportunity costs do not show up in the final project accounts, being absorbed in the general financing. Thus, in the example above of the piece of equipment brought on site early, the hiring cost will appear as one item. A declaration of the extra costs involved by bringing the equipment on site before it was needed is a statement which is outside the experience of either author. It is also true that opportunity cost may not be the sole criterion in making a decision. It may be that other commercial considerations outweigh the opportunity cost but it must always be taken into account.

ELEMENTS OF PROJECT PLANNING

The earliest attempt at a formal planning system was the *Gantt chart* which was derived from the simple *bar chart*. The use of the term 'bar chart' is now so universal for referring to either form that it has been used throughout this text, except in this chapter where 'Gantt charts' and 'bar charts' are discussed.

A project plan in its simplest form is an attempt at a timetable for all the activities which make up the project. It forms the first major step in the project management process, and sets out 'how', 'who does what' and 'when'. At the next stage of sophistication it will also state to 'what level of performance and quality' and at 'what cost'. At a yet higher stage of sophistication it will also be related to the availability of the resources required to carry out the activities. As each stage is considered, it may be necessary to reconsider and modify the preceding ones.

The process of creating a project plan is the responsibility of the project manager and the project team, with the advice and assistance of the project sponsor, the customer and other stakeholders. The preparation of a project plan is an iterative process. It needs to be reviewed and updated as information becomes available throughout the life of the project. It is never a static document and it forms the base against which all progress in the project is measured. It must therefore be as accurate and up-to-date as is possible. *No plan should ever be regarded as set in concrete – it is a working tool.*

There will always be several levels within the project plan. At the highest level it will be a summary showing key events and milestones in the project as an executive overview for senior management. In a consortium project, the plan will indicate the agreed division of work between the members of the consortium. The lower levels will have increasing amounts of detail with the lowest giving activity lists for task owners who are responsible for activities in a particular cost centre or function.

The plan will always have a timetable for the work to be done. This may only be in bar chart form but should preferably be a network, which has been analysed to obtain the start and finish data for all the activities. As the project proceeds the planning documents will also contain progress information showing the current state of the project against the plan. In a long duration project the amount of detail included in the plan should vary with time. In the short term, which may be three to six months or in some cases more, there should be the full expansion of detail with progressively less from there on. The short-term horizon is, of course, moved forward at each update or at pre-planned times so that detail increases as the project moves forward.

The plan will include the budget for the project and financial statements showing expenditure, income and net cash flows adjusted to net present values. This part of the project plan may be restricted to certain levels of management, as may other parts if they contain confidential information.

Contained within the project plan there will also be plans for change and configuration management, for quality and for procurement together with a risk assessment showing both financial and technical risks and their possible impact on the project. These may be the work of separate groups within the parent organisation which specialise in the appropriate techniques, but for the project they report to the project manager who has to agree and approve their plans. If separate groups exist they will probably second a member to the project team to support the appropriate activities. If the project is large or is taking place physically distant from the originating organisation, there will probably be support teams, as part of the project team, for some or all of these aspects of the project plan.

THE WORK BREAKDOWN STRUCTURE

Concurrently with the time-based plan a *work breakdown structure* (WBS) should also be produced, which will provide all those involved in the project with a hierarchically structured division of the work required in the project. The WBS can be structured in a number of alternative ways depending on the use to which it is to be put. Common ways are by division of the product into major components which are then split into sub-assemblies and so on down to components, by a functional breakdown or by cost centre code. The way chosen is usually related to the type of project and the industrial or public sector in which it is taking place.

In all cases, the lowest level in the WBS comprises groups of activities – or single activities if they are large enough – which are the responsibility of a named individual – the task owner. The task owner is responsible for identifying, estimating, planning, executing and reporting progress on the work in accordance with the project plan. The task owner is also responsible for the quality of the inputs to the project plan and for ensuring the progress data is accurately obtained and provided on time as required in the plan.

For each task a 'statement of work' (SOW) is required which describes the activities in the task in sufficient detail to provide an unambiguous statement of the task owner's commitment to the project and thus enable the activity list data to be complete. The data required will include estimated durations together with the resources required, costs, measures of performance including how any stated quality requirements are to be assessed, any risks and uncertainties and details of reporting procedures.

When the identified task is a subproject in its own right so that the task owner becomes a supplier to the project, the statement of work may need to take the form of a legal contract. This will certainly be so if the task owner is external to the parent organisation.

The project manager must assess and discuss the statements of work supplied by the task owners before agreeing the assignment of the work. Implicit in the agreement is the ability of the task owner to fulfil the commitment, as defined in the statement, at the time specified in the project plan. The task owner is thus committed to provide the required resources at the right time without interfering with other work.

Concurrent with the WBS, the logical relationships between project activities should be planned through the use of bar charts (where the logical relationships are difficult to express) or, preferably, through network diagrams in which the inclusion of the logical relationships is a part of the technique, whichever of the two types of diagram – of activity-on-arrow (AoA) or activity-on-node (AoN) – is used. Both bar charts and project network techniques (PNT) are presented in detail in later chapters and discussed further below.

There are differences of opinion among practitioners as to which comes first, the WBS or the network or an activity list. Your authors do not feel strongly about it and would suggest that whichever is most convenient for the project is what comes first. Whatever happens, the result is the same – the project plan and all that goes with it.

INTRODUCTION TO PROJECT PLANNING TECHNIQUES

The bar chart

When attempting to determine the completion date for any project, whether it be the building of a bridge, the mounting of a sales conference, the re-layout of a shop, the designing of a new piece of equipment or any other project, it is necessary to timetable all the activities that make up the task, that is to say a *plan* must be prepared. The need for planning has always been present, but the complexity and competitiveness of modern undertakings now requires that this need should be met rather than just recognised. The first attempt at a formal planning system was the *Gantt chart*.

In the Gantt chart the time that an activity should take is represented by a horizontal line, the length of that line being proportional to the duration time of that activity. In order that several activities can be represented on the same chart, a framework or ruling is set up, giving time flowing from left to right, the activities being listed from top to bottom (*see* Fig. 4.1)

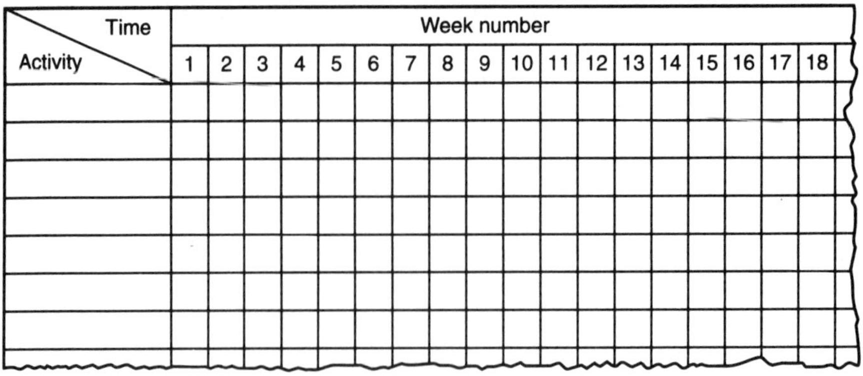

Fig. 4.1 GANTT (Bar chart framework.)

Assume, for the sake of simplicity, that there are three activities, A, B and C, which must be carried out in sequence and that the duration times are:

Activity A: 4 weeks
Activity B: 6 weeks
Activity C: 5 weeks

This is represented on the Gantt chart as shown in Fig. 4.2 and reveals quite clearly how work should progress. Thus, by the end of week 8, the whole of activity A and two-thirds of activity B should be complete.

To show how work is actually progressing, a bar or line can be drawn within the uprights of the activity symbol; the length of the bar representing the amount of the work completed. Thus, if 50 per cent of an activity is complete, a bar half the length of the activity symbol is drawn (*see* Fig. 4.3). This gives a very simple and striking representation of work done, particularly if a number of activities are represented on the same chart.

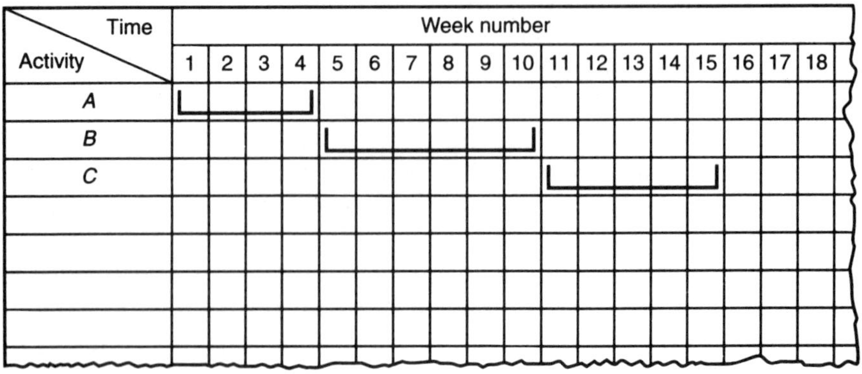

Fig. 4.2 Three sequential activities.

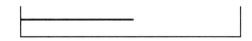

Fig. 4.3 Representation of 50% of activity complete.

If this chart has been correctly filled in and is viewed at the end of week 7, that is 'time now' (denoted by two small arrows at the top and bottom of the chart as shown in Fig. 4.4), then the following information is readily apparent:

Activity A   should be complete and, in fact, is so.

Activity B   should be 50 per cent complete, but, in fact, is only 17 per cent finished.

Activity C   should not be started and, in fact, is not started.

Activity D   should be 62 per cent complete and, in fact, is only 50 per cent finished.

Activity E   should be 17 per cent complete and, in fact, is 50 per cent finished.

Activity F   should be complete and, in fact, is not started.

Activity G   should be 87 per cent complete and, in fact, is complete.

Thus we see that incomplete bars to the *left* of the cursor line mean under-fulfilment, while those to the *right* mean over-fulfilment. By the use

Time / Activity	Week number																	
	1	2	3	4	5	6	7	8	9	10	11	12	13	14	15	16	17	18
A																		
B																		
C																		
D																		
E																		
F																		
G																		

Fig. 4.4 Representation of progress.

of codes and/or symbols the reasons for any delays can be displayed and the whole chart can be very succinctly informative, combining both planning and the recording of progress. For many tasks the Gantt chart is unsurpassed, and its use has been very highly developed.

Though valuable, the Gantt chart presents three major difficulties; one concerning the problem of interrelationships, the second that of needing to take several decisions simultaneously and the third the problem of modifying the chart.

The problem of interrelationships

Consider activity F in Fig. 4.4. It is shown here to start at the beginning of the project. However, it may be that there is another requirement, namely that it must be complete *before* activity C can start. This means that activity F can in fact 'slide' five weeks without detriment to the whole project. There may also be another activity, K (not shown in Fig. 4.4), which can start *only* when F is complete. How can these interrelationships be displayed? It is possible, in a small-scale work, to 'tie' bars by dotted lines but, if more than a few activities are concerned, the chart becomes so muddled as to be useless.

The problem of simultaneous decisions

Locating an activity on a Gantt chart requires three simultaneous decisions to be made:

- *Method (logic)*: activity C is shown to follow activity B, that is, a decision on the way the project is to be carried out has to be made – the *logic* has to be decided.
- *Time:* any activity bar has a *length*, that is, a decision has been made on the time each activity will occupy.
- *Resources:* locating an activity in position implies that resources are available to carry out the activity at that time.

All projects have these three dimensions – logic, time, resources – and each is important. To require a planner to make decisions on these three features at one time is to set an impossible task, yet this is what is required when a Gantt chart is drawn. In practice, the decisions must be taken serially.

The problem of modifying the chart

When changes to the plan are necessary – something which is inevitable even in the best planned project – the Gantt chart is virtually impossible to modify successfully both due to the physical problem of changing the chart and the lack of knowledge of the interrelationships which prevents the effect of a modification to one bar upon the other unmodified bars being reliably predicted.

The Gantt chart is now more generally referred to as a 'bar chart' – from which it was derived – and the latter term will be used in this text.

Project network techniques

These difficulties were resolved by the development of the family of *project network techniques* and their charts or diagrams.

Project network techniques (PNTs) were developed in the mid-1950s and early 1960s when two types of network diagram originated. Essentially, these involve representing the proposed project as a diagram (or 'model') built up from a series of *arrows* and *nodes* (boxes or circles). The original structure of the model depends only upon the proposed method of carrying out the project and is drawn in such a way that the logical structure of the plan is easily observed and tested. It must be realised that as with any plan, the network model does not represent the 'best' or 'only' way of carrying out the project at any stage in its development. It represents the way the project has been planned on this occasion and forms a model for understanding and, when necessary, modifying the plan.

Once the diagram is believed to show an acceptable logic, times are set for the various constituents of the diagram (the duration times). A calculation is then carried out to discover the total duration of the project. If this is satisfactory, then no further action is necessary at this stage. If the total project time needs to be reduced then the activities dictating this time – the 'critical activities' – are examined to see whether they can be adequately shortened by using a different method or by changing the logic of the plan. It is foolish, indeed it should be impossible, to change an activity duration unless it is achieved by method or logic changes. Unfortunately, this is often unacceptable to senior executives who believe that issuing a fiat will solve a problem. 'I don't care what your plan says, the job has got to be done in less time with the resources you've got' is a cry which every planner must have heard many times. The exchange between method, logic and time continues until an acceptable situation is obtained.

Time and logic having been considered, it may be necessary – in some fortunate cases it is not – to consider the resources required by the plan as it now stands and the resources available. This can be done by moving through the network and adding up ('aggregating') the resources required in each time period. The aggregated resources ('loads') are compared with the resources available ('capacities') and, if requirement exceeds availability, the network is re-examined to see if any manipulation can take place to 'spread' the load satisfactorily. If not, then clearly either the available resources or the total project time (TPT) or both must be increased.

It should be realised that the 'time analysis' of the network sets all activities at their earliest time and that the resource aggregation forms an 'early start aggregation' so that any manipulation of the network to reduce the load must, inevitably, delay activities, but not necessarily the project completion date. The resulting interactions with other activities and their resource requirements can become extremely complex and, except for very small projects or simple situations, such manipulations should not be attempted without an appropriate computer program.

One of the very useful by-products of drawing a network is that the diagram forms a useful means of communication. It demonstrates how a project is to be completed, or it can enable an executive to pass on information to a successor or a subordinate. It is quite certain that the network will be seen and used by persons other than those who prepared it. With this 'communicating' aspect in mind, it is important from a practical point of view that activities should be *unequivocal* statements in *positive* terms that have *significance* within the context of the task being considered. Furthermore, wherever possible, constituents should be chosen in such a way that the responsibility for carrying out the activity can be explicitly assigned. When desired, networks can be easily transformed into bar charts, with the facility for incorporating change or being manipulated when required.

Broadly, there are two PNT families: the activity-on-arrow (AoA) family, where an activity is represented by an arrow; and the activity-on-node (AoN) family, where an activity is represented by a box or node. These two families each have their own advantages and their own adherents. The authors have used both extensively and believe that neither shows an overwhelming advantage over the other. It is necessary for some organisations to have both families available to meet the needs of their customers/clients. Care must be taken to avoid confusing the two families. There are currently many excellent computer programs available for both AoA and AoN. Both families have the characteristics of a good plan – namely, they are:

Explicit – often uncomfortably so: their clarity is uncompromising;

Intelligible – with education they are very intelligible – it is often easy to deduce the way in which the planner's mind was working;

Capable of accepting change – changes are easily made to a network: a working network that does not incorporate change is a rarity;

Capable of being monitored – The progress of the project as a whole and of the constituent parts can be very easily deduced *providing that the information on performance is fed back to the network with appropriate speed.*

PNT can be used in situations where the start and finish of the task can be identified: continuous or flow production is not susceptible to planning by PNT *although the setting up or pre-production work is.* The size of the project is of no consequence – networking has been used to plan a simple test procedure just as successfully as to plan the construction of a new town or the launch of a space ship.

As with any other new management tool, PNT will require to be introduced into an organisation with care. It is suggested that the following points should be observed:

- PNT is not a universal tool – there are many situations where it cannot be usefully employed. These situations are, in general, those where activity is continuous, for example, flow production. A PNT-type situation is characteristically one that has a definable start and finish.

- PNT is not a panacea – it does not cure all ills. Indeed, in itself it does not solve any problems, but it does expose situations in a way that will permit effective examinations both of the problems and the effects of possible solutions. However, the formulation and implementation of any solution will remain the responsibility of the appropriate manager.

- Networking must not be made a mystery, known only to a chosen few. All levels require to appreciate the method and its limitations and an extensive educational programme will be necessary to ensure that knowledge is spread as widely as possible.

- The person introducing networking into an organisation must be of sufficient stature and maturity to be able to influence both senior and junior personnel.

- Wherever possible, the early application of PNT should be to simple situations. If networking is first employed on a very difficult task it may fail, not because of the difficulty of networking but because of the difficulty of the task itself. However, the failure is likely to be attributed to PNT and the technique will be discredited.

- The first application of networking will undoubtedly excite considerable interest and attract many resources, both physical and managerial. This may starve other non-PNT-planned tasks to their detriment and it may produce exceptionally good results on the 'PNT job' that cannot be reproduced on later jobs. While it is impossible to avoid this 'halation' effect completely, its existence needs to be recognised.

- PNT will involve committal to, and the acceptance of, responsibilities expressed in quantified terms. Many supervisors find this difficult to accept and will often try to escape by creating unreal problems. It is vital to make it quite clear that PNT is not a punitive device: it is a tool to assist, not a weapon to assault.

- The purpose for which the network is to be used must be known in advance. A 'feasibility' network is likely to be different to a working network. A network designed to control at one level in the organisation will differ from that used to control at a different level.

● Excessive detail must be eschewed. The authors have found, both in their own work and in talking to hundreds of network planners, that *excessive detail in the network is the most common cause of failure to use the network, and thus of the failure of the project.* A *very* approximate guide, for the majority of projects, is that few activities should be of less duration than 1 per cent of the total project duration. In addition, any network with more than a few hundred activities – say 400 at most – *must* be broken down into subprojects as part of the hierarchical planning and control process.

It must be realised that the duration time of an activity is the time that should be *expended* in carrying out the activity. It is not *necessarily* the time between the preceding and succeeding activities; for example, the preceding activity may finish in week 10. The succeeding activity may start in week 20 but the duration time of the activity itself may be only 4 weeks, in which case, the activity is said to possess *float* (in this case 6 weeks). This matter will be discussed more thoroughly later.

As with all scheduling techniques, the times assigned to activities must be realistic, that is to say they must take into account all current local circumstances. Using the work study officers' *standard* times is quite inappropriate here, since the actual work may not be performed 'at standard'. 'Actual' or 'observed' times are much more appropriate although the conditions then and on the current occasion should be checked for comparability. Unfortunately, in many cases the actual times are not available. It is extremely useful for performance data on resources and tasks to be collected, since time and resource performance may interact in unpredictable ways. Once recorded, these will assist the estimator in considering *current* circumstances and will lead to better duration estimates. Whatever the situation, however, the principle is clear: the duration times need to be *realistic* rather than *desirable*, and they should be accepted by those held responsible for their achievement.

THE NETWORK AS A BUDGET

A financial budget is defined as:

> **A financial and/or quantitative statement, prepared prior to a defined period of time, of the policy to be pursued during that period for the purpose of attaining a given objective.**

This is a definition also of a network – indeed of any comprehensive project plan – and it is often very helpful to consider the network as *a budget in terms of time*. The cost accountant has developed much skill in the assembly and use of financial budgets and it is prudent to consider this experience when drawing and using networks. The authors have found this parallel particularly valuable when considering the detail that should be incorporated into a network. A hierarchy of networks is just as appropriate as a hierarchy of budgets: it will enable problems to be identified without a mass of unnecessary detail and it can locate responsibility at an appropriate point in the structure of a company.

Again, the experience of the cost accountant is pertinent: costs should be agreed with, not imposed upon, the manager concerned. *The Cost Handbook* (Ronald Press, New York) contains the following (Section 20.20):

> **Primary responsibility for preparation of the budgets should rest with the supervisors of the various segments of the business. For example . . . the sales manager should participate actively in the development of the sales budget, since he will be the individual primarily responsible for the execution of the sales plan. This general procedure is equally applicable to every other segment of the business and should be vigorously pursued . . .**
>
> **In this connection Francis (*Controller*, Vol. 22) points out that: 'Budgets are frequently developed by one or two key individuals . . . sometimes management without the prior knowledge or approval of the operating executives in the (various) departments. This is the worst type of budget procedure and quickly defeats the objectives of forward planning.'**

These comments would hold exactly if 'project plan' were substituted for 'budget'.

It cannot be too heavily stressed that the assessment of durations, resources and costs is a vital aspect of planning. Deductions from the network plan can be no better than the information used in the calculations; consequently it is imperative that the managers responsible for carrying out activities *must* be involved in the assessment. If they are not consulted they may well ignore the plan as totally unrealistic, with disastrous results for the project.

The time and resource data are essential for scheduling and, between them, form the basis for the costing of activities which then forms the project budget. For many organisations, particularly those in manufacturing industries, for whom project resource control is difficult since resource availabilities for project work are virtually unknown in advance, the project budget is the principal means of control for the project.

CARD NETWORKING/BAR CHARTING

In an organisation which has networking/bar charting for project planning well established, it is possible to significantly reduce the time required for the preparation of such plans. In this approach, the basis of which is described in 'Speeded methods of network planning', by J.A. Larkin (*The Production Engineer*, February, 1968), plain cards are issued to each functional group concerned in the current project. These cards are used, one per activity, to record the details of all the activities for which the functional group is responsible in the project. The necessity for the use of the technique to be previously well established becomes apparent at this stage when it is realised that each group must plan at the same level of detail and use the same time units for durations.

When each functional group has completed its consideration of the project activities a meeting is convened to which it is essential that senior functional staff attend, since decisions taken at the meeting will affect the whole implementation of the project plan. The meeting should be held in a planning room equipped with magnetic or soft wallboards to which the activity cards can be stuck or pinned. The chair of the meeting guides a discussion of the project and as activities are discussed the cards representing them are added to the wallboards and the dependency interactions drawn in.

In this way the logic of the project is very rapidly established and any unforeseen problems emerge and can be discussed at once. It is said that in an experienced group a large and complex project can be set up in one day rather than the six to eight weeks it normally takes. The greatest virtue of the approach, other than the time saving, is that the functions discuss the problems of interaction directly with each other, rather than through the third party of the planning engineer, and are usually more co-operative in solving them at the senior level. The high level plan which results can be converted to the formalism of either AoA or AoN or to a bar chart as is required, and lower level plans with more detail can be prepared with confidence.

CHAPTER 5

Projects and quality

The need to achieve 'quality' affects all areas of industry including projects and project management. Appropriate quality possibly has even more significance for the product of a project than for a volume consumer product. A defective, say, alarm clock is a nuisance which can readily be replaced. A defective project product can probably only be restored to acceptability, if it *can* be so restored, at great cost and inconvenience. Project managers would claim that they have always been aware of the need to achieve the requisite quality in the project product(s), and that good project management is good quality management. While this may be true, what has not been done, till recently, is to formalise even this aspect of the impact of quality requirements.

There is, however, another aspect to the application of quality to projects which is seldom, if ever, considered – that of the quality of the project management process itself. Quality improvement in a management process requires a continuity of operation of that process and, in most cases, this is what does not happen in project management – the team is set up for the project and dispersed on its completion. In such cases the maintenance of a project log and the compilation of a project history becomes of even greater importance than it was in the past in order to maintain continuity within the organisation.

With more organisations seeking certification to BS:5750 in the UK and to EN:29000 in Europe there has come the requirement to show that they are correctly applying the quality management principles involved in such certification – which includes fully documenting all procedures to ensure traceability when required. For project management it means, among other things, a specific requirement for a quality plan as part of the project plan.

THE QUALITY CONCEPTS OF PROJECT MANAGEMENT

Five main quality concepts have been identified as critical to the achievement of quality in projects and project management. These are detailed below and summarised in Table 5.1.

Table 5.1 The quality concepts of project management

1. Maximising the satisfaction of customer and stakeholder needs is paramount.
2. All work is carried out as a set of planned and interlinked processes.
3. Quality must be built into both products and processes.
4. Management is responsible for creating a climate for quality.
5. Management is responsible for continuous improvement.

Maximising the satisfaction of customer and other stakeholder needs is paramount.

Satisfying customer needs means identifying and understanding those needs, both stated and implied, translating them into requirements and ensuring that all work in the project contributes to them. It also means establishing good communication links with the customer. Other stakeholders should also be identified and their needs should be understood and, where possible, taken into account. Where these needs are in conflict with the customer's needs the latter must, of course, take precedence.

All work in a project is carried out as a set of planned and interlinked processes

The processes within a project create value for the stakeholders. Through the tasks in the project processes, input from suppliers is transformed into output to fulfil the project objectives. Managing the project processes properly is therefore essential and entails:

- *planning,* which includes identifying and documenting the processes and their quality requirements as part of the project plan;
- *co-ordinating and integrating* the interlinked processes;
- *ensuring that the processes* have the right skills, processes, material, equipment and specifications;
- *monitoring and controlling* the processes.

Quality must be built into both products and processes

Quality does not just happen, nor can it just be inspected into a product; it is a matter of prevention, not of detection. It requires the combination of planned and controlled activities with competent and quality conscious personnel.

Management is responsible for creating an environment for quality

The creation of an environment for quality is the responsibility of the management of both the parent organisation and the project organisation and entails:

- setting quality objectives which can be quantified;
- providing an organisational structure and support which is conducive to meeting quality objectives;
- providing for quality assessments and follow-up;
- involving all personnel in achieving quality.

Management is responsible for continuous improvement

An organisation originating projects is responsible for continuously seeking to improve the project management process by learning from experience. Project management in the organisation should be treated as a process, not just as an isolated activity, and a system should be established to collect and analyse information from projects for use in a continuous improvement programme. Equally the project organisation is also responsible for seeking to continuously improve the quality of its own processes and activities. The price of quality is eternal vigilance.

PROJECT QUALITY AND THE HOST ORGANISATION

If the parent company, which may be a consortium, is new to project management, the project team may well find, when it comes to setting up the quality system for the project, that the company quality management system, even if it exists, is difficult to adapt to the different style of management required for projects. The quality management function in the parent organisation may be reluctant to change its standard approaches but must be persuaded to do so, where necessary, if the quality system is to be usable by the project team. It may be that a separate quality system has to be set up specifically to meet project requirements; if so, the interface between it and the main system will need careful management.

One of the main problems with 'quality' is defining what is meant in a particular case in measurable terms. If it cannot be measured or quantified in some way, then there is no way of saying whether it has been achieved or not. The quality plan has, therefore, to set out exactly how 'quality', at each stage or milestone in the project's progress, is to be defined in measurable terms and how those measures are to be applied. In some projects the aesthetic aspects of the product may be of importance and a very real problem arises in defining how it is to be assessed.

PROJECT PROCESSES AND QUALITY

The five quality concepts affect all the strategic, interlinking and operational processes in a project.

Strategic processes

The strategic processes set the direction for the project. They require the identification and documentation of all the stated and implied needs of the customer which, again, might be a consortium and other stakeholders and their conversion into a product specification for the project. Should the customer requirements be in conflict with other stakeholders' requirements these must be resolved if at all possible. However, in the final analysis it is the customer's needs that are paramount and these *must* be formally documented once agreed. The process of identifying new stakeholders and their needs has to continue throughout the life of the project.

Policies for the operational processes have to be set, in particular for the procurement of goods and services, for the product and process quality and for risk assessment and mitigation. These policies should support the operational processes and should specify:

- the performance measures to be used to monitor progress;
- the timing of regular management reviews.

The reviews ensure that the project objectives remain valid and provide for preventative or corrective action when required by changes in circumstances. Policies for the proper closure of the project should also be set up; these will be a function of the type of organisation and whether the project team is remaining as a unit or not. In all cases they should ensure that both good and bad aspects of the project provide lessons for future projects.

Interlinking processes

The project manager is responsible for the interlinking processes which are required because all projects consist of a number of interrelated processes. Changes in actions in one process will always affect several others and this needs to be recognised and managed if unfortunate consequences are to be avoided. The three main processes involved are:

- development of the project plan;
- interaction management;
- change management.

The project plan

The development of the project plan requires the integration of all the subsidiary plans, including the quality plan, into a coherent project plan. The degree of detail in the plan will, of course, be related to the size and complexity of the project, but there should always be a plan. It will require identifying all the internal and external interfaces and interlinks, and, if the project host is a consortium, the division of work between the members of the consortium. It should be noted that it is usually at these points that problems occur. The schedule of management reviews and audits should also be part of the plan.

Interaction management

Interaction management is concerned with minimising the adverse effects of actions in one process on others by arranging for interfunctional meetings to resolve any difficulties and to assign responsibility for actions to mitigate any adverse risks involved. The project communication system is a vital aspect of this process.

Change management

Change management includes any changes both to the configuration of the project product and to the project processes. It requires that a formal system be set up for assessing all requests for change within the project for whatever reason and for preventing unauthorised changes. The effects of all changes should be evaluated and costed and all changes *must* be authorised *before* implementation. When a change has been authorised the change management process should monitor its implementation and resolve any unforeseen conflicts which arise. There is a very real danger in most projects of design staff wanting to improve the existing design – 'one can always do it better the next time' – and thus exceeding the specified performance of the product. This must be prevented unless it can also be shown that there is a significant cost saving in the proposed changes which, in most cases, is unlikely. The old adage that 'the best is the enemy of the good' should be remembered.

Operational processes

The operational processes relate to the project scope, time, costs, resources, communication, personnel, procurement and risk and, in each case, the effect of applying the quality concepts needs to be considered.

Scope

The scope related processes aim to translate the stakeholders' requirements into activities to achieve the product and any other objectives of the project. They also aim to ensure that work in the project remains within the defined scope, that is, it achieves the specification and not something which exceeds or falls short of it, and that if changes are required that they are properly managed. To carry out these aims requires the development of the basic concept into a formal statement of the product specification which can be agreed by the customer. It will include measures, in quantifiable terms, of how all aspects of the product are to be assessed on completion of the project. It will therefore set out, in as much detail as is possible, the work breakdown structure, the activities in the plan and how the control system will work.

The full scope definition will usually be developed after the conception phase of the project since the feasibility studies will affect much of the detail of the specification and the activities required to achieve it. If the project is for a customer outside the parent company it will, in most cases, be then that a formal contract is agreed, although there may also have been a separate agreement on funding for the feasibility studies. A further expansion of the detail in the scope documentation will of course occur in the development phase, in particular in the project plan.

The *time, cost, resource, risk and procurement* related processes are dealt with in detail in the next and later chapters.

Communications

Communications in any organisation are critical to its success, and this is certainly true of projects. The aim of the process is to ensure that the information necessary for the management of the project is collected and exchanged or distributed on time and that, when required, it is adequately stored for traceability. This requires a communications plan, as part of the project plan, which specifies what information will be collected and when, who will be responsible for the collection and analysis of the data and to whom and how and when it will be distributed. The plan should also set out the schedule of meetings with formalised procedures for attendance lists, minutes and agenda, both within the project organisation and with the customer. As with any plan, procedures for its control also need to be set up, which will interact with the document control procedures.

Personnel

People are the most important part of any organisation. On them the success or failure of the organisation and the quality of its products depends. The project personnel-related processes aim to create an environment in which people can contribute effectively to the success of the project. They may well differ from the processes in the parent organisation because of the, usually, short-term needs of the project to build and motivate a team. Despite this, the project processes must not conflict with those of the parent company. A particular difficulty may arise here when a consortium exists to perform a project; usually it is the processes of the major partner which take precedence.

A structure for the project organisation must be set up and tailored to the needs of the project, which will change as the project proceeds. People must be selected or recruited to fill the positions in the organisation. There should be clearly defined job descriptions, which should include responsibilities and authority as well as the level of competence and experience required.

A significant part of the process for any major project is team building and development. It will be important in any but the smallest projects but becomes critical as the size of the project increases and particularly when the team is drawn from the members of a consortium with possibly different cultures and languages. The performance of any team is related to the opportunities offered to the team members for personal involvement, satisfaction and development and will have significant effects on the quality and success of the project. These opportunities are enhanced by creating a co-operative and positive approach within the team so that team members are encouraged to raise problems, which can then be properly discussed and resolved if they are personal, or appropriate action initiated if they concern the project. In a functional organisation, they will also be enhanced by the recognition of good work in the project which is also reported to the function from which the individual was seconded.

In building a team attention must be given to the provision of appropriate training to bring personnel up to the required level of knowledge. In an organisation with a new quality system, or one in which the project system differs significantly from that of the parent organisation, early training will be essential to ensure that the quality plan is properly prepared, as part of the project plan, and tailored to the project needs.

CHAPTER 6

Projects and procurement

Procurement is a vital element in the success or failure of many projects, particularly those concerned with a hardware product. The commitments for materials, goods or services with a long lead time may have to be made before either the project team or the project manager are in place. These in themselves can, for good or ill, set the course of a project. Procurement therefore is deserving of more attention than it is usually given in texts on project management.

PROCUREMENT PROCESSES

The procurement processes aim to acquire hardware, software, processed materials, services or combinations thereof which are necessary for the completion of the project. Thus the word 'procurement' is more generally used in project management than 'purchasing' or 'buying' since project procurement involves much more than just purchasing. In addition to purchasing, a project will often require the procurement officer to organise:

- the transport of material to a location distant from the parent company, possibly overseas;
- the organisation of transport and documentation;
- the arrangement of accommodation for staff away from home;
- the hiring of specialists or consultants or other services;
- the renting of plant and equipment not available in the parent company.

While it is essential for the project manager to be involved in the selection of plant and subcontractors, it is sensible for the procurement executive to carry out the initial searches and discussions with potential suppliers/subcontractors. In arriving at final decisions, the selection and contract conditions may require skills and knowledge other than those of the project manager or procurement executive. Certainly the human resource department should be involved in the selection of personnel, the engineering departments in the selection of plant and equipment and the legal department in the drawing up of contracts. Experience from previous projects, as recorded in the project logs, should be used to assess how services have performed, suppliers delivered or rented plant behaved, as part of the procurement process.

Of the various functions which have to be undertaken in a project, procurement is probably that which fits least easily into the project organisation. The difficulty arises from four sources:

1 single items can form a very significant capital investment in themselves, often of such magnitude that a main board decision is required before a contract can be placed;

2 often material is particular to the project and not held in stock in the parent company;

3 processed material may only be available at a location distant from the project;

4 there may be political or contractual reasons for procuring material in a country in which no procurement has previously been made, and in which therefore there is no experience of culture, methods or regulations.

The consequence of these difficulties is that the autonomy of the project group is severely curtailed: much of the effort and many of the decisions involved in procurement must take place in the parent company which may be geographically distant from the project. It would obviously be foolish not to obtain material locally to the project if it is possible to do so and often it is a contract requirement that a certain percentage of material used in a project must be obtained locally.

Thus there may well be two procurement groups, one at base and one at the project site. In such circumstances it is usual to find that the project group has a limit to the amount it can commit on any one order or on any one item, and good communications between the two procurement groups is essential. The management of this situation requires care: the channel between the two groups must not become a second project progress reporting channel. This having been said, it cannot be emphasised too strongly that the procurement executives *must* be involved in the project planning from the outset since the early commitments often decide the success or failure of the project. In addition, the feasibility of many projects will often depend on the delivery dates of goods and services.

SOURCES OF INFORMATION

The procurement group will draw information from a number of internal sources in addition to their own records:

1 The design/engineering departments which will specify the material required by the project.

It is imperative that before any specifications are acted upon that they should be as watertight as possible. The quality of these specifications will significantly affect the quality of the product and, by reducing the uncertainty inherent in any material, will reduce any risks involved in using the materials. A frequent cause of cost overruns in hardware projects is the extra charges made by subcontractors arising from 'changes in design during manufacture'. One of the authors recalls working for a company which employed a group whose sole task was to make claims under this heading. This group was an imaginative and robust generator of profit.

2 The project team itself.

The relationship between the procurement group and the project team should be formed as early as possible in the project. Representatives of the procurement group should be present at all project planning meetings as the availability of goods and services will often determine project completion dates.

3 The finance department.

This will provide information on the availability of finance and the financial stability of potential suppliers.

TASKS OF THE PROCUREMENT GROUP

The procurement group has a number of tasks to perform, some of which are particular to projects. These are discussed in detail below and summarised in Table 6.1.

1 Finding and approving suppliers.

In this context, 'suppliers' must be taken to include both those who supply goods and those who supply services. While some of this can be done by letters or discussion with representatives, the very nature of projects will dictate that meetings at the possible supplier's premises are essential. For hardware, it is not only important that the supplier has the design and technical capabilities to produce to the required quality, but also has the financial stability and resources to support the contract from start to delivery. Where there are several alternative suppliers a quantitative vendor

Table 6.1 Tasks of the procurement group

- Finding and approving suppliers.
- Ensuring the availability and use of adequate material specifications.
- Purchasing at least total cost.
- Vendor surveillance – ensuring delivery of goods or services at the right time.
- Warning all concerned if delivery promises are not going to be met.
- Secure storage and accurate control of material.
- Organising all discussions with actual and potential suppliers.
- Advising on prices.
- Acting as a 'window on the world'.
- Post-project disposal of unrequired material and equipment.

rating system can be a useful means of reducing the subjectivity which can result from a particularly persuasive supplier's representative. In such a scheme the qualities demanded of a supplier are listed and a weight indicating the importance of each quality to the project is assigned to each. Each supplier is then 'marked' across one quality at a time. From the product of this marking and the weight previously assigned a total 'score' can be obtained. Possible qualities may be:

- design competence;
- technical competence;
- previous experience;
- financial stability;
- perceived quality;
- delivery promise;
- price;
- terms of payment.

Such a list should not be taken as definitive, nor can any weights be suggested as each project will have different requirements. The construction of such a list will often be found to be a valuable exercise in itself.

2 Ensuring the availability and use of adequate material specifications.

All goods and material used in a project should be covered by an appropriate standard. If possible this should be an international (ISO) or national standard or written specially for the project. The importance of a comprehensive specification cannot be overstated. Materials or goods, even those which are apparently trivial, which are inadequate in design or quality when delivered on site can wreak havoc with the project completion time and with costs.

3 Purchasing at least total cost.

Wherever possible the supplier should be determined by competitive tender. While purchase price is important, other factors, such as those listed above, should also be taken into consideration. In some cases life-cycle costing should also be considered as an appropriate measure. A target price is often a useful criterion against which to judge the validity of a supplier's offer. A low price which is combined with, say, poor quality may well result in a high total cost. An unexpectedly low offer should be treated with extreme caution.

4 Vendor surveillance – ensuring delivery of goods or services at the right time.

Placing an order does not necessarily guarantee its satisfactory completion. Bitter experience insists that orders need to be chased (progressed). In some cases this may be done by letter or telephone, but where key items are concerned a visit to the supplier's plant is essential, a visit which must include a sight of the manufacturing floor. Experience says that promises made over the telephone tend to be optimistic. When a subcontractor is supplying heavy or complex items of plant it is vital to ensure that the process of its manufacture is carried out correctly (a key rule of quality control is 'get it right first time'). This is best done by a series of visits. If the procurement group is unable to undertake these then they should arrange for a competent specialist to do so.

5 Warning all concerned if delivery promises are not going to be met.

If the procurement group learns that any delivery date will not be met, then the project manager *must* be informed. It may be that the project plan requires that an apparently trivial item has to be available by a particular date, and failure to meet this date can have serious effects. On the other hand, early delivery of material should be discouraged. It may deteriorate in storage and can involve the company in payments earlier than had been planned.

6 Secure storage and accurate control of material.

Hardware projects depend on material and often that material is in short supply at the project location. It is important therefore that its storage should be secure, and that there is good documentation on issues and quantities of material available.

7 Organising all discussions with actual and potential suppliers.

It will often be found that designers, engineers and project planners need to have discussions with suppliers. It is wise for the appropriate procurement executive to arrange and usually to attend these meetings. Suppliers are very happy to make a 'contact' within a company avoiding the procurement group, hoping thereby to obtain a commitment to purchase a product. This commitment may not be in the long-term interest of the company. Less important, but considerably more irritating, 'contacts' are likely to be inundated by all the supplier's documentation and advertising. This is a nuisance in itself, but may also mean that the information is not sent or passed to the procurement office where it should be collated. Equally, it is foolish of the procurement group to have meetings with suppliers in the absence of the appropriate technical specialist.

8 Advising on prices.

In the feasibility stage of any project, prices for goods and services will be required without involving any suppliers. The procurement group should be best placed to advise on such prices.

9 Acting as a 'window on the world'.

Procurement brings continual contacts with outside organisations, and these can provide valuable channels whereby information on new products, materials, processes, services and equipment can be brought into the company and the information distributed to interested groups.

10 Post-project disposal of unrequired material and equipment.

At the completion of a project there are often items of equipment and material which are surplus to requirements. The disposal of these items must be conducted under strict control as many items will be 'useful' to persons outside the company.

CHAPTER 7

Projects and risk management

All work contains an element of risk in that it may not proceed according to plan. However, in most of industry, which is relatively stable and dealing with that which is knowable, risks tend to be small, known and accepted as part of the task of management. Projects, on the other hand, are concerned with change and, therefore, carry with them considerable uncertainty, and with uncertainty comes risk. If there is no uncertainty there is no risk. Project risks are consequently often novel, with little to guide the manager. Even where they *are* known the probabilities of occurrence are likely to be quite different from those which occur in 'normal' work situations.

Risk management includes the identification and assessment of risks together with the development of strategies to minimise them, and when they do occur, to mitigate any adverse effects or take advantage of beneficial ones. As a process it must be a key element in the formation of the project plan which must continue throughout the life of the project. No project plan will be realistic unless account is taken of that which could go wrong and contingency plans prepared to counteract them. This aspect of project management has been increasingly recognised as one of the most important features of the project manager's task in planning and controlling a project. The use of a project network, combined with any of the project management programs now available, allows the ready testing of alternative contingency plans. This is not possible with other planning methods.

UNCERTAINTY AND RISK

'There are two things in life which are certain, death and income tax.' Any other statement about that which is due to happen in the future must, by virtue of the uncertainty inevitable in a plan or forecast, be implicitly qualified by a statement of 'risk'. All projects are therefore 'risky' since they are planning for a future outcome. A project customer cannot be absolutely certain that the anticipated benefits from the project will be realised, no matter how successfully the project has been run. For instance, the market need may have changed for a commercial project designed to produce some new artifact. The customer is usually, therefore, the primary risk-taker, but the project manager also faces risks in the form of the inevitable uncertainty in the project processes and the project environment.

Reducing uncertainty reduces risk

For the project manager and the project team a risk is usually viewed as a hazard, something malign, which may adversely affect the project so that the achievement of the objective becomes more difficult, if not impossible, within the constraints of the project requirements. The project manager and the team should therefore take steps to identify, assess and manage all the risks inherent in the project as an integral part of the project management process. In the process of identifying and assessing risks it is possible that beneficial opportunities will also be identified, the process must be organised to take advantage of these, not just to react to identified hazards.

Risk in projects is not limited to accidents, technological failure or unsound commercial and managerial practices. Differing views of what constitutes risk to the project on the part of the project team, the parent company, the customer and other stakeholders forms a significant area of risk in itself for the project manager. For instance, a failure to identify the implied, as well as the stated, needs of the customer can lead to misunderstandings and even conflict, for which the project manager will not be prepared.

SOURCES OF RISK

Risk can arise from a number of aspects of a plan.

Timing

A statement (plan) which says that so-and-so will happen at a particular time is making a prediction which will always carry a degree of uncertainty. A task which is in the open air will be subject to weather conditions unless appropriate precautions are taken. One which is distant, or worse – overseas – from the organisation, will be subject to uncertainty in transport, communications and local politics.

All project activities are concerned with time. For the purposes of risk assessment and minimisation it is convenient to divide them into two categories: internally and externally timed activities.

Internally timed activities are those where the work is internal to the project, where the estimation of activity duration is made by the project team in conjunction with the task owner who will be *held responsible for carrying out the activity*. Clearly they will draw on various sources of information:

● past experience of similar work – the value of the project logs of previous projects can not be overstated here;

- the experience/knowledge/hunches of the task owner and of the project team(s) – good communications in the company are essential for this purpose;
- external sources – published papers, meetings of professional groups, specialist consultants – can sometimes provide useful information. It is not recorded how much information passes at professional meetings in the informal pre- and post-discussions. The authors suspect that these 'chats' are usually the most valuable part of many meetings.

Externally timed activities are those where some outside body sets the duration time – that is, those matters which are the responsibility of the procurement executive. Thus, good procurement techniques are essential. The procurement function does not begin and end with the placing of an order. Potential suppliers must be vetted to discover, as far as is possible, how reliable they are with regard to the quality and reliability of their product, the reliability of their delivery dates and the facilities for providing a good after-sales service. These matters are further discussed in Chapter 6 on projects and procurement. The order, having been placed, must be systematically monitored by telephone, letter and personal visits. Again, delivery performance must be recorded in the project log.

Technology

The newer the technology of a job the greater the uncertainty that it will be completed as planned. Even with well tried technology there is still an element of uncertainty, particularly if the application is novel. Where proven designs can be used, considerable uncertainty is removed, that which remains being due to poor performance. Again, where the work is being carried out by an external supplier, the procurement officer plays an important part by ensuring that an explicit and comprehensive specification for the work is provided. Clearly the supplier should have been thoroughly vetted before the placing of a contract, and competently inspected during its performance.

People

People carrying out any job must introduce an element of uncertainty based on their skill and experience. This uncertainty can be reduced by the following:

1 *Good training.* The first and second levels of the project team must be prepared to devote considerable time and effort to the training of the 'coal-face' staff. This is particularly true of a newly constituted team, and one employing indigenous labour in overseas projects.

2 *Clear definition of tasks.* Methods need to be clearly and simply communicated to those who have to carry them out, preferably in writing. A simple misunderstanding can lead to disaster. It is said that the tragedy of the 'Light Brigade' arose from a misunderstanding of a command to attack a part of the enemy.

3 *Good communications.* Where information has to be passed it is essential that it is done clearly and concisely. This is not a skill which comes easily to many people. It is a skill which has to be developed and then used. It is also a particularly difficult skill to acquire when the project is in a consortium involving several countries.

In addition, a project may suffer because of the degree of importance assigned to it by the parent company. Should it be deemed to be of little value there may be attempts to 'pass off' 'difficult' employees to the project.

Finance

The availability of adequate finance to both parties to the contract to complete the contract is a matter which should be thoroughly investigated by the parent company before the contract is signed, and as such is not a matter which concerns the project team. The financial stability of potential suppliers, however, is a matter which should be investigated by the procurement executive as the items in a capital project may require considerable investment on the part of the supplier.

Managerial

The parent organisation may not delegate the necessary authority to the project manager to deal effectively with the problems of cross-functional areas of the project, or may intervene in the management of the project in other ways.

Delegation involves trust. Some executives 'delegate' a task, then intervene because the delegatee is carrying out the task in a manner which is different to that which the delegator had imagined. They find difficulty in accepting that somebody else's way can be equally as good as their own.

Political

The internal politics of the parent organisation, as well as external national and international politics may have significant effects on the success or failure of a project. An assessment of the political situation within an overseas location should be sought from the Commercial Counsellor in the overseas embassy, or from the Foreign Office.

RISK ASSESSMENT

Since projects are always concerned with the introduction and management of change, the 'uncertainty' aspects of projects need to be carefully considered. This has led to the introduction of techniques for 'risk' assessment and 'risk' mitigation as a major part of project planning once the risks have been identified. Unfortunately there are two separate components to risk: that aspect which can be quantitatively assessed and that which is subjective assessment. In addition, in projects, there is the added complication of the perception of risk of both the project manager and the sponsor of the project. For each of them it will be coloured by past experience and their personal views of what constitutes risk in the present project and may well be at variance.

Until recently, risk assessment, if considered at all, concentrated on quantifiable risks using ever more sophisticated statistical analyses. Statistical analysis is usually based on past data to establish the underlying model. This then assumes that what happens tomorrow will be a continuation of the past, to establish a 'probability' for a risk occurring. The identified risks are then 'managed' or 'mitigated' by insurance, contingency factors, subcontracting, etc. The identified risks are in most cases those which are seen as hazards rather than the more general concept of uncertainty. Uncertainty can give rise to benefits as well as adverse effects and a full analysis should consider both. In many cases of projects failing to meet their objectives because of unforeseen event occurrence, the necessary information and knowledge were available within the project team but were not passed on or sought out by management. As stated earlier in the discussion on personnel, the provision of an environment in which people are encouraged to raise problems is a requirement for good project management. It is vital for good risk identification, assessment and management.

RISK IDENTIFICATION

The essential first step in risk management is the systematic identification of as many of the possible risks of problems occurring in the life of the project and of areas of uncertainty which may develop into risks. Only when this has been done can the risks be ranked in order of seriousness and plans prepared to mitigate or eliminate them.

Risk analysis should attempt to obtain answers to three fundamental questions:

1 What could go wrong?
2 How likely is it?
3 How will it affect the project?

The project team and others connected with the project can be encouraged to recognise the potential areas of risk and of beneficial effects by:

- brainstorming;
- using experience and lessons from past projects;
- using the project networks to model possible risk events.

The use of the networks to structure the analysis allows the team to concentrate both on the risks associated with particular activities and on the interfaces between functions, suppliers and other external factors where high levels of risk may also occur. It also reveals activities with considerable spare time (float) which may be useful in mitigating risk.

Technical risks are relatively easy to identify, can in most cases be quantified and usually relate to particular activities. In such cases, breaking the activity down into smaller segments for assessment may help to pinpoint the problem area and aid the mitigation procedures.

Once risks have been identified and listed as primary risks, each should be assessed for the nature and extent of the damage it could cause to the project if it occurs. These primary risks should then be quantified by assessing the probability of the problem occurring, and simply ranking them as 'high', 'medium' or 'low' will do much to indicate the size of the problem. More sophisticated techniques may be developed when it is necessary to be more accurate. Secondary risks arise because efforts to deal with the primary problem or undesired event, if it occurs, often creates further difficulties. These can sometimes be of greater magnitude than the primary risk and must not be overlooked in risk management.

Once quantified, some risks may turn out to be unacceptable to the customer or to the parent company, raising doubts about the viability of the project or, at least, some of the objectives. The risk assessment may also raise questions about the use of particular methods or technologies which must, of course, be answered before the project proceeds.

THE RESPONSE TO RISK

A plan for dealing with each identified risk should be part of the project plan. Risk analysis and management are central to the project manager's understanding of the project and the difficulties to be faced in achieving the agreed project objectives. If these difficulties are severe enough, one extreme response might be to modify the project objectives; another might be to find alternative methods or technologies or alternative ways of managing the project. Other less drastic solutions might be to increase management strengths in the project, to reduce the dependence of one technology or task on another, or to increase the flexibility and scope in the project plan for management intervention so that potential problems and obstacles to progress are avoided rather than being left to be dealt with when or if they occur. These responses are summarised in Table 7.1.

Risk management strategies should impact on every area of the project plan but are especially relevant to procurement and contract management.

Table 7.1 Response to risk

- Modify the project objectives
- Use alternative technologies or methods
- Use alternative ways of managing the project
- Increase managerial strength
- Reduce interdependency
- Increase resources
- Avoid obstacles by increasing flexibility

RISK MITIGATION

Risk mitigation can take a number of alternative forms:

1 *Risk transfer.* The transfer of the risk to someone who is more capable of dealing with the problem, e.g. a specialist subcontractor, or by passing the risk to someone who is paid to deal with it, for example an insurer.

2 *Risk deferral.* Risks can be deferred by moving the activities to a later date in the project when any adverse effects may be reduced. For example, it may be possible to move outside activities which are subject to weather problems to a different time in the year.

3 *Risk reduction.* This aims either to reduce the probability of the risk occurring or to reduce the adverse impact on the project if it does occur, or a combination of both. This is the main thrust of most risk assessments in projects.

4 *Risk acceptance.* Some risks have to be accepted. Once they have been identified and the adverse effects assessed, a reserve or contingency plan may be developed in case the risk occurs.

5 *Risk avoidance.* When risks have been identified they can in some cases be avoided, for instance by changes in design or methods, which may involve additional costs.

These methods of risk mitigation are summarised in Table 7.2.

Table 7.2 Risk mitigation

- Risk transfer
- Risk deferral
- Risk reduction
- Risk acceptance
- Risk avoidance

Subjective risks are harder to identify since they usually concern people and their interaction in the project, and, as such, are much more difficult to quantify. Subjective judgement of 'high', 'medium' or 'low' risk is normally all that is possible even when risks have been considered. All too often the risks which relate to people are included in the 'management of human resources' and ignored as risk factors. These 'soft issues' are discussed by A. Oldfield and M. Ocock in a paper presented at the INTERNET world congress at Oslo in 1994, in which they rightly point out that this therefore ignores a large element of risk analysis in projects. Their paper also includes a useful bibliography on risk analysis techniques for these soft issues and the managerial issues affecting risk in projects.

CHAPTER 8

Examining the project

Managing anything essentially requires information for decision making. For a project this means monitoring the project to discover:

- that which *has* happened;
- that which *is* happening;
- that which *should have* happened;
- that which *should be* happening.

Where differences occur, action must be taken to return the project to the plan together with the explicit incorporation of those measures which will take advantage of any beneficial differences. This totality of collecting information and taking action based on that information is what is meant by control rather than supervision or direction.

The monitoring of progress requires plans to have been prepared with those measures which will be used for assessing progress explicitly incorporated. These will include time, cost, resources and quality. Time is the base against which all progress has to be measured as any schedule must relate to time. However, in this case what is referred to is the actual timing of activities, *when* they are to be performed and how long they should take. The cost and resource schedules are derived from the activity schedule, although, because of constraints on the availability of resources or for cash flow considerations, they may also have had an effect on the scheduling of the activities. Quality is not a time-based measure; it will be assessed at pre-defined points in the project plan – usually at milestones, but also when required for individual activities.

TIME-RELATED PROCESSES

The time-related processes are basically concerned with the activities in the project plan. They include the determination of the logical interactions between activities and the estimation of their durations, and extend to the development of schedules and the control of activities. The schedules should identify the critical and near critical activities in the plan. They should define the *key events* in the plan – milestones – and a separate *key event schedule* should be produced and agreed with the customer. These key events may also indicate the times when part-payments are made. Chapters 12 and 13 discuss in detail time analysis and the preparation of schedules.

As the project proceeds the schedules will need to be updated to reflect the actual progress. This updating should be planned to occur at regular intervals throughout the life of the project. The frequency of these updates will be a function of the level of control required and this will in turn affect the level of detail in the plan. Thus, for example, if progress is to be assessed once every two weeks there is little point in having activity durations expressed in hours – even days may be too small a time unit. If many activities are started and completed between updates there is no possibility of exerting any control – it is only possible to influence the future, not the past. If this happens the control process often degenerates into a recording system. However, the information may be needed for the project log and may in turn affect future projects.

There must, of course, be a consistent unit of time used throughout the plan, although it is possible that subprojects may be planned and controlled, as projects in their own right, at a different level of detail using different time units but still reporting to the main project at the scheduled progress intervals.

COST-RELATED PROCESSES

The cost-related processes aim to complete the project within the financial budget and include both forecasting and managing costs. They require the estimation of costs of activities which will be based on man-hours, labour rates, materials, services, set-up charges, rental charges and overheads. The budget is based on those estimates, and forms the basis for the control of costs throughout the project. For many projects cost control is the principal means of project control and for a customer it is almost certainly the only means of control. Much more detail on costs and cost analysis is given in Chapter 10.

RESOURCE-RELATED PROCESSES

The resource-related processes aim to plan the use and control of resources. Resources as a term covers much more than the 'four Ms': men, money, machines and material. 'Resources' include anything that is required for carrying out an activity and which may, by its availability, constrain when the activity can be performed. For example, in many hardware projects working space can be so limited that activities, which have no logical sequential interaction, have to be scheduled sequentially so that space to carry out the work is available to each in turn.

Resource planning can vary from a simple summation (aggregation) of the requirements for a resource or resources in each period in an activity schedule to sophisticated computer-based systems for scheduling activities with time or resource constraints. Many projects are often severely hampered in this area for lack of the basic information on the future availability of resources to the project from the parent company, which has its normal business to carry out using those same resources. The problem is that the work in the normal business is unlikely to be planned with sufficient detail or accuracy to reveal when particular resources could be made available to a project without causing a disruption to the normal business schedule. Resource analysis and scheduling are discussed in Chapters 17 and 18.

Resource control is, of course, only applicable if a resource-based schedule has been produced. As will be discussed later, the activity schedule produced by the time analysis sets activities at their earliest start time since the only constraint being considered is that of the logical interactions. However, given that a schedule is available, the control procedures should monitor the usage of resources in the plan and report on any deviations from the plan so that corrective action can be taken and a report included in the project log to assist future planning. In particular, care should be taken to ensure that when resources alternative to those originally planned are used, as they often are for availability reasons, there will be no increase in time or costs or reduction in product quality.

PLANNING AND THE PROJECT DURATION

Plans to achieve an objective can be prepared in many different ways. The authors firmly believe that the use of network techniques as the model for any plan are the best tool a planner can have. This belief is based on a wealth of experience over the last three decades. A network sets out the sequence of activities and events in the plan in a clear and unambiguous way and enables much essential information on the plan to be derived from the activity data. It will form a statement of policy and a budget and is certainly a first-class communication tool. A policy is sometimes defined as the means whereby an objective is to be achieved, and in this sense a network can be assumed to be a formal and explicit statement of policy. This concept will be found quite useful when considering the amount of detail which should be displayed.

The work breakdown structure

As discussed in Chapter 4, the preparation of any plan requires that the logic of the plan be established, that is the *logical* sequence of activities and events which are needed to achieve the objective of the plan. In this, the division of work that is the preparation of a work breakdown structure (WBS) and the formation of a hierarchical set of network plans go hand in hand. A network showing the logical interactions of the tasks at each level should be prepared as the objective is decomposed level by level down to the point at which an individual can be allocated personal responsibility for managing the tasks. The WBS may be by physical grouping, by functional grouping, by cost centre or any other convenient decomposition of the product; no one way is necessarily the best, except in the context of the project being considered. In many cases more than one breakdown will be used.

The network of the tasks at the lowest level of the WBS will usually be capable of a further level of expansion to include the individual activities which make up the tasks at the previous level. Once the logical structure of the plan has been set down, at any level of the hierarchical set of networks the durations of the activities must be obtained and added to the network. It is quite usual to find that these durations have to be modified as more information is obtained at the next level down and is aggregated back up the levels, and that the estimated total project duration may also change and become too long.

Examination of the plan

As already stated, a network is a statement of policy. It is extremely rare for only one acceptable policy to be formulated; further, it is equally true that almost any policy can be improved. This is very clearly recognised by anyone in work study where the basic tenet of faith is 'there is always a better way'. It is unlikely that any plan to achieve anything is necessarily the 'best' way, and certainly it will not be the 'only' way – it is just the way that has been thought of this time.

This being so, it is desirable that when a plan has been drawn it should be very carefully and critically examined. In complex projects, the difficulty in examining all activities is so great that frequently no examination takes place at all, or alternatively only those activities in which the examiner has a particular interest are inspected. Project network techniques (PNTs) have the tremendous advantage that, by isolating the *critical* activities, i.e. those which determine the total project time, examination can be directed towards those areas that most significantly affect the overall time. In reducing the times of the initially critical areas, new critical paths may be created which, in turn, must be scrutinised.

It is the experience of both authors that, almost always, the total project time deduced from the first (relatively) complete plan is unacceptably long, so that it must be shortened to meet the objectives of the project. Clearly, the duration times of some activities on the critical path(s) must be reduced, but it is a fatal mistake to believe that simply altering durations will achieve the required reduction. Even if those responsible for carrying out the activities have agreed under pressure to the shortened durations, they are unlikely to be achieved unless additional resources are made available. Quite apart from the fact that resources cost money, those promised under pressure have an uncomfortable habit of disappearing or being committed elsewhere as the project proceeds. Should they not become available when needed, since the original duration was the *normal*, that is, the *usual* time for carrying out the activity, it is likely that it is the *original* time which is in fact achieved. Project time reduction by increasing some activity resource requirements should only be adopted when a full resource analysis is available.

REDUCING THE TOTAL PROJECT TIME

As with any other task, it is sensible to approach the problem of reducing the project time systematically. It is suggested that the process should take place in several stages. First activities on the critical path(s) should be subjected to the *questioning technique* to see if there is a quicker way to carry out an activity which does not involve an increase in resources or capital expenditure. One often finds that to the question 'Why that way?' the answer is 'That's the way we've always done it!' Alternatives are seldom considered unless the right questions are asked. Second, can the logic of the plan be changed or the project modified by overlapping or paralleling activities? This is a very potent way of reducing the total project time (TPT). Third, is it acceptably possible to increase the risks taken in the project? Fourth, if resource analysis is being undertaken, can any resources be moved or can any increase in costs for increasing resources be tolerated? As pointed out above there are dangers in this as increased costs/resources promised at the start of a project can vanish as the project proceeds. Table 8.1 summarises the type of questions to be asked when reducing the project time.

The questioning method

In order that the examination of the various activities will be consistently useful, it is desirable to employ the well-tried work study technique of systematic questioning. In this, a number of questions are set up, and these questions are asked of every activity. By asking the same questions in this apparently rigid way it is possible to ensure that a thorough examination is made of *all* alternatives. For a full discussion of this method, reference should be made to any one of the many textbooks on work study. The following should be considered only as an introduction to the method.

Activities can be considered to be of two kinds:

1 'do' activities, where time is consumed in a task which, in itself, advances the project; and

2 'ancillary' activities, where time is consumed in tasks which support 'do' activities.

For example, if a project involves the making of a component, the act of making is a 'do' activity, and the acts involved in setting up and breaking down the plant to carry out the making are 'ancillary' activities. Clearly, it is the 'do' activities which should be examined first, since if they can be reduced or eliminated, the 'ancillary' activities may either vanish or be reduced. (One of the authors recalls a project that involved an activity 'assemble refrigerated tank', along with its associated activities of 'place orders', 'obtain materials', 'test lagging,' and so on. Discussion had centred on the problem of reducing purchasing time, until the 'do' activity – 'assemble refrigerated tank' – was examined, when it was discovered that in fact this was an unnecessary activity, and with its elimination, the 'ancillary' activities disappeared.)

Once these 'do' items on the critical path have been identified, they can be tested against a series of questions, which are dealt with more fully in R.M.Currie's *Work Study*:

1 *Purpose*   What is being done?
              Why is it being done?
              What else could be done?
              What should be done?

2 *Place*   Where is it being done?
              Why there?
              Where else could it be done?
              Where should it be done?

3 *Sequence* When is it done?
              Why then?
              When else could it be done?
              When should it be done?

4 *Person*   Who does it?
              Why that person?
              Who else might do it?
              Who should do it?

5 *Means*   How is it done?
              Why that way?
              How else can it be done?
              How should it be done?

Should *these* questions, having been applied to the critical activities, not produce the desired result by changes in methods, then other approaches must be considered as follows.

Reduction by overlapping activities

A sequence of activities which follow each other immediately, as in Fig. 8.1, can sometimes be overlapped or paralleled as in Fig. 8.2, with a consequent reduction in total time. This overlapping is represented much more clearly in PNT as a time-based network than in the conventional bar chart where the interrelationships are not so obvious. This technique is discussed in Chapter 11 (AoA) and Chapter 12 (AoN), and Questions 25, 26 and 41 (on pp. 258) illustrate the method. It should be noted that the greater the degree of overlapping of activities which occurs in a project, the more difficult the managerial task of controlling those activities becomes since the interactions become more complex.

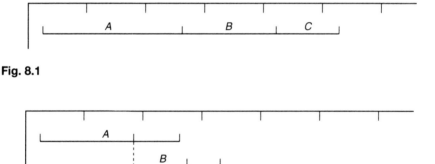

Fig. 8.1

Fig. 8.2

Reduction by increased risk

Can an activity be reduced by increasing the *risk*? For example, it may be that the initial network has in it a 'testing', 'checking' or 'proving' activity. Such activities can often be reduced, but with an increase in the risk of failure; thus, after drawings are completed, checking is often carried out, and if this is thorough then the checking time can be great – a substantial part of the drawing time. If this checking time is reduced, there is a greater chance that errors will slip through, with all the consequent undesirable results. To reduce this time, therefore, will increase the risk, and this decision must be squarely put to management for acceptance or rejection.

Reduction by the transference of resources

The non-critical activities in a network can sometimes be used to obtain resources that can be applied to critical activities to reduce their durations. This is sometimes known as 'trading off' resources.

Reduction by increased cost

All other methods having failed, a reduction in time may have to be obtained at an increased cost, usually by increasing the resources that are employed. If the costs to reduce times are known, then a table can be set up showing the relative costs for the reduction in time of each activity by a constant amount. The cost of reducing duration time by unit time may be defined as the 'cost-slope', thus for activity B in the example network in Chapters 13 and 14:

Normal duration time of 20 weeks costs £2000

Reduced duration time of 19 weeks costs £2200

hence the cost-slope = £200 per week.
For the example network the table of cost-slopes might be:

Activity	Duration	Float	Cost-slope (£/week)
A	16	8	300
B	20	0	200
C	30	21	100
D	15	0	450
E	10	9	1200
F	15	8	600
G	3	1	100
H	16	0	150
K	12	1	950

Clearly, of the critical activities (those with zero float), activity H has the smallest cost-slope, and it is desirable to investigate the practicability of reducing it first. These investigations may show not only that it can be reduced by one week, at an increased cost of £150, but that further reductions are readily obtainable. Inspection of the other activities which are due to be worked on at the same time (in parallel), however, shows that two activities (G and K) will become critical if activity H is reduced by one week and, in fact, two critical paths:

B–D–H and B–D–G–K

will be formed. This can be clearly seen if the network has been laid out on a time base as is discussed in Chapter 16. Thus, in order to further reduce total project time (TPT), *either* the common part of these two paths, that is B–D, must be reduced *or* the two branches, H and G–K, must be reduced simultaneously. Considering these alternatives, for the two branches the least cost is incurred by reducing activity G at £100/week *and* activity H at £150/week. This will produce an effective cost-slope of £250/week, which is greater than the cost-slope of reducing activity B at £200/week, so that it would probably be desirable to investigate the reduction of activity B first.

Dangers of the cost-slope concept

The concept of 'cost-slope' is appealing in its apparent simplicity. However, the following must be pointed out.

1 It is frequently extremely difficult to obtain reliable figures for the changes in cost resulting from changes in duration time. These difficulties are so great that in practice the cost-slope technique is unusable. The authors have never found any examples of the useful application of the technique.

2 The relationship between cost and time is not a simple one. Multiplying labour time by wage cost is obviously inaccurate and, moreover, to 'extend' the resultant labour cost by a constant overhead factor can be equally misleading since the reduction in time may be obtained, for example, by the hiring of special plant that has a non-linear hiring rate.

3 The technique assumes that *all* resources are freely convertible to cost and are freely available. This is not true: some resources may already be at their limit of availability or not included in the costing, for instance space.

These difficulties make it dangerous to try and deduce general *time–cost* curves, or, to put it another way, to assume that cost-slopes are constant. For short time intervals this assumption can be reasonable, but it is desirable to examine it very closely. All this, of course, is true whether PNTs are used or not, but employing PNTs has the great advantage that investigations can be directed to the critical activities.

Effect of *increasing* duration times

Just as it is possible to reduce duration times by increasing costs, so it may be possible to reduce costs by increasing times. For example, an activity C as planned has a duration of 30 weeks and a float of 21 weeks. Examination of C may show that its duration time could be extended to, say, 40 weeks, while at the same time reducing the cost. Such a reduction in cost would not change the overall project time, but the savings might help to offset the increased costs of shrinking other activity durations.

By means of this sort of approach, the overall project time *can* be reduced and total costs minimised. In a simple project no great problems will arise, but in larger or complex projects the number of alternatives to be considered escalates very rapidly and a 'what-if' approach using a computer will be needed. This rapidly becomes very tedious in practice.

The relationship between time and the labour employed

As noted above, durations cannot be reduced indefinitely by increasing resources. For example, in digging a hole it may well be that two men can carry out the work in less than half the time one man can carry it out, since work can be efficiently divided. However, three men may not show the same reduction in performance time, and a fourth man may well slow up

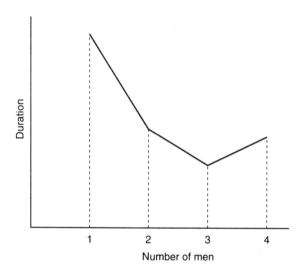

Fig. 8.3

the work since his physical presence may impede the other workers (*see* Fig. 8.3). There is thus a minimum time below which it is not possible to reduce the duration time of the activity using the same methods.

THE FINAL NETWORK

The final network, after a reduction process has been carried out, may well be considerably different from the initial network. The logic may have changed, duration times altered and new critical paths created. Illogicalities may have been introduced, and it is worth retesting the network by checking every activity once more against the two questions:

1 What had to be done before this?

2 What can be done now?

Check especially at any 'cross-roads' situations to ensure that *all* emerging activities do depend on *all* entering activities.

Once a project is under way with an acceptable TPT it will be found that, unless a comprehensive resource schedule has been prepared – and even then it can still happen – on many occasions the resources required to carry out the activities at their scheduled times are not available and that the activities have to be delayed. While delays can be tolerated on some activities without extending the TPT, for those that are critical any delay affects the TPT by at least the amount of the delay. If the network plans are being properly used by the project team they will have recognised which areas of the project may have problems of this nature and will have prepared additional contingency plans to further shorten the TPT if, or when, the problems occur.

It should be noted that in the absence of a resource schedule the TPT reduction should always be pursued to the point where it is significantly shorter than the time to the project due date. *Project durations always extend!*

As will be discussed later in Chapters 17 and 18, if a full resource schedule has been produced a different situation exists. What may appear to be free movement, which would apparently allow the delay of an activity in the schedule, may not in fact exist since the resource required by an activity may well be committed for use elsewhere at that time in the schedule.

As a general rule, it is always best to gain time early on in the life of any project. There is more opportunity then for alternative approaches – the degree of freedom diminishes as the project proceeds – and it will certainly be cheaper than trying to gain the same amount of time later in the project.

Table 8.1 Questions to be asked when reducing the project time

- Purpose?
- Place?
- Sequence?
- Person?
- Means?
- Overlapping?
- Risk?
- 'Trade-off'?
- Cost?

CHAPTER 9

Controlling time

Any industrial control system appears to have six essential features:

1 A plan must be made.

2 This plan must be published.

3 Once working, the activity being controlled must be measured.

4 The measurements must then be compared with the plan.

5 Any deviations must be reported to the appropriate person.

6 A forecast of the results of any deviations must then be made, and corrective actions taken to cause the activity to continue in a way that will produce the original desired result, or, if this is not possible, a new plan must be made.

The above six features appear to be general to any organisational control system including project control. Project network techniques (PNTs) satisfy completely these needs of a control system. On the other hand, a bar chart plan is made and published, performance is compared with the plan and deviations reported. However, it is often extremely difficult, if not impossible, to forecast the results of the deviations and take appropriate corrective actions whose effects, in the short term can be forecast, but whose long-term effects are unknowable. This supreme difficulty arises from the inability of the bar chart to show interrelationships clearly, if at all.

Looking at PNT it will be seen that inherently it contains the first two basic features, planning and publishing, most adequately. In many tasks it is the only possible planning technique available, and its use as a means of communication has already been commented upon; it is an excellent means of publishing a plan. As with a bar chart, measurements are taken and deviations reported. The power of PNT lies in its ability readily to forecast the effects, both short term *and* long term of any corrective action which is proposed.

MEASUREMENT OF ACTIVITIES

There are, again, a number of general features of control measurements that have emerged from other control situations which appear to apply when setting out to control a project. These are as follows.

1 *The measurement should be appropriately precise.* Any measurement can be increased in precision by an increase in the cost of making the measurement. PNT indicates very clearly which activities need to be precisely measured (those on the critical path) and those which do not need such a high precision (those which can tolerate delays). For example, in a project in which the durations are measured in weeks, activities which are critical might need to be monitored to the nearest day, whereas for an activity which can tolerate considerable delay the nearest week will probably be adequate and to increase the precision would be needlessly expensive.

2 *The measurements should be pertinent.* This is quite self-evident, yet the files of industry bulge with data that have been collected and never used. It is essential to question the use that will or can be made of the data.

3 *The speed of collection of the information must be rapid compared with the time-cycle of the system as a whole.* In a project lasting two years, collecting information and processing it every two weeks is probably adequate, since it will allow corrective action to be taken. No general rule can be laid down here, but it must be remembered that, as a project progresses, the time remaining for completion diminishes and, hence, the speed of collection may need to increase. Thus it is quite usual, at the outset of a long project, to receive reports once a month but, as time advances, to reduce the reporting interval to two weekly, later to once a week and eventually it may become daily. The essential thing to remember is that measurement must be taken frequently enough to allow useful action to be taken. Collecting progress information is both difficult and expensive.

4 *Measurements need to be accurate or of consistent inaccuracy.* As with the degree of precision, so with accuracy; accuracy can be bought with increased cost. It is frequently cheaper to accept a measuring technique which is known to be inaccurate but consistent than to attempt to obtain a very high accuracy. Consistent inaccuracies can be allowed for; high accuracy inevitably results in increased cost. Here again, PNT indicates where a high accuracy measurement should be made and where a low accuracy measurement is tolerable. Thus, for an activity which can tolerate little delay, an accuracy of ± 10 per cent is required, while for an activity which can tolerate considerable delay, an accuracy of ± 50 per cent could be acceptable in the early stages of a project. (*Note:* Although

accuracy and precision are related, they are quite separate concepts, and should not be confused.)

5 *The number of data processing points should be kept as small as possible.* Once a measurement is made, it should be passed through as few processing departments as possible. Not only will handling delay the using of the information, but it will inevitably cause distortions that are very difficult to eliminate.

The monitoring and analysis of project data should enable the project manager to address problems at an early stage and also to take advantage of opportunities which may benefit the project. The aim should always be to pre-empt situations and prevent problems occurring rather than responding once they have developed. Good communications throughout the project system will ensure that the project team and those carrying out activities are working with the same information and that they are aware of the project status, so that when potential problems occur they are quickly dealt with.

COMPARING AND REPORTING

Some of the ways in which this can be carried out are given below. While it is possible to devise many other methods, it is sensible to avoid letting the ingenuity of the method become an end in itself. The authors have observed many clever techniques in which the mechanics of the method have obscured the results. *The simplest method is always the best.*

1 *The bar chart/network itself.* As work progresses, the bar chart/network itself can be marked in some way to indicate that work has been done, although this tends to be unsatisfactory since the location of an activity on the drawing is not related to the time when it should be performed unless the network has been translated onto a time base in bar format, as is discussed in Chapter 16. This can be a very useful manual control tool for small projects. Modern computer software for project management often has the ability to display and print out a bar chart in various arrangements. Some also use plotters to draw the network and can usually present it on a time base.

2 *Re-analysis.* In large or very complex projects it becomes difficult to present the situation graphically in a way that enables the complete picture to be seen. This is particularly difficult with a bar chart, but PNT here demonstrates its inestimable value. By taking the original network and inserting into it the *actual* times instead of the expected duration times, it is simple to re-analyse the network and see the effects of the actual work. Care is needed with activities which have been delayed past their calculated latest start time, and a new delay activity will need to be incorporated to account for this. Another alternative, which obviates the need for delay activities, is to redraw the network, leaving out all those activities which are complete and using the time remaining for those in progress, and then re-analysing in the normal way, substituting the actual date for the date of the new first event. This will have the effect of gradually collapsing the network from the left, and in large networks a progressive simplification will result. Some computer systems will do this by assuming that when durations are set to zero the activities – other than dummies in AoA – are completed, and will re-analyse the network as of 'time-now'; this has the same effect.

3 *Negative float.* If the network is large or complex, another alternative is to fix the end date of the project as a scheduled date, insert the actual durations for activities and re-analyse the network. This is a technique which is not applicable to the bar chart. Any activities which are running late will appear with negative float, which shows up the amount by which they are late and where corrective action must be taken. This matter is discussed in detail in later chapters.

The computer is of particular value in 'updating' PNT networks since it is happy to carry out repeated calculations. (*Note:* In any form of the analyses discussed above, it is essential in the AoN technique to modify not only the duration times but also all the affected dependency times.) Single and multiple dependency times in AoN networks are discussed in Chapter 15.

One continually recurring problem in 'updating' project plans is the difficulty of obtaining useful statements from the operating points where work is being performed. It is impossible to give simple solutions to what is a very complex problem. Two things can be said:

1 Avoid recrimination. If an activity overruns, be careful not to use this as an opportunity to create a fuss. The past is dead – take steps to *avoid* a recurrence of whatever failed. A respected networker once referred to PNT as a 'do-it-yourself hangman's kit'. Let PNT be a tool to assist, not a weapon to assault.

2 Progress should be reported in the form 'not complete' or 'complete'. Thus to the question: 'Is activity X complete?' the response should be either 'Yes' or 'No' and if 'No' then a second question: 'How much time is required to complete activity X?' should be asked. Statements such as: 'Nearly finished', 'Almost finished', 'Just a little to do', 'It'll soon be done!' and so on should be eschewed. They both inculcate a sloppiness of mind and an avoidance of responsibility.

The authors have found that, when using PNT, a useful way of progressing work is by employing the latest start times and latest finish times derived from the analysis of the network. Thus it is possible by scanning the analysis to determine for a number of weeks into the immediate future which activities 'must' be started and which activities 'must' be finished. At progress meetings it is then possible to identify exactly which activities must have been started by the date of the meeting and which must have been finished. This sorting of activities into 'must start' and 'must finish' categories is very easily carried out by the computer.

FORECASTING AND TAKING CORRECTIVE ACTION

When performance does not conform with plan, and it is necessary to take corrective action, it must be clearly understood that while PNT indicates very clearly where problems are likely to occur, PNT does not remove any responsibility from the manager concerned; indeed, by causing areas of authority to be clearly distinguished, it reinforces and emphasises the manager's position. PNT is neither a prophylactic nor a panacea, and any failures to achieve an agreed plan must not be laid at the door of PNT; they will rest, as always, with the manager.

This having been said, it must be pointed out that PNT has a particular use in this field, namely that it will enable predictions of resultant actions to be deduced from present or past action. This, in other than small or very simple situations, is virtually impossible with a bar chart. For example, any 'slip' in a critical activity will result in the whole project 'slipping'. To correct this it may be possible to transfer resources from other non-critical activities, and the consequent effects of this can be clearly seen by considering the network, or by reprocessing the data if a computer is being used. This predictive value of PNT is probably unique among planning systems, and certainly is of great value in real-life situations in testing alternative solutions to problems.

A forecasting example using PNT

Consider a network with a planned TPT of 1000 days. Four hundred days after the project start it is found that the planned network time – that is to say, the time derived from the network at the start of the project – for the activities actually completed is 350 days. What is the best estimate for the time to completion?

To merely rerun the network, inserting the actual times for the completed activities while using the existing planned times for the uncompleted activities, assumes that there will be a significant change in performance . . . all new activities after day 400 will be performed to their planned time while those completed before day 400 took $400/350 \times 100$ per cent longer than planned.

It is reasonable to assume that unless there is a *guaranteed* change in project performance after day 400, then:

Current estimated time to complete	$= (1000-350) \times 400/350 =$	743 days
Current estimated TPT	$= 400 + 743$	$= 1143$ days
Current time slip	$= 350 - 400$	$= -50$ days
Total current estimated time slip	$= 1000 - 1143$	$= -143$ days
Current schedule performance index	$= 350/400$	$= 0.875$

These parameters can form the basis for managerial control and decision-making. Is a slip of 143 days acceptable? What penalty will be incurred if this takes place? How much can be expended to avoid such a slip?

The above can be generalised as follows:

Let:

Actual time for work performed be	ATWP
Planned time for work performed be	PTWP
Planned TPT	PTPT

Then:

Time slip	$=$ PTWP – ATWP
Current schedule performance index (SPI)	$=$ PTWP/ATWP
Planned time to complete (PTC)	$=$ PTPT – PTWP
Estimated time to complete (ETC)	$=$ PTC/SPI
Estimated total project time	$=$ ATWP + PTC/SPI

A useful presentation of performance against plan is obtained by plotting *planned* time against *actual* time as in Fig. 9.1. In an ideal world, *actual* would coincide with *planned* performance, giving the 45 degree straight line OP. In practice this rarely happens and the line OP divides the space into two: the upper *fast* sector and the lower *slow* sector. Plots such as the (400,350) point indicate a project which is running slower than planned. If it is decided that there is an acceptable level of departure from plan – say 20 per cent – then control limits can be included on the graph showing the acceptable boundary. In Fig. 9.1 both overrun and underrun limits have been shown, though it must be said that it is outside either author's experience for an underrun to occur except in the case of projects with a considerable bonus opportunity.

OTHER CONTROL SYSTEMS

The discussion here has considered project progressing in isolation as a means of control. In practice the data used in, and the information derived

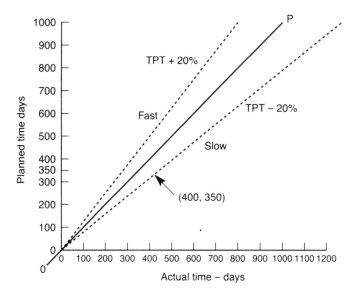

Fig. 9.1

from, project progressing should be integrated with all the other systems which contribute to the project planning and control process. The time taken to perform an activity is of interest not only to the project team but also to the costing department, the wages department, the material control section, and so on. Failure to co-ordinate the work of various departments will lead to duplication and dissipation of effort, and will also prevent those cross-checkings that can do so much to make up for other inadequacies. Not only this – a number of imperfect systems acting in parallel can often produce a total accuracy, which one highly perfected system cannot attain, and this can enable economies to be made that do not result in any degrading of information. It is therefore highly desirable that project progressing is used *as a control technique* as well as a planning technique, and that its work here should be integrated as closely as possible with all other management controls.

The other control systems with which the project progress system interacts and with which it must be integrated will include:

- financial control
- progress control
- change control
- configuration control
- document control
- quality control
- resource control

- procurement
- risk management
- personnel management.

As discussed in Chapter 4 the integration of all these control and management systems is provided by the project plan which is in effect, and fact, the project bible. The parent company will in most cases have all or most of these systems as part of the company management systems, but as again noted in Chapter 4, they may need to be adapted for the project purposes. Any such adaptations must of course be agreed with the managers of the company systems since they will always have to interact.

CHAPTER 10

Controlling cash

Many projects justify the setting up of semi-automonous project teams to manage and execute the projects. In these cases it must be remembered that there will probably be two cost control systems operating side by side. The first is the costing system that all organisations must provide to satisfy the requirements of their financial auditors. This collects and uses data on a historical basis, is totally accurate, as it must be for company and tax purposes, has no predictive element and it normally presents results far too late to be of use to the project manager as a control tool.

The second system is that set up by the project team to collect and use cost data for its own purposes. The essential aspect of such systems is speed of response. This is of far more importance than accuracy – within 5 per cent is quite good enough for most purposes.

In this chapter it has been assumed that network or bar chart techniques will be used to plan and control the project. However, some of the discussion, for example the use of 'hammock' activities, is applicable only to network techniques and saves much work relative to the use of other procedures to collect and use information.

CONTROL DURING THE LIFE OF A PROJECT

Cost control *during the life of a project* is probably of greater importance than the control of any other resource. A cost overrun will result in, at best, a reduction in profit, or at worst bankruptcy, unless it is a 'cost-reimbursable plus a percentage fee' project, and here the client is likely to investigate the cash control and recording systems very thoroughly indeed. The procedures exercised by an organisation will clearly be influenced by the type of contract being carried out. In a 'cost-plus' contract the emphasis will be on controlling costs rather than reducing them, considerable attention being paid to comprehensive recording. A 'fixed-price' or internal project will merit a great deal of interest being shown in both the accurate estimation of costs and in choosing methods which keep those costs as low as possible. Given acceptable alternatives the cheapest will always be chosen.

It should be noted that costs can occur in a number of ways in a project and that the availability of 'money' can equally be expressed in a number of alternative ways. The cost of an activity may be purely labour plus overheads; it may also be plus materials as a cost spread throughout the duration of the activity, or as a lump sum at the start of, or at some stage through, the activity. The first two will probably require the use of hammocks to collect the relevant information; the third, depending on the system, may require alternative input as a special resource.

Chapter 9 suggests that control systems have six features:

1 plan;

2 publish;

3 measure;

4 compare;

5 report;

6 forecast and correct.

In relation to cost control, 'earned value analysis' has replaced traditional performance analysis methods that compare the actual cost incurred to a given date with the budgeted or planned expenditure to that date. Earned value analysis should introduce a measure of the project achievements for the costs incurred and can be used with other techniques to identify and correct problems. The basis of earned value analysis is a continuous comparison of actual project data with the plan to determine the work done and correct adverse variations.

Therefore the plan which is published is the budgeted cost analysis of the project, the monitoring system measures and compares, while control is exerted by action taken on the reports to provide forecasts which enable corrective action to be taken. The need for accuracy and speed of action discussed on page 68 is as valid in cost control as in any other type of control system. The present chapter discusses how a project budget may be created, how monitoring is set up and how data collected by the monitoring system may be used within the earned value concept.

BUDGET PREPARATION

Data collection

Much of management is concerned with the control of situations where work is stable enough for forecasts to be derived from past experience of similar work. Project management, which is essentially 'one-off' management, is concerned with novel situations where the data must be derived from estimates of work new to the organisation. These estimates are therefore usually prepared from a more detailed breakdown of the project than may be usual in a traditional budgeting system.

It is often easier to derive realistic estimates for small parcels of work – activities – than for groups of activities forming a subproject. In setting up a project the time data – activity durations – will have been obtained as a matter of course and it is useful to extract resource data at the same time. Indeed, in some cases it is easier to derive a duration time from a knowledge of the work content of the activity and of the likely availability of the required resources, though it must be remembered that subsequent resource analysis and allocation may cause these resource availabilities to change with possible effects on activity duration times. Cost data is then deduced from the resource and time data.

The work breakdown structure

Both when extracting and controlling costs the project should be divided into clearly defined and manageable parts (work packages) for each of which responsibility for execution must be clearly defined. The definition of a work package will include all relevant information on labour, equipment, material and overhead rates. The activity list is then ordered into these work packages to give the work breakdown structure (WBS). It is this which is used as the basis both of the budget preparation and the subsequent cost control. In a functionally organised company, groupings will tend to be functionally orientated, while in a project organised company they will tend to be by subproject. The difficulty of preparing the WBS, which tends to be industry specific, should never be underestimated.

Cost centre codes

Each activity in a work package will be given a cost centre code unique to that package. Within a package there may be subgroup codes, just as the package cost code may itself be a subgroup to a higher level cost centre code. The organisation of these cost centre codes is crucially important to the success of the cost control system. It is essential that the code element at any level should be unequivocally the responsibility of a single person, and that it should be possible in the reporting system to identify all the elements with the persons responsible for them. The larger the project the more carefully the coding system must be organised since, as all costs must eventually be aggregated for management reports, the search procedures needed may overload the computing system.

The company's organisational structure will have a significant effect on the coding system. A company new to project management may have an existing system which is inappropriate to project cost control, and it is unwise to try to force such a system on to the project management team.

It should be noted that there is some disagreement in the literature on the order in which the various aspects of the procedure are tackled. Some writers suggest that the activity lists and work breakdown structure are prepared before drawing the network/bar chart, while others suggest the reverse, namely that the network/bar chart is prepared first. While there can be no firm recommendation on this the authors are of the opinion that the network/bar chart *should* come first. However, it is very much a matter of 'doing what comes naturally' in an organisation and the truth probably lies between the two extremes, modifications to whatever is done first arising from that which follows. None the less, whatever the procedure, the result is the same, namely:

- a network/bar chart endorsed with the costs associated with each activity;

- a code defining the cost centre to which each activity is assigned;

- a statement of the name of each person responsible for the control of each activity cost, this control probably being exercised by the actual control of the activity.

Indirect expenses – the use of hammocks

All the costs so far discussed are *direct* costs, that is they are assignable directly to activities. There are always other costs which are not so assignable, and which must be spread over a number of activities – the *overhead costs*. PNT allows overheads to be spread over cost centres, and the reader is referred to pages 77 and 105 for a discussion on this matter.

THE BUDGETING SYSTEM

Once the data produced above is available, the next stage, generating the project budgets, can proceed. It is generally assumed that for any activity the spend rate with respect to time is constant. Thus, if an activity has a duration of 3 time units and requires a total expenditure of £15 000, each time unit will be assumed to consume £5000. While this may not be true, consequent inaccuracies are likely to be trivial compared with the inaccuracies caused by estimation errors! Should significant errors result in the final budget, these may be reduced by breaking the activities into smaller portions until the 'constant spend rate' assumption becomes acceptable. The build-up of the budget then proceeds by cost centre, subproject or any other grouping desired, up to the total project budget.

This procedure is normally carried out by setting the network/bar chart at a defined time condition, usually with all activities at 'earliest start' unless a specific schedule, such as a resource allocated one, has been produced, when the scheduled times are used. Costs are then aggregated (summed) for all activities in each time interval throughout the life of the project. Aggregation can be by cost codes within cost centres and a variety of reports are possible for each level in the organisation. Where required, the figures at each level can be displayed as tabulations or graphs.

It should be remembered that not all cost generating tasks will necessarily have been included in the network/bar chart. For example, many activities consume materials, the ordering of which may be one or many tasks and which may not have been included in the network/bar chart. In addition, the way in which the costs of materials are allocated to the project must be regularised. There are normally three possibilities in the way the costs can be allocated to the project. These are when material is:

1 ordered;

2 received into the organisation;

3 deployed on the project.

Conservative accounting will commit the cost to the project at the time the order is placed so that the charge on the budget can be seen as early as possible. The project activity costing system may well allocate these same costs to the individual activities so that there will be a discrepancy between the project spend curve and that generated from the company's accounting system. Once the reason for such differences is known, they need cause no difficulties. Some project costing systems maintain three sets of figures:

1 the budget;

2 committed costs;

3 actual costs.

The 'actual' and 'committed' costs should ultimately agree as the materials are consumed by the project.

The mechanism whereby all project cost data are collected is a 'charge' or 'booking' number, which should agree with the code taken from the WBS. Whenever hours are worked, materials used or services paid for, the appropriate costs *must* be booked against the 'charge' number. Two potent sources of error occur here:

1 The charge number does not agree with the WBS code. Translation must then take place with all the consequent potential for mistakes to be made.

2 Legitimate charges are not booked to the charge number.

In relation to the second source of error it should be realised that there is a deeply ingrained reluctance to provide feedback on both performance and costs, particularly if either appear unfavourable. It is important to convince all concerned that the *accurate* and *timely* completion of all documentation is not just a bureaucratic whim serving no useful purpose, but a means to the satisfactory completion of the project. (*See also* 'Improving the data' below and Chapter 20 'Some practical considerations'.)

A well organised system will arrange for all the:

- time sheets;
- purchase orders;
- invoices;
- stores issue notes;
- goods received notes;
- etc.

to be forwarded to a central collection office where they are loaded with overheads and any other charges to the project. This is a complex operation since, for example, labour hours have to be converted into pay, pensions, holiday pay, bonuses if paid, and so on. The charge to the project will include not only the above but also appropriate overhead recovery.

BUDGETED AND ACTUAL COSTS

Every control system involves the comparison between that which is and that which should be – the error. In budgetary and cost control the error, which is the difference between the budgeted cost and the committed cost, is known as the *variance*:

> **Budgeted cost – Committed cost = Variance**

The variance is one error which can be considered, although it requires careful analysis since the simple conclusion that 'positive variance means unconsumed budget, negative variance means cost overrun' may be misleading. Consider the following report;

Account B345

	Budget	Commitment	Variance
	£20 000	£16 250	+£3750

Only if all work on B345 has been completed does the positive variance suggest a highly desirable situation, namely that the budget has been well underspent. However, the variance could have arisen from three alternatives:

1 good control;

2 some outgoing not recorded;

3 some activity/material costs overestimated.

Either of the last two can, of course, have serious commercial consequences particularly for future tenders.

If, however, the work is only partly completed, then all that is certain is that £3750 remains with which to complete the work. If the proportion of the work to be done equates with the proportion of the budget remaining then the situation is not yet disastrous.

If the variance is negative, then some action is necessary. Thus, consider the following report:

Account B345

Budget	Commitment	Variance
£20 000	£23 750	–£3750

This is a serious enough situation even if all the work on B345 has been completed. This negative variance could again have arisen from three alternatives:

1 poor control;

2 extra unbudgeted work was included;

3 some activity costs were underestimated.

All of these could have very serious commercial consequences, both immediately and in the future.

In neither of the above cases is there enough information to determine what, if anything, was wrong, or what action to take, a most undesirable situation. What is required is a statement which brings together both the budget and the progress of the project.

IMPROVING THE DATA

In an attempt to overcome at least some of these disadvantages additional data should be required. Instead of merely using progress reports, reports on the percentage remaining for the activity are needed. For instance, the following data is reported:

Account B345

Budget	Commitment	% of activity remaining
£20 000	£14 500	50%

Simple arithmetic reveals that for 50 per cent of the activity £20 000 × 0.5 = £10 000 should have been committed; in fact £14 500 has been committed, a negative variance of £4500. This reveals rather more than before:

- the activity is half completed and overspent;
- if the remaining work is completed to budget the total overspend will be £4500;
- to complete the project within budget means saving £4500 on this or some other activity.

The additional information is useful but still not enough, as it has not actually revealed *why* the budget has been exceeded. As noted on page 80 there is a reluctance to provide information at any time and particularly when it is unfavourable. In this case it is not unknown for managers to work the information backwards and claim an increased percentage completed. This practice conceals the problem until it is too late for action to be taken, and, what is worse, some managers compound the problem by reporting diminishing progress with time. This merely ensures that it will definitely be too late for action.

The best way of dealing with the data to ensure accuracy of knowledge is to integrate the time reporting aspects of the network and the cost collection system of the WBS, bringing together progress and costs. It should be noted that the dual meaning of *actual* costs – committed/collected – can cause confusion. For example, materials may have been ordered and thus a commitment incurred but no actual payment has yet been made with a charge against the project, i.e. 'collected', but the system may well report this as an 'actual' cost. However, the terminology is common usage, so that any possible confusion needs to be resolved within an organisation at the outset of each project.

COST AND SCHEDULE VARIANCES

For any instant in the life of a project there should be the following information available:

1 the known cumulative budgeted cost of work performed, 'the budgeted cost of work performed' – BCWP;

2 the known cumulative actual cost of work performed, 'the actual cost of work performed' – ACWP;

3 the total budgeted cost of the scheduled activities, 'the budgeted cost of work scheduled' – BCWS.

These three parameters yield two useful variances which give an indication to management of the magnitude, location and reasons for current and future problems:

- the schedule variance (in cost terms)   = BCWP – BCWS
- the cost variance   = BCWP – ACWP

Considered together these two variances yield a lot of useful information about the project. For example:

- a negative schedule variance with zero cost variance suggests a project running late with no over-spend;
- a negative cost variance with zero schedule variance suggests a project on time with an overspend;
- a negative schedule variance with a negative cost variance suggests a project running late which is also overspent.

If the data is plotted as shown in Fig. 10.1 it can be very revealing as it will display:

- the planned costs – the BCWS curve;
- the incurred costs – the ACWP curve;
- the budgeted (earned) value of the work actually performed – the BCWP curve.

Used in combination with the WBS, it can also be used to track down *where* in the project the variance comes from and *who* is responsible. In projects of any size a computer-based system is essential. It must be remembered that while the project team is collecting, analysing and using the project cost information, the organisation, of which the project team is a part, will also be collecting the same information. However, it is likely to be collecting it more slowly than the project team, and analysing it in a different way using different conventions, so that its output is likely to be of limited value for project control purposes.

It should be noted that the BCWS curve shown is the 'baseline' for the account for which the data has been generated – it may be for a single activity, a work package, the project or even a group of projects. In practice this baseline is not fixed, as it changes each time a modification is made to the project plan. These changes may be design or engineering changes but may also be because people have a bad habit of adding in work as the project proceeds which was not included at the original planning stage. The total cost to completion *may* be unaltered – though that is unlikely – but the shape of the curve *will* change. What is, however, essential is to keep track of all changes and to incorporate them into the baseline if there is to be any hope of maintaining control of the project.

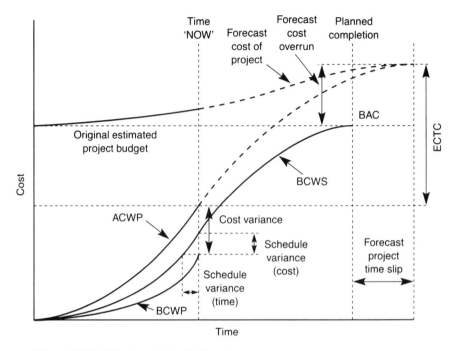

Where ECTC is Estimated Cost To Complete
BAC   is Budget At Completion (Current)
BCWS is Budgeted Cost of Work Scheduled (Current)
BCWP is Budgeted Cost of Work Performed (Earned Value)
ACWP is Actual Cost of Work Performed

Fig. 10.1

In all except small internal projects – and even there it is desirable – a formal system for recording and incorporating change *must* be set up. This system must record:

● the authorisation for the change, together with the date at which it will be incorporated;
● the budget change involved;
● the reasons for the change.

The objective of the system is to ensure that the baseline, against which all control measures are derived, is at all times as accurate as is possible.

As an illustration of the calculation and use of these parameters, consider Project B79, which for simplicity is assumed to have 10 work packages with the following data.

Work package	A	B	C	D	E	F	G	H	J	K
Completion time	t_1	t_2	t_3	t_4	t_5	t_6	t_7	t_8	t_9	t_{10}
Budgeted cost '£'	50	50	100	150	150	150	150	120	60	50

At time t_6 it is reported that the situation is as follows:

Work package	A	B	C	D	E	F
Per cent complete	100	100	100	100	60	40
Actual cost (£)	60	80	120	160	100	100

At time t_6 it is easy to see that:

The budgeted cost of work scheduled (BCWS)
$$= £(50 + 50 + 100 + 150 + 150 + 150) \qquad = £650$$

The budgeted cost of work performed (BCWP)
$$= £(50 + 50 + 100 + 150 + (0.6 \times 150) + (0.4 \times 150)) = £500$$

The actual cost of work performed (ACWP)
$$= £(60 + 80 + 120 + 160 + 100 + 100) \qquad = £620$$

From this:

- the schedule variance (in cost terms) $\quad$ = BCWP – BCWS
  $$= 500 - 650 \qquad\qquad = -150$$
- and the cost variance $\qquad\qquad\qquad$ = BCWP – ACWP
  $$= 500 - 620 \qquad\qquad = -120$$

Since both of these are negative it is apparent that the project is running late and is overspent.

A full tabulation of the data for Project B79 throughout its life is given in Table 10.1 and presented in Fig. 10.2. The plot assumes that no changes occur to the basic BCWS curve.

VARIANCE ANALYSIS

To explore a variance more thoroughly it may be broken down into a set of sub-budget variances, a technique known as *variance analysis*. For example, estimates of expenditure are made up from:

- labour costs;
- material costs;
- overhead costs.

Variances for each of these can be prepared as in Fig. 10.3.

Table 10.1 Life of Project B79

Work Package	t1		t2		t3		t4		t5		t6		t7		t8		t9		t10		t11	
	%	£	%	£	%	£	%	£	%	£	%	£	%	£	%	£	%	£	%	£	%	£
A	90	50	100	60	100	60	100	60	100	60	100	60	100	60	100	60	100	60	100	60	100	60
B			75	70	85	75	100	80	100	80	100	80	100	80	100	80	100	80	100	80	100	80
C					65	75	100	120	100	120	100	120	100	120	100	120	100	120	100	120	100	120
D							90	150	100	160	100	160	100	160	100	160	100	160	100	160	100	160
E									0	0	60	100	80	150	100	200	100	200	100	200	100	200
F											40	100	75	150	85	180	100	210	100	210	100	210
G													60	100	80	200	100	250	100	250	100	250
H															50	100	75	150	100	200	100	200
J																	60	50	100	100	100	100
K																			50	100	100	100
BCWS	50		100		200		350		500		650		800		920		980		1030		1030	
BCWP	45		87.5		167.5		335		350		500		672.5		819.5		926		1005		1030	
ACWP	50		130		210		410		420		620		820		1100		1280		1480		1580	

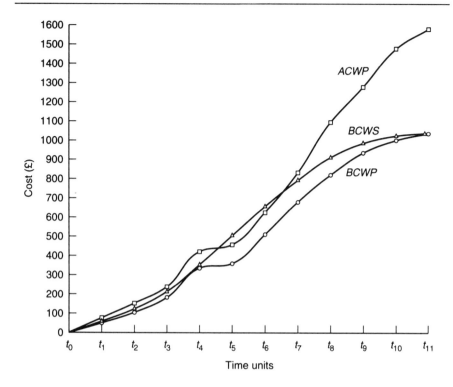

Fig. 10.2

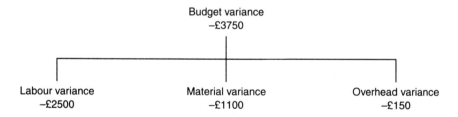

Fig. 10.3

This immediately indicates where the main problem is, namely in an overspend on labour costs. The labour variance may itself be split into:

- labour hours variance;
- labour rates variance.

Either or both of these can be split further if required, as can the material and overhead variances. The budget itself may have been changed during the course of the project and a budget revision variance may also be appropriate. In this way a complex triangle of variances can be built up.

While variance analysis is an invaluable technique which enables investigation to be focused on trouble areas, care must be taken to carry the analysis no further than is useful. It is tempting to erect a highly detailed triangle displaying every possible sub-variance but this may well clutter up the information system. It is better to start small and enlarge only when it seems useful. Experience is the best guide here.

FORECASTING

Reports on performance indices and variances are required at all levels in the management system, those at any one level being built up from those at lower levels. It must be appreciated that both favourable and unfavourable reports will flow upwards and that these may apparently 'cancel' themselves out and not appear in the higher level report. It is important therefore that reports should be framed in such a way that no masking of unfavourable information takes place so that appropriate investigations can be made. Equally, it is important, in motivational terms, that achievement and favourable variances should be recognised and rewarded.

The project team may be asked at any time to forecast the time and cost to completion of the project. In particular, when unfavourable performance indices and variances are being consistently reported, top management will need to decide on whether to proceed, to refinance or to cancel the project. Unfortunately there can be no wholly mathematical techniques which can guarantee a reliable forecast. Mathematical techniques assume that the future will behave in a manner determined by the past, but if there have been external influences which were not allowed for in the original plan, the past may be a very poor guide to the future. A forecast therefore should be based on the best mathematical analysis but modified by managerial judgement.

The time to completion is of course obtained by carrying out a new analysis of the network, the result of which is modified in the light of the best available information derived from the performance index to date. (*See also* Chapter 9 on forecasting.) The cost to completion is not obtained so directly. Two expressions, one involving the budget at completion (BAC), are of assistance here:

- Cost performance index to date (CPI) = BCWP/ACWP
- Budgeted cost to completion (BCC)   = BAC – BCWP

Then:

- Estimated cost to complete (ECC)   = BCC/CPI
- Forecast cost at completion (FCC)   = ACWP + ECC

This forecast can be built up at all levels of the budgeting system and will include all individual cost accounts which have been opened. Thus the forecast will take into account all activities and cost accounts which have been started with a factor based on the performance to date from the cost performance index. It cannot be emphasised too strongly that all forecasts *must* be modified in the light of any information currently to hand and which was not available at the start of the project. In particular, as much use as possible should be made of graphical displays since any trends can be seen at an early stage and corrective action taken.

For example, continuing the analysis of Project B79 at time t_6:

The cost performance index (CPI) $= BCWP/ACWP = 500/620$
$= 0.81$

The schedule performance index (SPI) $= BCWP/BCWS = 500/650$
$= 0.77$

Both of these being less than 1.0 indicates a poorer performance than planned in each case.

Based on these figures the estimated total cost of the project will be :

Budgeted cost to complete (BCC) $= BAC - BCWP = 1030 - 500$
$= £530$

Estimated cost to complete (ECC) $= BCC/CPI \quad = 530/0.81$
$= £654$

Forecast cost at completion (FCC) $= ACWP + ECC = 620 + 654$
$= £1274$

and the estimated project duration will be $= 10/0.77 = 12$ time periods.

In practice the total cost of the project turns out to be £1580 and the actual duration 11 time periods.

The interested reader may care to calculate the measures at stages through the life of the project from the full tabulation of the data for Project B79 which is given in Table 10.1 and presented in Fig. 10.2. The plot assumes that no changes occur to the basic BCWS curve.

COMPARING PROJECTS

Within any organisation there is often a requirement to compare the performance on several projects, and, as these may be of different sizes, simple financial or time statements may not be appropriate. In such cases, it is useful to extract two non-dimensional performance indices:

- Cost performance index (CPI)   = BCWP/ACWP
- Schedule performance index (SPI) = BCWP/BCWS

A performance index greater than 1 represents a better than planned performance, an index equal to 1 indicates an 'on-time' or 'on-cost' performance, while one less than 1 represents a performance poorer than planned. For instance, Table 10.2 shows three projects for which data on time and cost performance are compared, where:

Table 10.2 Project comparison

Project	Time			Cost		
	SPI	FTC	PTC	CPI	FCC	BCC
4836	0.78	34	26	0.68	4.1	3.7
4837	0.96	25	24	0.98	2.01	2.0
4838	0.46	62	50	0.51	13.5	10.0
4839						
4840						
4841						
etc.						

SPI = Schedule performance index   = BCWP/BCWS
                            or = PTWP/ATWP
PTC = Planned time to complete   = PTPT – PTWP
FTC = Forecast time to complete   = PTC/SPI

CPI = Cost performance index   = BCWP/ACWP
FCC = Forecast cost at completion = ACWP + ECC
BCC = Budgeted cost to completion = BAC – BCWP

From these figures it can be easily seen that all the projects are running late and over budget. Although project 4837 is apparently close to being in control it would also be useful to know the percentage completion of each of the projects. In a full managerial report this and other information would of course be provided.

THE TIME VALUE OF MONEY

The value of money depends upon its availability, £1 available *now* being worth more than £1 available *later*, since the 'present' money can earn some return.

Present value

Assume that £1 is available now, and that it can be immediately invested to produce an annual income of 10 per cent. The £1 would grow as follows:

		Value (£)
Now, beginning of year 1	1	1
End of year 1	$1 + 1 \times 0.10$	1.1
End of year 2	$1.1 + 1.1 \times 0.10$	1.21
End of year 3	$1.21 + 1.21 \times 0.10$	1.331
End of year 4	$1.331 + 1.331 \times 0.10$	1.464
End of year n	$1(1 = 0.10)^n$	

It is thus possible to say that £1.464 in four years' time at an earning rate of 10 per cent has a *present value (PV)* of £1, or that £1 in four years' time at an earnings rate of 10 per cent has a present value of $1/1.464 = £0.683$.

Tables of PV factors are readily available for a variety of circumstances (invested immediately, or invested each month and so on). Alternatively pocket calculators with built-in programs can be easily and cheaply obtained.

Projects may have both cash outflows (expenditures) and inflows (payments); the *net present value (NPV)* is the sum of *all* cash flows. By comparing the NPV of competing projects it is possible to appraise the values of the various projects to the organisation.

Discounting

An alternative way of appraising projects is to *discount* the cash flows, discounting being the inverse of compounding. Any project will generate a series of in- and outflows of cash. It is possible to discover the earnings rate that allows the PV of the inflows and outflows to balance. This rate is the *internal rate of return (IRR)*, the *time adjusted return* or the *project rate of return (PRR)*. Discovering this rate allows competing projects to be compared, the most desirable project having the highest rate of return.

The technique is probably best illustrated by an example which, for the purpose of clarity, is greatly simplified. A project has the following characteristics: annual costs are committed at the beginning of each year, and these are the only costs during the year.

Cost at the beginning of year:	*Value (£)*
1	2 500
2	3 000
3	6 500
4	4 500
5	4 000
	Total £20 500

It is anticipated that when the project is completed at the end of year 5 it will generate an income of £32000. What would be the PRR?

The PRR is calculated by a trial and error procedure:

Earnings rate 15 per cent:

	Cash flow (£)	PV factor	PV (£)
Beginning of year 1	2500	1	2500
Beginning of year 2 (after 1 year)	3000	0.870	2610
Beginning of year 3 (after 2 years)	6500	0.756	4914
Beginning of year 4 (after 3 years)	4500	0.658	2961
Beginning of year 5 (after 4 years)	4000	0.572	2288
		NPV	£15273

A cash inflow of £32000 after five years has an NPV of £32000 × 0.497 = £15904.

Earnings rate 20 per cent:

	Cash flow (£)	PV factor	PV (£)
Beginning of year 1	2500	1	2500
Beginning of year 2 (after 1 year)	3000	0.833	2499
Beginning of year 3 (after 2 years)	6500	0.694	4511
Beginning of year 4 (after 3 years)	4500	0.579	2605
Beginning of year 5 (after 4 years)	4000	0.482	1928
		NPV	£14043

A cash inflow of £32000 after five years has an NPV of £32000 × 0.402 = £12864

Earnings rate 25 per cent:

	Cash flow (£)	PV factor	PV (£)
Beginning of year 1	2500	1	2500
Beginning of year 2 (after 1 year)	3000	0.800	2400
Beginning of year 3 (after 2 years)	6500	0.640	4160
Beginning of year 4 (after 3 years)	4500	0.512	2304
Beginning of year 5 (after 4 years)	4000	0.410	1928
		NPV	£13004

A cash inflow of £32000 after five years has an NPV of £32000 × 0.328 = £19496.

Given these three sets of figures it is possible to sketch (Fig. 10.4) the NPVs of the in- and outflows at various discount factors, the intersection

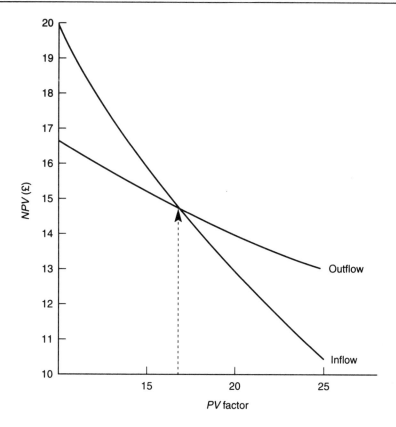

Fig. 10.4 *NPVs* of cash inflows and outflows of various *PV* factors.

of the two curves indicating the balancing point and hence the PRR of, effectively, 17 per cent. Alternatively a series of 'homing-in' calculations can be carried out. Clearly, attempts at high accuracy are time-consuming and unnecessary.

This value is then used for comparison with other competing projects.

Appraising not costing

It must be emphasised that the above techniques and their variants are methods of judging the desirability of alternative projects – *they do not form the basis of any costing system.*

The application of network techniques

It is quite impossible to list all the applications of networks since the technique is now used extremely widely. However, to give some idea of the 'spread', the following is a brief summary of where PNT has been used to plan and control the use of time, materials and other resources, of which the authors or their colleagues have personal knowledge. It must be emphasised that this list is not exhaustive: new applications are continually being found.

1 *Overhaul:* plant, equipment, vehicles and buildings, both on a routine and an emergency basis.

2 *Construction:* houses, flats and offices, including all pre-contract, tendering and design work.

3 *Civil engineering:* motorways, roads, bridges, road programmes, including all pre-contract, tendering and design work.

4 *Town planning:* control of tendering and design procedures and subsequent building and installation of services.

5 *Marketing:* market research, product launching and the setting up and running of advertising campaigns.

6 *Shipbuilding:* the design and building of ships.

7 *Design:* the design of cars, machine tools, guided weapons, computers, electronic equipment, aero engines and aircraft.

8 *Pre-production:* control of production of jigs, fixtures, tools and test equipment.

9 *Product changeover:* the changing over from one product or family of products to another, for example 'winter' to 'summer' goods.

10 *Commissioning and/or installation:* power generation equipment of all types, and data processing plant.

11 *Modification programmes:* the modification of existing plant, equipment or retail shops.

12 *Office procedures:* investigations into existing administrative practices (for example the preparation of monthly accounts) and the devising and installation of a new system.

13 *Consultancy:* the setting up and control of consultancy assignments.

14 *Plant layout:* the layout or re-layout of production or other facilities, including service systems.

15 *Emergency planning:* preparation of contingency plans to deal with all types of emergency situations.

BS 6046 Part 1 also gives a list of areas of applications of network techniques together with an indication of the use of the techniques in those areas.

CHAPTER 11

Drawing the activity-on-arrow network

As already stated, in the activity-on-arrow (AoA) system, more generally known as critical path analysis (CPA) or program evaluation and review technique (PERT), a project is represented by an *arrow diagram*.

ELEMENTS OF AN ACTIVITY-ON-ARROW DIAGRAM

The diagram is made up of two basic elements:

1 *An activity*, which is an element of the work entailed in the project. In some instances the 'work' is not real in the sense that neither energy nor money is consumed, and in some cases (*see* dummy activities below) no time is used. However, ignoring these last cases, an activity is a task that must be carried out. Thus 'waiting for delivery of component X' is an activity, just as much as 'making component Y', since both are tasks which must be carried out. This 'non-work' aspect of some activities is sometimes found difficult to accept until the test of *needfulness to the project* is applied. Once this test is applied it is clear that 'waiting for delivery' is an activity in the sense in which the word is used in drawing networks.

2 *An event*, which is the start and/or finish of an activity or group of activities. The essential criterion is that a definite, unambiguous point in time can be isolated – a broad band of availability is of no use. The word 'event' may be misleading here, since there may in fact be a concurrence of a number of separate events, and for this reason some authorities prefer the terms 'node', 'junction', 'milestone' or 'stage'. In general 'milestone' is reserved for particularly significant events that require special monitoring. 'Node' is possibly the most generally used term when referring to the network diagram and will be used subsequently for this purpose, while 'event' will be used when time is concerned with the same point. It must be remembered that a 'node' in AoA has a different significance to a 'node' in activity-on-node (AoN).

CONVENTIONS ADOPTED IN DRAWING AoA NETWORKS

There are only two conventions usually adopted in drawing networks and, like all conventions, they may be ignored if circumstances warrant. In the early stages of network drawing, it is suggested that the conventions be respected until sufficient experience has been gained to warrant dropping them. The conventions are:

- *Time flows from left to right.*
- *Head nodes always have a number higher than that of the tail node.*

This allows activities to be referred to simply and succinctly by their tail and head numbers, so that 'activity 3–4' means only 'the activity that starts from node 3 and proceeds to node 4'; it *cannot* mean 'the activity that starts from node 4 and finishes at node 3'. Most modern computer programs do not require this convention to be followed since they can accept randomly numbered and alphanumeric labels, but experience has shown that it is nevertheless a useful one, particularly for newcomers to the technique. It will also be found to sound better. Since alphanumeric identifiers are often used, it is better to refer to 'node or event *labels*' rather than 'node or event *numbers*'.

For beginners, it may be convenient to remark here that it is not necessary for all numbers to be in sequence, that is numbers need not follow each other in natural order. In fact it is sometimes useful, when labelling events, to leave gaps in the normal sequence or use only odd or even numbers so that, if it is necessary to modify a drawing, it is not also necessary to relabel all nodes – a tedious task. No inconvenience will be found to result from this, and it is the practice of one of the authors to initially label the nodes using only multiples of five. It is useful to realise that the head and tail labels of the activities effectively specify the logic of the diagram, and that from a list of head and tail labels the network can be constructed.

The graphical representation of events and activities in AoA

Nodes are represented by labels within convenient geometric shapes – usually circles. Activities are represented by arrows, the arrow-heads being at the completion of the activities. The length and orientation of the arrow are of no significance whatsoever, being chosen only for convenience of drawing. The activity of digging a hole can equally well be represented by Figs 11.1 and 11.2.

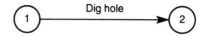

Fig. 11.1

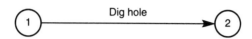

Fig. 11.2

These both have, within an arrow diagram, precisely the same significance, namely that to proceed from event 1 to event 2 it is necessary to carry out activity 1–2. It is equally not essential that arrows should be straight, although it will be found that the appearance of the whole diagram will be improved if the main portion of each arrow is both straight and parallel to the main axis of the paper on which the diagram is drawn. This will often require that arrows are 'bent', as in Figs 11.3 to 11.5. The description of the activity should always be written upon the straight portion of the arrow.

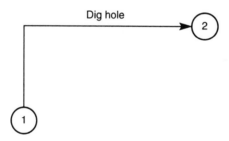

Fig. 11.3

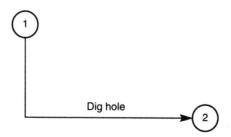

Fig. 11.4

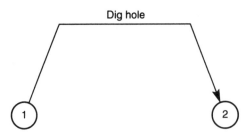

Fig. 11.5

It is strongly recommended that wherever possible this method of drawing should be adopted. There is often a temptation to substitute a code letter for an activity description when drawing a network. This should never be done as it makes the checking of the network extremely difficult if not impossible. It also destroys the 'communicating' ability of the network.

The representation of time

The expected time that will be required to carry out an activity (the duration time) is written as a central subscript to the activity. Thus, if it is anticipated that it will require six days to dig a hole the activity would be as shown in Fig. 11.6. It should be noted that *more* than 6 days might be *available* for digging. This matter will be dealt with later in Chapter 14.

Fig. 11.6

If an activity must, for some reason external to the network, be completed by a given date, then an inverted triangle can be drawn above the node at the head of the activity arrow. For example, if the digging of the hole must be completed by day 20, then the diagram would be as shown in Fig. 11.7.

Fig. 11.7

Identification of activities

The node at the beginning of an activity is known as a 'tail' or 'preceding' node, while that at the conclusion of an activity is known as a 'head' or 'succeeding' node. Some writers refer to tail and head nodes as *i* and *j* nodes, this deriving from the generalisation of an activity as in Fig. 11.8.

Fig. 11.8

This usage is extremely convenient when drawing up tables, where the single letters *i* and *j* are simpler to use that the words 'preceding' and 'succeeding', which are recommended in BS 4335:1987, or 'tail' and 'head'.

Fundamental properties of events and activities

Basically, the representation of nodes and activities is governed by one, simple, *dependency rule* which requires that an activity which depends upon another activity is shown to emerge from the head of the activity upon which it depends, and that *only* dependent activities are drawn in this way. Thus, if activity B depends upon activity A, then the two activities are drawn as in Fig. 11.9, while if activity C is also dependent upon activity A, but is *not* dependent on activity B, then the three activities are drawn as in Fig. 11.10.

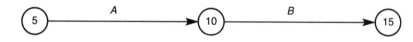

Fig. 11.9

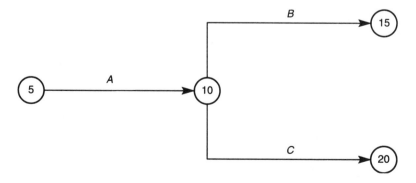

Fig. 11.10

This dependency rule gives rise to two fundamental properties of events and activities:

1 *An event cannot be said to be realised (or 'be reached' or 'occur') until all activities leading into it are complete.* For example, in a network such as Fig. 11.11, event 10 can only be said to occur when activities 3–10, 4–10 and 5–10 are all complete.

2 *No activity can start until its tail event is realised.* Thus, in Fig. 11.12 activity 10–11 cannot start until event 10 is realised.

These two statements can effectively be combined into a single comment, namely that 'all activities entering a node *must* be complete *before* any leaving it can start.' It must be understood, however, that this single statement has two facets as set out in points 1 and 2 above.

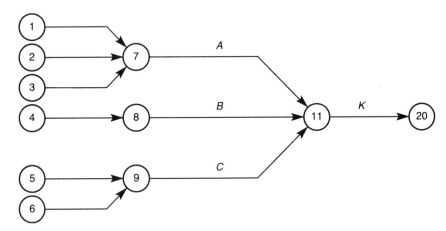

Fig. 11.11

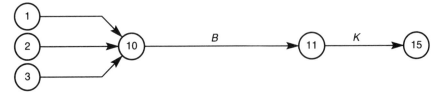

Fig. 11.12

'Merge' and 'burst' nodes

Events into which a number of activities enter and one (or several) leave (*see* Fig. 11.10) are known as 'merge' nodes. Events that have one (or several) entering activities generating a number of emerging activities are known as 'burst' nodes (*see* Fig. 11.13).

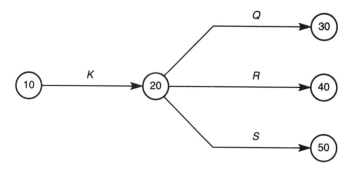

Fig. 11.13

Two errors in logic

Two errors in logic may come about when drawing a network, particularly if it is a complicated one. These are known as *looping* and *dangling*.

Looping

Consideration will show that the loop in Fig. 11.14 must not occur since this would represent an impossible situation: 'activity R depends on activity Q which depends on activity P which depends on activity R which depends on activity Q . . .' If looping like this appears to arise, the logic underlying the diagram must be at fault, and the construction of the diagram must be re-examined. Adherence to the convention that no activity can start until its tail event is realised reveals the existence of a loop very easily.

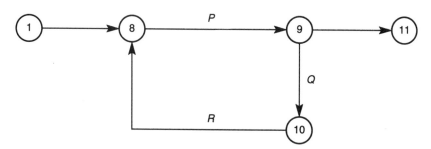

Fig. 11.14

Dangling

Similarly, the situation represented by Fig. 11.15 is equally at fault, since the activity represented by the dangling arrow 9 – 11 is undertaken with no result. Such arrows often result from hastily inserted afterthoughts. Two rules can be enunciated which, if followed, will avoid dangling arrows, namely: 'all nodes, except the first and the last, must have at least one activity entering and one activity leaving them' and 'all activities must start and finish with a node'. There are special occasions when 'dangling' activities can be accepted but any appearance of a 'dangle' should be very carefully considered to ensure that it does not arise from an error in logic or an inadequate understanding of the task being considered. (*See also* 'Multiple starts and finishes' below.)

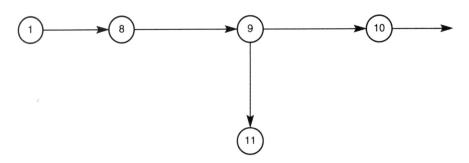

Fig. 11.15

When set out in isolated form as above, both errors are quite obvious. However, in a complex network these errors (particularly looping) can arise; a loop, for example, can form over a very long chain of activities. Before finalising a network it is wise to examine for both the above logical errors. If the network is being processed by computer, the computer program itself will have built in diagnostic checks for these and other errors, and will produce appropriate reports, if errors exist, before further calculations are undertaken.

Interfacing

If an event is common to two or more subnetworks it is said to be an 'interface' event and is represented by a pair of concentric circles in place of the usual single circle.

Milestones

These are events which have been identified as being of particular importance in the progress of the project, and are identified in the diagram by an inverted triangle over the event node. There may also be an imposed time for the event to occur.

Multiple starts and finishes

Most modern computer programs do not require networks to have a single start or finish node. However, those that allow multiple starts or finishes require that all start or finish nodes are suitably identified (usually as given in the program manual) or they report a start or finish 'dangler' as discussed above. In carrying out the time calculations it is assumed that, unless otherwise specified, all the start events can occur at the start of the project and all finish events will occur at the end of the project.

Hammock activities

Where a network is to be used for cost control, it is extremely useful to introduce into it *hammock* activities. It is simplest to assign to activities the *direct* costs, that is costs which are directly assignable to the activity, for example materials. There are always other costs which are not so assignable, and which must be spread over a number of activities, the *overhead* costs. The burden of these costs are borne by artificial hammock activities which are inserted into the network. A hammock will embrace activities which are linked and belong to the same cost centre. Hammocks are assigned no duration time and play no part in the time analysis. During cost analyses a hammock is assumed to have a duration determined by the time elapsing between the start of the first hammocked activity and the point at which measurement is being made, which may be 'time now' or the end of the activities concerned. The overhead rate is assumed to be constant over the life of the hammock.

DUMMY ACTIVITIES

In some cases it is necessary to draw 'dummy' activities, that is activities which do not require resources but may in some cases take time. They are drawn as broken or dotted arrows as in Fig. 11.16.

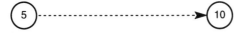

Fig. 11.16

A dummy activity *is always subject to the basic dependency rule* that an activity emerging from the head node of another activity depends on that activity.

There are three occasions when dummies are used:

1 identity dummies;

2 logic dummies;

3 transit time dummies.

Identity dummies

When two or more parallel independent activities have the same head and tail nodes, the identity of the activities, as given by the node numbers, could be lost. For example, if in making a cup of instant coffee two activities 'boil water' and 'heat milk' could proceed simultaneously, then the diagram shown in Fig. 11.17 might appear. This would result in two activities having the same head and tail numbers.

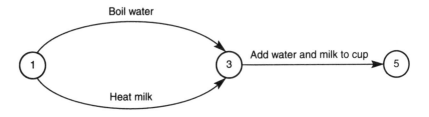

Fig. 11.17

Although some computer programs will accept this situation, but require the addition to the activities of uniqueness identifiers, it is preferable to avoid confusion by the introduction of a dummy which can be either activity 1–2 (Fig. 11.18) or activity 2–3 (Fig. 11.19).

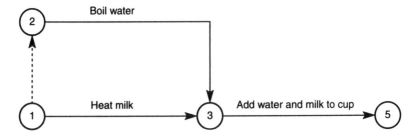

Fig. 11.18

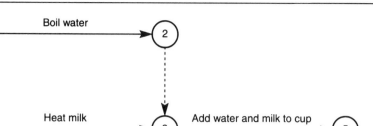

Fig. 11.19

Note: In Fig. 11.18 the 'Boil water' activity has been opened to accept the dummy. The other activity could equally well have been chosen, giving four possible diagrams. Which activity is in fact broken is a matter of indifference, though it is usual to insert the dummy at the head of the activity with the shorter duration.

Logic dummies

When two chains of activities have a common node yet they are in themselves wholly or partly independent of each other, then an error in logic could unwittingly arise. Consider the situation:

Activity K depends on activity A.   (1)
Activity L depends on activities A and B.   (2)

At first sight the diagram might appear to be as shown in Fig. 11.20. Unfortunately an error is displayed in this diagram. Activity L is, quite correctly, shown to be dependent on activities A and B. However, activity K is also shown to be dependent on both activities, whereas it depends only on activity A. To resolve this a new activity (a dummy) is introduced to separate K from B (Fig. 11.21).

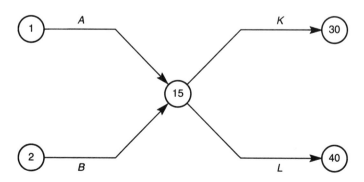

Fig. 11.20

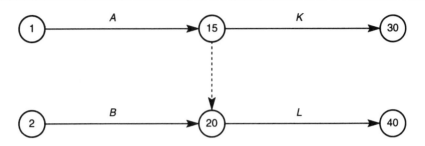

Fig. 11.21

Examining Fig. 11.21 it will be seen that:

K depends on A.
K does not depend on the dummy.

Hence K depends only on A. (1)

L depends on B.
L *does* depend on the dummy.
The dummy depends on A.

Hence L depends on A and B. (2)

(1) and (2) are the situations which the diagram is required to represent.
It must be noted that multiple dummies may be necessary to maintain logic. For example, the situation:

Activity K depends on activity A
Activity L depends on activities A and B
Activity M depends on activity B

is represented by the diagram given in Fig. 11.22

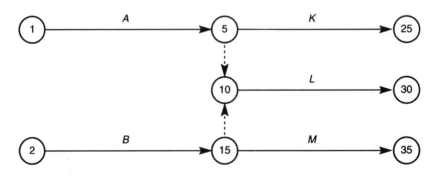

Fig. 11.22

Helpful hint

It is highly desirable to examine any 'crossroads' (Fig. 11.23) that arise in the drawing of a network to ensure that the dependence of activities upon one another is quite clearly understood and represented. This is not to say that 'crossroads' may not occur, but that the logic which is displayed must be very carefully scrutinised.

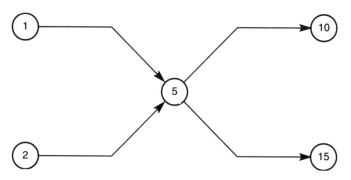

Fig. 11.23

The direction of dummies

Trouble is often encountered in assigning a direction to a dummy activity. If the purpose of the dummy is quite clearly understood, then the direction of the dummy becomes clearer. Thus if, in Fig. 11.21, the dummy exists to release activity K from activity B then the dummy emerges from the tail node of activity K; on the other hand, if activity K depended on activities A and B and activity L depended only on activity B and *not* on activities A and B, the general configuration would remain unaltered except that the dummy arrow-head would point the other way, i.e. from node 20 to node 15. Reference should be made to an earlier discussion on 'Fundamental properties of events and activities' (page 101), and it should be clearly understood that the situation shown in Fig. 11.24 represents activity X being dependent on both activity R and activity S, while Fig. 11.25 represents activity X being dependent only on activity R and *independent* of activity S.

The authors have found it useful to consider the dummy as a 'one-way dependency street' – dependency can flow from the tail of the dummy to its head, it *cannot* flow from its head to its tail.

Transit time dummies

On many occasions a delay must occur after the completion of an activity before the activity which is dependent on it can start. In Fig. 11.21 activities

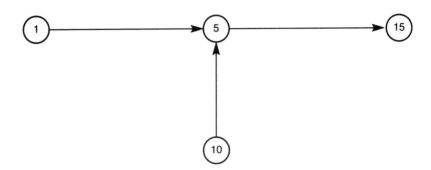

Fig. 11.24

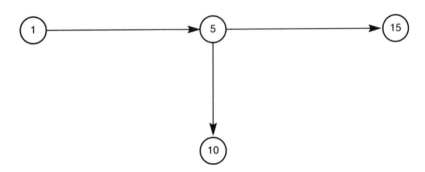

Fig. 11.25

K and L are dependent on activity A and it may be a requirement that a specified time must elapse between the end of A and the start of L. In such a case the dummy shown would carry a duration which is known as a 'transit time'. This transit time is the minimum time which *must* elapse between the ending of the activity and the start of an activity dependent on it.

OVERLAPPING ACTIVITIES

In all that has been said so far, it has been assumed that activities are quite discrete, the start of a succeeding activity being delayed until a previous activity is complete. For example, if a large number of plants are to be lifted in a large garden and relocated some distance away, it might be thought that the diagram would be as in Fig. 11.26.

However, this would indicate that *no* plant can be relocated until *all* plants were lifted. This may not in fact be so; it may well be that relocation can start when some of the plants have been lifted, and that thereafter the relocation of the plants can go on while the lifting proceeds. The relocation

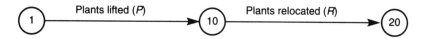

Fig. 11.26

will eventually be completed after all the plants have been lifted and moved. This can be represented by breaking both activities into two portions P1, P2 and R1, R2, as in Fig. 11.27.

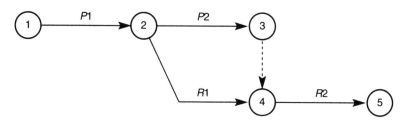

Fig. 11.27

This diagram shows that it is not possible to start Activity R until some of Activity P is completed. The dummy activity 3–4 allows the parallel activities 2–3 and 2–4 to be identified. Once lifting (P) and relocation (R) are under way it may be considered desirable to rake the soil (S) around the newly moved plants. If this activity can proceed concurrently with activities P and R, then this can be represented by 'breaking' R1 into two parts R1/1 and R1/2, thus permitting S to start part way through R1 (Fig. 11.28).

Alternatively, it may be decided that S1 cannot start until the *whole* of R1 is completed and a first attempt at a diagram might be as in Fig. 11.29.

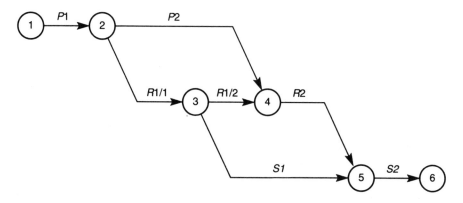

Fig. 11.28

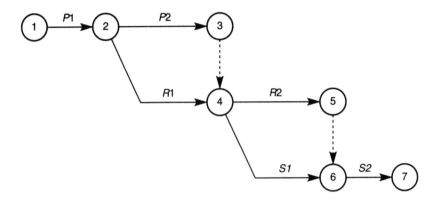

Fig. 11.29

However, Fig. 11.29 shows S1 depending on P2 through the dummy activity 3–4. If this is not so and S1 can start with R1 complete and P2 incomplete, then a dummy between the junction of R1 and S1 and the junction of activity 3–4 and 2 will release the dependency. It will also remove the necessity for dummies 3–4 and 5–6 (Fig. 11.30).

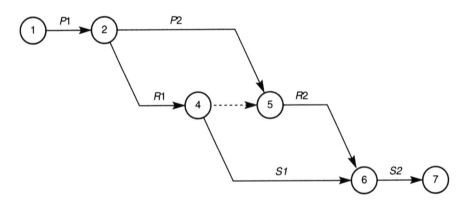

Fig. 11.30

All these diagrams represent similar situations, namely a resultant activity starting before its originating activity is complete. Care must be exercised in using and analysing these networks, since some combinations of duration times can result in subsequent activities apparently being capable of finishing earlier than physically possible. To overcome this it is necessary *either* to examine the results of analyses and eliminate any impossibilities, *or* to impose a restriction on the 'breaking' of the various activities – for example, ensuring that all concurrent activities are broken into the same fraction. Thus, if

$$P1 = P2, R1 = R2 \text{ and } S1 = S2$$

the physical meaning of the above diagram is 'When P is half-completed, R is started; the *second* half of R is not started until the *second* half of P is completed. The *first* half of S is only started when the *first* half of R is completed, and the *second* half of S is only started when the second half of R is completed.' Of course, this may result (apparently) in tasks proceeding in a 'jerky' manner, if the work content of the overlapping activities so dictate. The analyst must ensure that, if the activities are in fact necessarily continuous, the numerical analysis does not indicate a discontinuity. It is often most useful to break the activities into three parts – for example, Start P, Continue P and Finish P (Fig. 11.31).

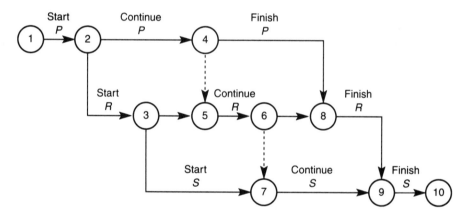

Fig. 11.31

By adjusting the resources used on the activities, their duration times can be modified, and this, in conjunction with careful choice of the Start and Finish components, enables control to be exerted over the way resources are deployed. The whole of the problem of overlapping depends upon the most careful disposition of resources.

A number of modern programs allow the use of a 'negative transit time'; this can in some cases simplify the drawing of a string of overlapping activities. In such cases the negative transit time ($-t$) specifies the time by which the two activities are overlapped and is given on the dummy activity inserted between two sequential activities (Fig. 11.32).

Activity	Duration	Activity	Duration
Start P	2	Continue P	10
Finish P	2	Start R	3
Continue R	15	Finish R	3
Start S	1	Continue S	5
Finish S	1		

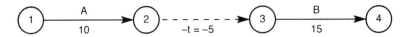

Fig. 11.32

This drawn to timescale would be as in Fig. 11.33.

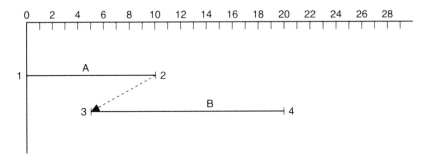

Fig. 11.33

DRAWING THE NETWORK

Policy is sometimes defined as the means whereby an objective is to be achieved, and in this sense a network can be assumed to be a formal and explicit statement of policy. This concept will be found useful when considering the amount of detail that should be displayed. In general, as one descends the hierarchy of an organisation, the detail given in a policy statement increases, while its scope decreases; the same thing is true of plans.

The idea of the network as a statement of policy is useful, and its implications are substantial. Policy denotes *known* objectives; it is not possible to lay down sensible policy unless the purpose for which it is in being is clearly known and explicitly stated.

The first action, therefore, when drawing a network is to *define the purpose* of the project being considered. Stated thus baldly, the statement appears trite and, indeed, in some cases the objectives are very clearly known. Even in construction and manufacturing, however, where 'purpose' may appear obvious, some thought on the subject is valuable. A 'feasibility' network is likely to be very different from an operating network, a 'resource' network may well be different to a time network and so on.

It is in design and development, an area where project network techniques (PNT) can be very usefully employed, that the understanding of the task is often least well understood. Every development department must at some time have been faced with a request to design something that either has no target specification or else an extremely vague one. By agreeing very clearly with the 'customer' what is required, enormous savings can be achieved. Time spent on preparing a design specification is *never* wasted.

It is very rare that development work is undertaken at the frontiers of knowledge, and an unequivocal specification can be of inestimable value in allowing the designer to draw upon experience and in enabling the preparation of realistic plans.

When drawing an arrow diagram of a project, the major activities are fairly readily identified, and these should be approximately located in their correct positions relative to each other and the start and finish events on a large sheet of paper. While it is possible at this stage to prepare a list of activity descriptions, it is always more convenient to write the descriptions on the diagram itself. For this reason it is unwise to try to make the arrows or nodes too small. Descriptions may well be abbreviated ('fnds' for 'foundations', 'cmpnts' for 'components'...) and some organisations set up a list of approved abbreviations.

A list of activities, amplifying the descriptions and specifying times and resources used, is often useful, but this is probably best prepared once the network has been tidied up and tested. Some writers recommend that the first task to be undertaken is to prepare an activity list and from this prepare the diagram. The authors have found this process to be inhibiting. The list once prepared takes on a rigidity from which it is difficult to depart, and a feeling is inculcated that once all the activities on the list are 'fixed' into the network the planning is complete. It is often the act of preparing the network and debating the logic which clarifies the activities.

It is also unnecessary at this stage to try and make arrows straight, or always moving from left to right. Work on the diagram can proceed from both the start and finish; it is sometimes found that the project divides into a series of interrelated chains, and completing one chain at a time can be very helpful. The most useful pieces of equipment at this stage are a pencil and a good eraser: chalk and a blackboard are excellent alternatives.

The major activities having been drawn, the network can be completed by filling in the minor activities. A problem that repeatedly arises is to decide when to stop writing down minor activities. If too much detail is written into a diagram it becomes excessively large, and the subsequent analysis increases in complexity without usefully increasing in value. There is, furthermore, the danger of losing sight of the physical realities underlying the diagram, so that the whole analysis declines into a mathematical exercise. Rules on this do not seem to emerge, but it is suggested that three lines of enquiry can usefully be pursued:

1 Can separate resources be shown with separate arrows?

2 Does any single arrow cover responsibilities assignable to more than one person?

3 Is the detail greater than that which is necessary for the person employing the network to make sensible decisions?

Almost certainly too little detail is preferable to too much. No more detail should be incorporated than is required for the level of control which is to be exercised.

It must be remembered, of course, that the definition of a resource, and the accountability for a responsibility, will apparently change with the level at which the plan is being made.

The first rough diagram may now be redrawn, and the straightening up and disposition of arrows checked in accordance with the conventions described above. It should be realised that, as arrows are not vectors, their lengths and orientations are determined *only* by the convenience of drawing and the logic behind the project. The properties of activities must be written into the diagram, but the location of an activity, by considering that which takes place *previously*, *concurrently* and *subsequently*, will also be found very helpful. It is also wise to investigate the need for dummies in ensuring that, where necessary, they are inserted.

The authors have found the following practice invaluable: once a network has been drawn, start from the final node and move up each activity, asking the question:

● What had to be done before this activity could take place?

Having reached the first node, move down each activity asking the question:

● What can now be done after the completion of this activity?

Carefully and systematically carried out, this procedure will be found to be of very great assistance in ensuring logical cohesion.

As pointed out earlier, the network is a statement of policy and, consequently, once a network is adopted, it commits the organisation to a course of action, along with all the concomitant administrative procedures. Numbers of people – for example, departmental managers, site foremen, section leaders – are thus committed to *and will be held responsible for* carrying out tasks laid down in the network. If for no other reason, therefore, it is very wise indeed for the planner drawing the network to enlist the aid of the appropriate executives when drawing each part of the diagram. This may mean that the planner has to sit down separately and in conference with all the interested parties while individual responsibilities are being painfully worked out and agreed. It is often a temptation for a planner to try to carry out the whole operation by him or herself. This temptation should be resisted except in the case of very simple or frequently repeated tasks.

In order to locate responsibility and authority quite unambiguously, it is helpful to redraw the diagram so that it is divided horizontally into responsibility areas, and vertically into broad time areas. This will result in a diagram for an AoA network appearing as shown in Fig. 11.34.

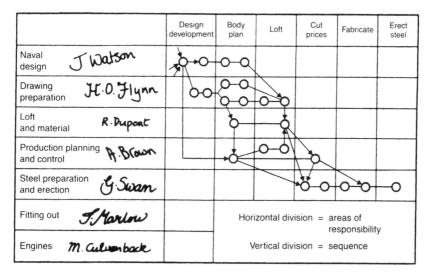

Fig. 11.34 Refinements of a network
(By permission of International Computers & Tabulators Ltd.)

To ensure that responsibilities are understood *and accepted*, the signatures of the appropriate officers are required to appear on the diagram itself. This type of technique can prove of considerable benefit to the structure of the company, and some of the results obtained will be:

- a clear understanding by all managers of the work they are committed to do;
- the delineation of responsibilities between managers;
- an investigation into the organisation of, and procedures used in, the company;
- the application of current experiences to the planning function.

CHAPTER 12

Drawing the activity-on-node network

The term 'activity-on-node' (AoN) networking implies not a single system of networking but a family. Of these AoN systems the best known and most widely used are '*precedence diagrams*', which was originated by IBM, and '*method of potentials*' (MoP), which was originated by Mons. B. Roy, and was the first AoN system. Since MoP is the simpler technique it will be described here in some detail; its family resemblance to the precedence diagram system is so great that translation from one to the other is not difficult.

ELEMENTS OF AN AoN NETWORK

The network diagram is made up of only two basic elements:

1 *An activity:* an element of the work entailed in the project. This activity has precisely the same characteristics as the activity in AoA, namely that it is an element of the work entailed in the project. While resources may not be used ('wait for paint to dry'), an activity is essentially that which is necessary to the project. It is represented, however, by a *node*, usually drawn as a rectangle. Thus an activity A would be shown as in Fig. 12.1. (Within the AoN family there are slight differences concerning the other information which is placed in the node. Reference will be made to these later.)

Fig. 12.1

2 *A dependency or sequence arrow:* that shows the inter-relationship between various activities. Thus, if activity B depends upon (that is, *must* follow) activity A the diagram would be as given in Fig. 12.2.

Fig. 12.2

These two symbols alone allow the representation of a project without the need for the dummy of AoA (*see* p. 105). Thus, if activity K depends on activity A and activity L depends on activities A and B the diagram would be as in Fig. 12.3.

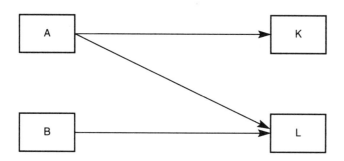

Fig. 12.3

Similarly:

Activity K depends on activity A
Activity L depends on activities A and B
Activity M depends on activity B

would give the diagram in Fig. 12.4.

While:

Activity K depends on activity A
Activity L depends on activities A and B
Activity M depends on activities B and C

would give a diagram as in Fig. 12.5.

Freedom from the need to introduce dummies is one of the most frequently cited advantages of AoN networking. While accepting this considerable benefit it must be pointed out that an AoN diagram is likely to be larger, and appear more complex, than the equivalent AoA network diagram.

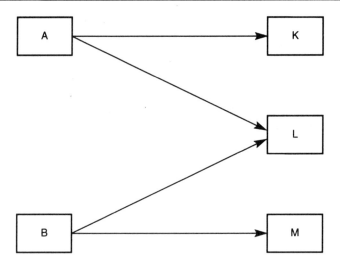

Fig. 12.4 K depends on A, L depends on A and B, M depends on B.

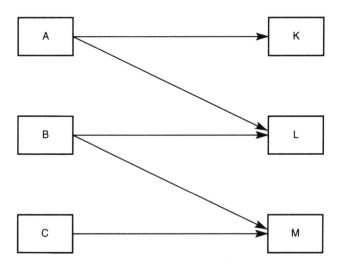

Fig. 12.5 K depends on A, L depends on A and B, M depends on B and C.

Representation of dependency time

While CPA uses a subscript to the activity arrow to represent the duration time of the activity, MoP uses a subscript to the dependency arrow to denote the dependency time, that is, *the time that must elapse between the start of an activity and the start of the succeeding dependent activity.* This permits considerable flexibility in showing the time relationships between activities and constitutes one advantage of MoP over CPA.

Negative constraints

The above dependency time may be said to form a *positive* constraint upon the start of a succeeding activity. A different sort of constraint, the so-called *negative* constraint, may be incorporated in the diagram. Thus, if the interval between the completion of A and the start of B may not exceed X the diagram would appear as in Fig. 12.6. The value of this negative constraint in practice is more apparent than real.

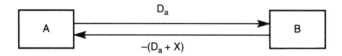

Fig. 12.6

Activity duration times

In AoN it is usual to include the activity duration time *within* the node. Thus, if activity A requires 16 units of time for its completion, then it will be represented as in Fig. 12.7.

Fig. 12.7

If now activity J can only start when activity A is complete, then the diagram becomes as given in Fig. 12.8.

Fig. 12.8

If, however, activity J can start 12 units of time after the start of activity A, then it will become as in Fig. 12.9

Fig. 12.9

Care must be taken in the use of dependency time to ensure that an unintentional absurdity does not result. For example, activity A, duration time 10, may precede activity B, duration time 5, and activity B may be capable of being started 1 unit of time after activity A. This might seem to give a diagram as in Fig. 12.10.

Fig. 12.10

This would give the situation:

	Start	Finish
Activity A	0	10
Activity B	1	6

that is, activity B would finish *before* its predecessor. This *may* satisfy the logic of the situation in which case the representation is valid. However, it could be that activity A must be complete before activity B can finish, in which case a false statement is being made.

Overlapping activities

A common situation is that where several activities 'overlap'. For example, assume there are three activities P, R and S. The diagram (Fig. 12.11) would imply that the *whole* of P was complete before any of R was started, and that the *whole* of R was complete before any of S was started.

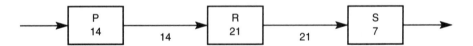

Fig. 12.11

Breaking each activity into three components 'start', 'continue' and 'finish' – would allow overlapping to be represented (Fig. 12.12). This may result in tasks proceeding in a 'jerky' fashion if the work content of the overlapping activities so dictates. In practice, either this jerkiness must be tolerated – by allowing work rates to change and accommodate delays – or resources must be adjusted to give 'smooth' working.

Multi-dependency AoN presents a different solution to this problem.

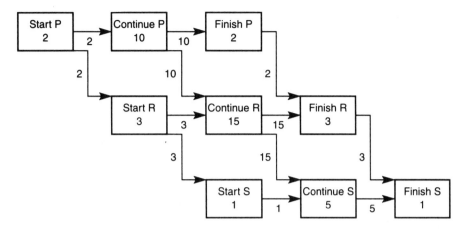

Fig. 12.12

Milestones in MoP

It is sometimes convenient in the life of a project to identify 'milestones' when particular decisions have to be taken or situations reviewed. Milestones usually represent the completion of a number of activities, and in CPA they are represented by events (nodes). In MoP, events do not exist as such: however, it is possible to represent a milestone in MoP by using a fictitious activity of duration 0 (Fig. 12.13).

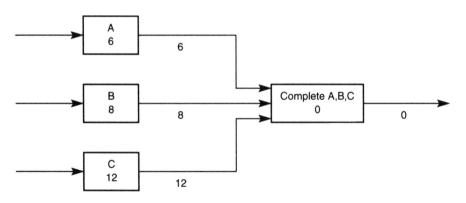

Fig. 12.13

If a specific date must be assigned to either an individual activity or to a milestone, this may be done by a triangular flag (Fig. 12.14).

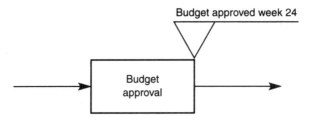

Fig. 12.14

Start and finish nodes

For convenience in manual calculations, all opening activities should emerge from a 'start' activity (node) of zero duration, and all finish activities should come together in a 'finish' activity (node), again of zero duration. Modern computer systems do not require this and multi-start and finish is acceptable, although these activities must be designated as required by the system being used.

The identification of nodes

Nodes (activities) are identified by their description, but it is convenient and succinct also to identify them by a label, usually placed at the front of the description. If a computer is being used to process the network this label will in any case be required by the system and must, therefore, be unique to the node. A useful convention to adopt is: 'Nodes at the head of a dependency arrow have a higher label number than those at the tail of the arrow.' This is a simple convention to implement: the network is drawn with *all* dependency arrows pointing from *left to right*. A ruler is then laid on the diagram at right angles to the axis and drawn from start to finish. As each node is exposed it is numbered, from the top of the diagram downwards. It is convenient to let the label number have some significance, either geographically, where it locates the node on the network, or organisational, where it indicates the organisational responsibility for the carrying out of the activity. Avoid, however, excessively long, cumbersome numbers which are inconvenient to handle. Again, modern computer systems will accept alphanumeric labels, the only requirement being, as noted above, that each node has a unique label.

Interfacing

A large network will cover several drawing sheets. Activities which appear on more than one sheet are said to be 'interface' activities and are represented as shown in Fig. 12.15.

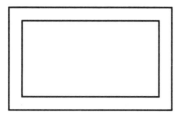

Fig. 12.15

Two errors in logic

Two errors in logic – *looping* and *dangling* – can occur in a network, particularly if it is a complex one.

Looping

Consideration will show that the loop in Fig. 12.16 must not occur, since this would represent an impossible situation: 'Activity R depends on activity Q which depends on activity P which depends on activity R . . .' Should such a loop apparently arise, either an arrow head has been misplaced or an error has been incorporated in the logic (*see* p. 118).

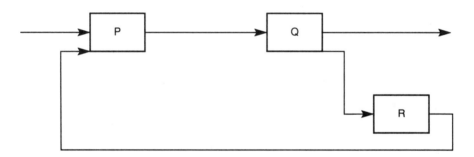

Fig. 12.16

Dangling

Similarly, the situation represented by Fig. 12.17 is also at fault since activity M is undertaken with no resulting successor. Such dangling nodes often arise from hastily inserted afterthoughts.

Hammock activities

Where a network is to be used for cost control, it is extremely useful to introduce into it *hammock* activities. It is simplest to assign to activities

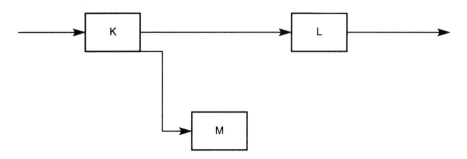

Fig. 12.17

direct costs, that is costs which are directly assignable to activities, for example materials. There are always other costs which are not so assignable, and which must be spread over a number of activities, the *overhead* costs. The burden of these costs are borne by artificial *hammock* activities which are inserted into the network. A hammock will embrace activities which are linked and belong to the same cost centre. Hammocks are assigned no duration and play no part in the time analysis. During cost analyses a hammock is assumed to have a duration determined by the time elapsing between the start of the first hammocked activity and the point at which measurement is being made, which may be 'time now' or the end of the activities concerned. The overhead rate is assumed to be constant over the life of the hammock.

DRAWING THE NETWORK

Policy is sometimes defined as the means whereby an objective is to be achieved, and in this sense a network can be assumed to be a formal and explicit statement of policy. This concept will be found useful when considering the amount of detail that should be displayed. In general, as one descends the hierarchy of an organisation, the detail given in a policy statement increases, while its scope decreases; the same thing is true of plans.

The idea of a network as a statement of policy is useful, and its implications are substantial. Policy denotes *known* objectives; it is not possible to lay down sensible policy unless the purpose for which it is in being is clearly known and explicitly stated.

The first action, therefore, when drawing a network is to *define the purpose* of the project being considered. Stated thus baldly, the statement appears trite and, indeed, in some cases the objectives are very clearly known. Even in construction and manufacturing however, where 'purpose' may appear obvious, some thought on the subject is valuable. A 'feasibility' network is likely to be very different from an operating network, a 'resource' network may well be different to a time network and so on.

It is in design and development, an area where project network techniques (PNT) can be very usefully employed, that the understanding of the task is often least well understood. Every development department must at some time have been faced with a request to design something that either has no target specification or else an extremely vague one. By agreeing very clearly with the 'customer' what is required, enormous savings can be achieved. Time spent on preparing a design specification is *never* wasted.

It is very rare that development work is undertaken at the frontiers of knowledge, and an unequivocal specification can be of inestimable value in allowing the designer to draw upon experience and in enabling the preparation of realistic plans.

When drawing a node diagram of a project, the major activities are fairly readily identified, and these should be approximately located in their correct positions relative to each other and the start and finish activities nodes on a large sheet of paper. While it is possible at this stage to prepare a list of activity descriptions, it is always more convenient to write the descriptions on the diagram itself. For this reason it is unwise to try to make the nodes too small. Descriptions will have to be abbreviated ('fnds' for 'foundations', 'cmpnts' for 'components'...) and some organisations set up a list of approved abbreviations.

A list of activities, amplifying the descriptions and specifying times and resources used is often useful, but this is probably best prepared once the network has been tidied up and tested. Some writers recommend that the first task to be undertaken is to prepare an activity list and from this prepare the diagram. The authors have found this process to be inhibiting. The list once prepared takes on a rigidity from which it is difficult to depart, and a feeling is inculcated that once all the activities on the list are 'fixed' into the network the planning is complete. It is often the act of preparing the network and debating the logic which clarifies the activities.

It is also unnecessary at this stage to try and make the dependency arrows straight, or always moving from left to right. Work on the diagram can proceed from both the start and finish; it is sometimes found that the project divides into a series of interrelated chains, and completing one chain at a time can be very helpful. The most useful pieces of equipment at this stage are a pencil and a good eraser; chalk and a blackboard are excellent alternatives.

The major activities having been drawn, the network can be completed by filling in the minor activities. A problem that repeatedly arises is to decide when to stop writing down minor activities. If too much detail is written into a diagram it becomes excessively large, and the subsequent analysis increases in complexity without usefully increasing in value. There is, furthermore, the danger of losing sight of the physical realities underlying the diagram, so that the whole analysis declines into a mathematical exercise. Rules on this do not seem to emerge, but it is suggested that three lines of enquiry can usefully be pursued:

1 Can separate resources be shown with separate activities?

2 Does any single activity cover responsibilities assignable to more than one person?

3 Is the detail greater than that which is necessary for the person employing the network to make sensible decisions?

Almost certainly too little detail is preferable to too much. No more detail should be incorporated than is required for the level of control which is to be exercised.

It must be remembered, of course, that the definition of a resource, and the accountability for a responsibility, will apparently change with the level at which the plan is being made.

The first rough diagram may now be redrawn, and the straightening up of dependency arrows and disposition of activities checked in accordance with the conventions described above. It should be realised that the positioning of activity nodes is determined *only* by the convenience of drawing and the logic behind the project. The properties of activities must be written into the diagram, but the location of an activity, by considering that which takes place *previously*, *concurrently* and *subsequently*, will also be found very helpful.

The authors have found the following practice invaluable: once a network has been drawn, start from the final node and consider each preceding activity node, asking the question:

● What had to be done before this activity could take place?

Having reached the first node, consider each succeeding activity asking the question:

● What can now be done after the completion of this activity?

Carefully and systematically carried out, this procedure will be found to be of very great assistance in ensuring logical cohesion.

As pointed out earlier, the network is a statement of policy and, consequently, once a network is adopted, it commits the organisation to a course of action, along with all the concomitant administrative procedures. Numbers of people – for example, departmental managers, site foremen, section leaders – are thus committed to *and will be held responsible for* carrying out tasks laid down in the network. If for no other reason, therefore, it is very wise indeed for the planner drawing the network to enlist the aid of the appropriate executives when drawing each part of the diagram. This may mean that the planner has to sit down separately and in conference with all the interested parties while individual responsibilities are being painfully worked out and agreed. It is often a temptation for a planner to try to carry out the whole operation by him or herself. This temptation should be resisted except in the case of very simple or frequently repeated tasks.

In order to locate responsibility and authority quite unambiguously, it is helpful to redraw the diagram so that it is divided horizontally into responsibility areas, and vertically into broad time areas. This will result in a diagram for an AoN network similar to that shown earlier in Fig. 11.34 (page 117) for an AoA network. To ensure that responsibilities are understood *and accepted*, the signatures of the appropriate officers are required to appear on the diagram itself. This type of technique can prove of considerable benefit to the structure of the company, and some of the results obtained will be:

1 A clear understanding by all managers of the work they are committed to do;

2 The delineation of responsibilities between managers;

3 An investigation into the organisation of, and procedures used in, the company;

4 The application of current experiences to the planning function.

CHAPTER 13

Analysing the activity-on-arrow network

The total project time (TPT) is the shortest time in which the project can be completed, and this is determined by a sequence (or sequences) of activities known as the critical path (or paths).

ACTIVITY AND EVENT TIMES

To calculate the TPT, carry out a *forward pass* whereby the *earliest starting times* (EST) for each activity are calculated. In the calculation it will sometimes be necessary to refer to the *earliest finishing time* (EFT) of an activity, given by:

Earliest finishing time = Earliest starting time + Duration

The critical path is then identified by carrying out a *backward pass* whereby the *latest finishing time* (LFT) of an activity and its associated *latest starting time* (LST) is given by:

Latest starting time = Latest finishing time – Duration

It is important to recognise that activity times are *indirectly* derived from the forward and backward passes which *directly* give the event times for the nodes. A node has two times associated with it: one, from the forward pass, its *earliest event time* (EET), the earliest time the event can be realised; the other, from the backward pass, its *latest event time* (LET), the latest time by which the event *must* be realised if the total project time is to be achieved. The EET is the EST of all emerging activities, whilst the LET is the LFT of all entering activities.

It is recommended in BS 4335:1987 that when manual calculations are to be carried out, or when the diagram is to be used as a communications device, the node circle is drawn trisected with a vertical line bisecting the circle, and a horizontal line bisecting the right-hand semicircle. The node (event) label (number) is set in the left-hand semicircle, the EET in the top right quadrant and the LET in the bottom right quadrant (Fig. 13.1).

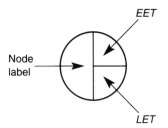

Fig. 13.1

While this recommendation will be followed hereafter in this text, other representations may be found, as shown in Fig. 13.2.

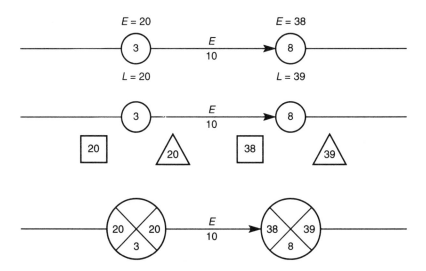

Fig. 13.2

Consider a part-diagram (Fig. 13.3) where node 15 has three entering activities K, L and M and the forward pass shows that:

Activity K, duration 16 weeks, tail-node 01 has an EET of 10 weeks

Activity L, duration 17 weeks, tail-node 05 has an EET of 20 weeks

Activity M, duration 18 weeks, tail-node 10 has an EET of 30 weeks

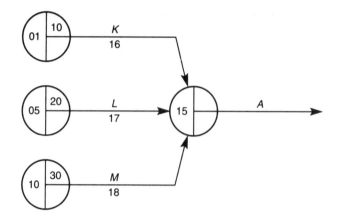

Fig. 13.3

Then:

Activity K has an EST of 10 weeks and hence an EFT of (10 + 16) weeks = 26 weeks

Activity L has an EST of 20 weeks and hence an EFT of (20 + 17) weeks = 37 weeks

Activity M has an EST of 30 weeks and hence an EFT of (30 + 18) weeks = 48 weeks

The fundamental property of events (page 101) states: 'an event cannot be said to be realised until all activities leading into it are complete.' The earliest time at which *all* activities entering event 15 are complete is week 48 so that the EET for event 15 is week 48, and the EST for *all* activities emerging directly from event 15 is week 48.

In reverse, consider a part-diagram (Fig. 13.4) where node 12 has three emerging activities W, X and Y and the backward pass shows that:

Activity W, duration 19 weeks, has a head-node 20 with an LET of 85 weeks

Activity X, duration 20 weeks, has a head-node 25 with an LET of 60 weeks

Activity Y, duration 21 weeks, has a head-node 30 with an LET of 72 weeks

Then:

Activity W has an LFT of 85 weeks and an LST of (85 − 19) weeks = 66 weeks

Activity X has an LFT of 60 weeks and an LST of (60 − 20) weeks = 40 weeks

Activity Y has an LFT of 72 weeks and an LST of (72 − 21) weeks = 51 weeks

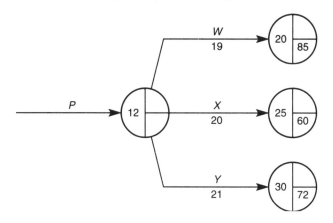

Fig. 13.4

The latest time by which event 12 *must* be realised is the *earliest* of the LSTs of all the emerging activities, that is week 40, so that the LET for event 12 is week 40.

A simple aid to calculation

The following simple rules may be found helpful:

EETs determine emerging ESTs.
LETs determine entering LFTs.

Or *more* succinctly:

Es look forward, Ls look back.

THE CALCULATIONS IN DETAIL

The calculations will be carried out as shown in Fig. 13.5 (where the durations are given in weeks).

The forward pass

Assign to the first node, here node 1, an EET: 0, that is activities A, B and C may start at the beginning of week 0. Then:

Node 2 has an EET of 16 weeks, that is activity J may start at the end of week 16.

Node 3 has an EET of 20 weeks, that is activities D and E may start at the end of week 20.

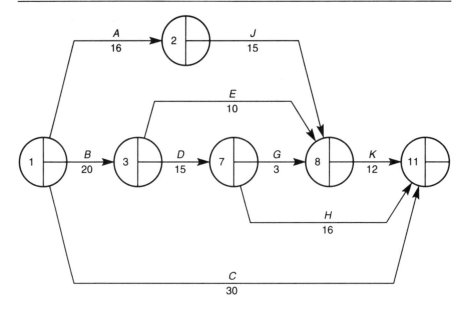

Fig. 13.5

Node 7 has an EET of (20 + 15) weeks = 35 weeks, that is activities G and H may start at the end of week 35.

When a node has several activities entering it, then its EET is determined by the *latest* of the EFTs of the entering activities. Node 8 has three activities (J, E and G) leading into it.

EFT for activity J is (16 + 15) weeks = 31 weeks

EFT for activity E is (20 + 10) weeks = 30 weeks

EFT for activity G is (35 + 3) weeks = 38 weeks

Of these, 38 weeks is the latest. Hence:

Node 8 has an EET of 38 weeks, that is activity K may start at the end of week 38.

Similarly, for node 11:

EFT for activity K is (38 + 12) weeks = 50 weeks

EFT for activity H is (35 + 16) weeks = 51 weeks

EFT for activity C is (0 + 30) weeks = 30 weeks

Of these finishing times, 51 weeks is the latest. The EET for node 11 is therefore 51 weeks. Since node 11 is the final node, this 51 weeks represents the minimum time in which the whole project can be completed – it is the TPT.

The backward pass

Assign to the final node, here node 11, an LET equal to the TPT just calculated – here 51 weeks, so that activities K, H and C may finish at the end of week 51. Then:

Node 8 has an LET of $(51 - 12)$ weeks = 39 weeks, that is activities J, G and E may finish at the end of week 39.

Node 2 has an LET of $(39 - 15)$ weeks = 24 weeks, that is activity A may finish at the end of week 24.

When a node has several activities emerging from it, then its LET is determined by the *earliest* of the LSTs of the emerging activities. Node 7 has two activities (G and H) emerging from it:

LST for activity G is $(39 - 3)$ weeks = 36 weeks

LST for activity H is $(51 - 16)$ weeks = 35 weeks

Of these, 35 weeks is the earlier. Hence:

Node 7 has an LET of 35 weeks, that is activity D may finish at the end of week 35.

Similarly for node 3:

LST for activity E is $(39 - 10)$ weeks = 29 weeks

LST for activity D is $(35 - 15)$ weeks = 20 weeks

Hence:

Node 3 has an LET of 20 weeks, that is activity B may finish at the end of week 20.

And for node 1:

LST for activity A is $(24 - 16)$ weeks = 8 weeks

LST for activity B is $(20 - 20)$ weeks = 0 weeks

LST for activity C is $(51 - 30)$ weeks = 21 weeks

Hence:

Node 1 has an LET of 0 weeks.

Since node 1 is the first node the LST of the *whole project* is week 0. This is to be expected: when the turn-round time at the final node is constant – that is, when the EET and LET of the final node are the same – the EET and LET of the first node must be the same since the forward pass adds up numbers that are then subtracted by the backward pass.

The sample network, using the recommended technique, would be as in Fig. 13.6.

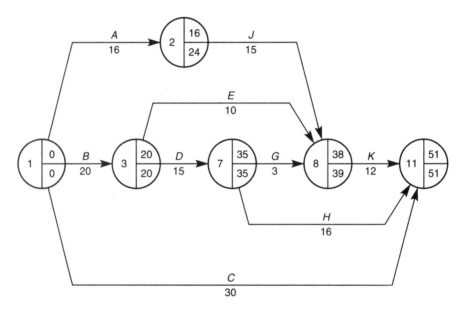

Fig. 13.6

THE CRITICAL PATH

Consider activity E. The calculations show that the earliest time it *can* start – given by the EET of its tail node – is at the end of week 20, while the latest time it may finish is at the end of week 39. Thus, the time that can be made *available* for the activity is (39 – 20) weeks = 19 weeks. The time *required* for this activity – that is, its duration time – is 10 weeks. There are, therefore, (19 – 10) weeks = 9 weeks 'spare' ('float') for the performance of

this activity. It may start 9 weeks late, finish 9 w
weeks extra time without increasing the TPT.
    Consider now activity D (Fig. 13.7):

LFT in weeks   = 35
EST in weeks   = 20
Time available in weeks = 15
Time required in weeks   = 15

    Spare time in weeks   = 0

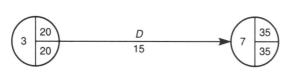

Fig. 13.7

Thus there is no 'spare' time in activity D – if it starts late or the duration
increases by any amount, the TPT will be increased. As with any dimension
affecting total performance activity D is said to be *critical* – it helps to
determine the TPT. It is one of a chain of activities that is critical – the *critical path*. In the network under consideration the critical path is activities
B, D and H. It will be seen that each of these has zero float.

Note: Newcomers to the technique sometimes make the error of assuming
that the critical path lies between nodes whose EET and LET are the same.
This is only partly true and is not a sufficient test. For example, activity C
(Fig. 13.8) lies between nodes whose earliest and latest times are the same.

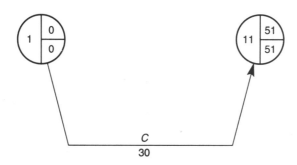

Fig. 13.8

LFT in weeks	= 51
EST in weeks	= 0
Time available in weeks	= 51
Time required in weeks	= 30
Spare time in weeks	= 21

Clearly, activity C is not critical. (If there is any further doubt on this matter the reader should insert an activity between – say – nodes 1 and 7 with a duration time of 1 and see if it is critical.)

Float is the only means of identifying the critical path.

The critical path is conventionally indicated by a pair of small transverse parallel lines across the activities concerned (Fig. 13.9).

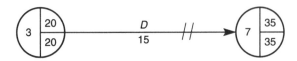

Fig. 13.9

Note: In practice, if a network is being calculated manually it is rarely necessary when identifying the critical path to calculate float on all paths. Four simple factors characterise the critical path:

1 It starts at the first node.

2 It is continuous.

3 It ends at the last node.

4 It has no float.

ACTIVITY TIMES – A RECAPITULATION

Since activities cannot start until their tail events are complete, and must not finish later than the time at which their head events must occur, the head and tail events can be considered to fix boundaries between which activities can 'move'. It is possible to describe these 'movements' by four simple 'times':

1 The EST is the earliest possible time at which an activity can start, and is given by the earliest time of the tail node. Thus, the EST for activity 2–8 is the earliest time for node 2 – that is, at the end of week 16.

2 The EFT of an activity is the earliest possible time at which an activity can finish, and is given by adding the duration time to the EST; again, for activity 2–8 this is $16 + 15 = 31$, that is the end of week 31.

3 The LFT is found by taking the LET of the head node; again, for activity 2 – 8 this is the LET for node 8, that is at the end of week 39.

4 The LST is the latest possible time by which an activity must start, and is given by subtracting the duration from the latest finish time; for activity 2–8 the LST is $39 – 15 = 24$ so that the activity can start at the beginning of week 24.

Summarising the above:

	Activity		Start time		Finish time	
Number	description	Duration	Earliest	Latest	Earliest	Latest
2–8	J	15	16	24	31	39

This can be done for all activities. The significance is that, considering activity 2–8, it must start between weeks 16 and 24 and must finish between weeks 31 and 39. An earlier start is impossible, while a later finish will increase the overall performance time for the project; in fact it will shift the critical path from 1–3–7–11 to 1–2–8–11.

Note: Do not confuse *event* times with *activity* times. The EST of an activity coincides with the earliest time of its tail node, and the LFT of an activity coincides with the latest time of its head node. However, the LST of an activity does not *necessarily* coincide with the latest time of its associated tail event, nor does the EFT *necessarily* coincide with the earliest time of its head event; such coincidences only apply to activities on the critical path. Thus, the LST and EFT in the table below *cannot* be read directly from the calculated diagram, but *must* be derived from the LFT and EST. It may be helpful to consider that event times E 'look forward' and event times L 'look backwards', so that in Fig. 13.10 E = 16 'looks forward' to provide one boundary for activity J, while E = 38 'looks forward' to provide a boundary for any activity emerging from node 8. Equally L = 39 'looks backwards' to provide a boundary for activity J while L = 24 'looks backwards' to provide a boundary for any activity entering node 2.

The earliest and latest start and finish times for the whole of the sample network are:

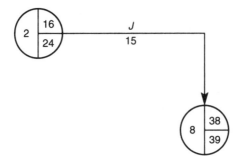

Fig. 13.10

	Activity	Duration	Start time		Finish time	
Number	description	weeks	Earliest	Latest	Earliest	Latest
1–2	A	16	0	8	16	24
1–3	B	20	0	0	20	20
1–11	C	30	0	21	30	51
2–8	J	15	16	24	31	39
3–7	D	15	20	20	35	35
3–8	E	10	20	29	30	39
7–8	G	3	35	36	38	39
7–11	H	16	35	35	51	51
8–11	K	12	38	39	50	51

FLOAT OR SLACK

BS 4335:1987 contains definitions of three types of float: *Total*, *Free* and *Independent*. Of these, total float is in general use and applies to both AoA and AoN; free and independent floats only apply to AoA. Independent float has declined in use and has been omitted from the discussion on float in this text.

As has already been described, the earliest tail and latest head event times form boundaries within which activities are able to move.

Total float

Looking again at activity J, as shown in Fig.13.11, it can be seen that the earliest possible time the activity can start (EST) is at the end of week 16, while the latest possible time it can finish (LFT) is at the end of week 39. Thus, it can be said that:

Maximum time available = 39 – 16 weeks
= 23 weeks

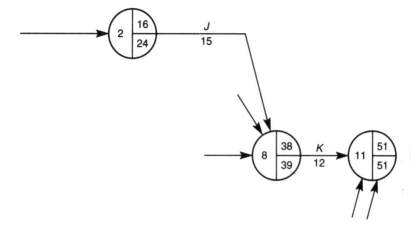

Fig. 13.11 Refer back to Fig. 13.6, page 136

Now the activity only 'needs' the duration time in which it can be completed, that is:

Necessary time = 15 weeks

Thus, the activity can be extended or delayed by (23 – 15) = 8 weeks. Any expansion or delay *greater* than this will change the critical path and increase the overall project time. This time of 8 weeks is known as the *total float* possessed by the activity (Fig. 13.12).

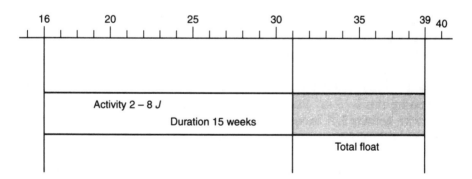

Fig. 13.12

Total float: the total amount by which an activity can be extended or delayed without affecting the total project time (TPT).

It must be realised that the total float is here shown as appearing as time at the *end* of an activity, but that is not necessarily the case. Float can appear at the beginning of an activity, that is, the starting of the activity can be delayed after the tail event is realised; or it can appear *in* the activity, so that the duration time is increased beyond that initially planned; or it can appear after the activity is finished, while other activities are being completed to realise the head event.

Free float

Examining activity K in the same way it will be seen that:

Maximum available time = $(51 - 38)$ weeks
= 13 weeks
Necessary time = 12 weeks
_____
Hence, float = 1 week
══════════════

However, if activity J actually absorbs all its float of 8 weeks, event 8 will be realised by week $(16 + 15 + 8)$ = the end of week 39. Thus, activity K cannot possibly start until the end of week 39, and:

Available time = $(51 - 39)$ weeks
= 12 weeks
Necessary time = 12 weeks
_____
Hence, float = 0 weeks
══════════════

so that, if activity J absorbs all its float, activity K has no float remaining. On the other hand, if activity J absorbs only 7 weeks or less of its float, the float in activity K remains unaltered at 1 week.

It can thus be said that activity J has 8 weeks' *total float*, of which 7 can be used without reducing the float in any succeeding activity. One way of expressing this is to say that there is an interference float of 1 week associated with activity J. A more common, and more useful, mode of expression is to say activity J has a *total* float of 8 weeks and a *free* float of 7 weeks.

> *Free float:* **the total amount by which an activity can be extended or delayed without affecting the start of any succeeding activities.**

In the planning stage it may be decided to increase the duration time of activity J (for example, by reducing the resources allocated to it and thus increasing its performance time). If this is done, then the float available in *previous* activities will be reduced, so that the term 'free' indicates only that use of the float which will not affect succeeding activities.

Negative float

It is sometimes convenient to compare the overall project time with a target or acceptable time, and this can be very conveniently done by 'turning round' at this target time. Thus, the target time is inserted at the final node, the latest event times (LETs) are then calculated from this final LET and the float again extracted. If the target time is greater than the TPT, then *all* activities will have positive float, while if the target time is *less* than the TPT, the critical path and possibly some other activities will have *negative* float. It should be noted that only total float has any meaning as a negative float. This negative float is the time by which activities on the path or paths concerned must be reduced if the TPT is to be met.

Slack

The term used to denote the difference between the EET and the LET for any event is *slack*. Thus, for event 2 in Fig. 13.13 where the EET is 16 weeks and the LET is 24 weeks, the slack is said to be 8 weeks, and for event 8 it is 1 week.

Note: Do not confuse float and slack. Slack refers to *events*; float refers to *activities*. Some (not all) US books use the terms as synonyms, while some reverse the usage prescribed here. The present terminology is that which is recommended by BS 4335:1987. In all the situations in which the authors have worked 'slack' has not been found to be a useful expression of available time.

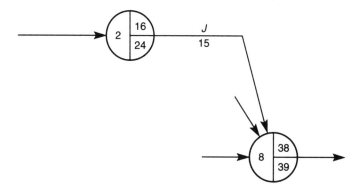

Fig. 13.13

Rules for calculating float

Total float

Subtract the earliest event time (EET) for the tail node from the latest event time (LET) for the head node and from this difference subtract the activity duration time (D).

Example: for activity 16–25:

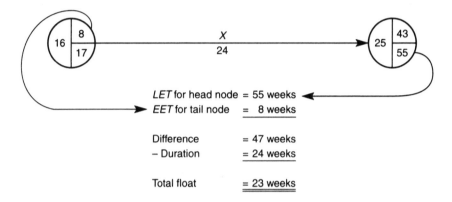

Note: When setting out an analysis in tabular form a useful alternative statement of the above rule is given by:

Total float: latest start date of activity minus earliest start date of activity (may be negative).

Thus for activity 16–25:

Latest start date   = $(55 - 24) = 31$ weeks
Earliest start date   =   8 weeks
                         = 23 weeks

Free float

Subtract the earliest event time (EET) for the tail node from the earliest event time (EET) for the head node, and from this difference subtract the activity duration (D).

Note: It is very difficult to derive free float from the tabulation, and it is always necessary to refer to the network on which the analysis has been carried out.

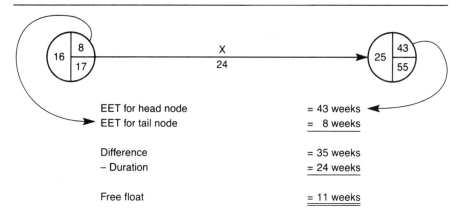

EET for head node	= 43 weeks
EET for tail node	= 8 weeks
Difference	= 35 weeks
– Duration	= 24 weeks
Free float	= 11 weeks

GENERALISED RULES FOR ANALYSIS

In mathematical terms for the generalised activity *i–j* of duration D (Fig. 13.14) where the tail node is labelled *i* and the head node *j*, the rules are:

Fig. 13.14

Earliest event time of node i = EET_i
Latest event time of node i = LET_i
Earliest event time of node j = EET_j
Latest event time of node j = LET_j

Then for activity *i–j*:

Earliest start time EST = EET_i
Latest start time LST = $LET_j - D$
Earliest finish time EFT = $EET_i + D$
Latest finish time LFT = LET_j
Total float TF = $LET_j - EET_i - D$
Free float = $EET_j - EET_i - D$
Event slack for event n = $LET_n - EET_n$

Using the above rules for the sample network already discussed (Fig. 13.15) we have the following:

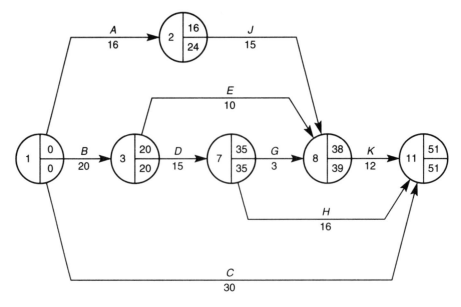

Fig. 13.15

	Activity	Duration	Start time		Finish time		Float	
Number	description	(weeks)	Earliest	Latest	Earliest	Latest	Total	Free
1–2	A	16	0	8	16	24	8	0
1–3	B	20	0	0	20	20	0	0
1–11	C	30	0	21	30	51	21	21
2–8	J	15	16	24	31	39	8	7
3–7	D	15	20	20	35	35	0	0
3–8	E	10	20	29	30	39	9	8
7–8	G	3	35	36	38	39	1	0
7–11	H	16	35	35	51	51	0	0
8–11	K	12	38	39	50	51	1	1

INTERMEDIATE IMPOSED TIMES

Circumstances sometimes require that events other than, or as well as, the final event should take place at particular times. Should this be so, then these 'scheduled' or 'imposed' times can be inserted into the network by means of an inverted triangle with the scheduled time included. For example, Fig. 13.16 indicates that event 75 'budget approved' must take place by time 100, that is, all activities with head number 75 must be completed by time 100. A triangle below the event number indicates that activities with tail number 75 cannot start until time 100.

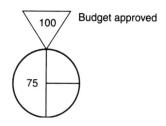

Fig. 13.16

The scheduled time having been inserted, analyses can now be carried out:

● between the beginning and end of the network, and

● between the beginning and/or end and the intermediate scheduled points, treating these points as if they were starts or finishes.

This can give rise to critical paths other than the main critical path, and these are known as secondary, tertiary and so on, each with its own set of floats. Once such an analysis has been carried out, the meanings of the various factors will become immediately obvious.

CHAPTER 14

Analysing the activity-on-node network

The example network used throughout this section of the text is in MoP (Method of Potentials) terms. It is shown in Fig. 14.2, and all calculations will be carried out on this network. The BS 4335:1987 recommended symbol for an activity (Node) in MoP is shown in Fig. 14.1.

Earliest start	Latest start
Label, Description, Resources, Etc	
Duration	Total float

Fig. 14.1

The significance of *total float* will appear later. Note that in the network used the dependency time is in all cases the same as the duration of the preceding activity, as pointed out on page 120; this need not be so. However, the method of calculation remains unchanged whatever the dependency times.

CALCULATING THE TOTAL PROJECT TIME

The total project time (TPT) is the shortest time in which the project can be completed, and this is determined by the sequence (or sequences) of activities known as the *critical path(s)*. To calculate the TPT a *forward pass* is carried out whereby the earliest start time (EST) of each activity is calculated. It is recommended that this EST is written into the top left-hand box of the node.

The forward pass

A forward pass is carried out as follows:

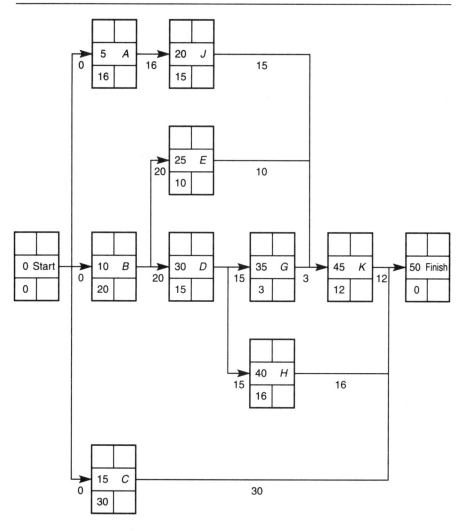

Fig. 14.2 Time in weeks

1 Start at the beginning of the network in Fig. 14.2, that is at the Start activity.

2 Assign to the Start node an EST of 0. This assumes that the whole project can start *now. Note:* if there is a known interval of time before the project can start – say X weeks – then an EST of X can be assigned to the start node. It is usually simpler, however, to assign an EST of 0 to the Start activity and then add X to all times subsequently calculated by adding it to the first dependency times.

3 Proceed to each activity in turn and calculate its EST from the EST of the preceding activity and the dependency time. For example, activity J is preceded by activity A which has an EST of 0. The dependency time governing the relationship between activities A and J is 16 weeks. Hence the EST of activity J is 0 + 16 weeks = 16 weeks. The partly calculated network appears in Fig. 14.3.

4 Three activities, J, E and G, converge on activity K. The EST of activity K is therefore given by the largest of the sum of the EST and the dependency time for each immediately preceding activity. Thus:

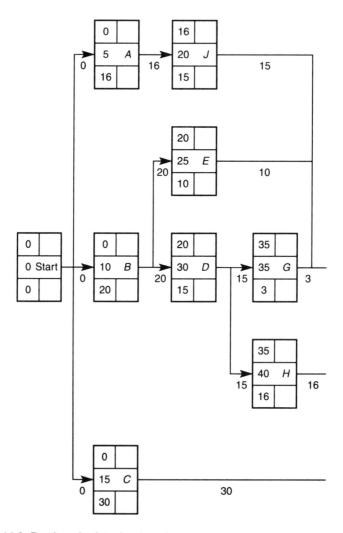

Fig. 14.3 Partly calculated network

If *only* J is considered, the EST for K is (16 + 15) weeks = 31 weeks.

If *only* E is considered, the EST for K is (20 + 10) weeks = 30 weeks.

If *only* G is considered, the EST for K is (35 + 3) weeks = 38 weeks.

Since J, E and G must *all* be considered the EST for K is 38 weeks. Similarly for the Finish activity:

If *only* K is considered, the EST for Finish is (38 + 12) weeks = 50 weeks.

If *only* H is considered, the EST for Finish is (35 + 16) weeks = 51 weeks.

If *only* C is considered, the EST for Finish is (0 + 30) weeks = 30 weeks.

Since K, H and C must all be considered the EST for Finish is 51 weeks. As the Finish activity has 0 duration, an EST for the Finish activity of 51 weeks means that the earliest time in which the project can be completed – the TPT – is 51 weeks.

5 If required, calculate the earliest finish time (EFT) for each activity from:

Earliest finish time = Earliest start time + Duration
$$EFT = EST + D$$

Thus, for activity K:

$$EFT = (38 + 12) \text{ weeks} = 50 \text{ weeks}$$

Since the EFT is such a simple and direct factor to calculate it is recommended that it does not appear on an MoP node.

6 It will be seen, in Fig. 14.4, that the EFT of the Finish activity is 51, which is therefore the TPT.

The backward pass

The critical path can be determined by carrying out a *backward pass* whereby the latest start time (LST) of each activity is derived. It is recommended that this LST is written into the top right-hand box of the node.

Note: This differs from the backward pass calculation in activity-on-arrow (AoA) where the latest *finish* time (LFT) of each activity is calculated. This difference arises from the fact that in MoP the dependency arrow time sets the difference between the start of an activity and the start of an immediately dependent activity.

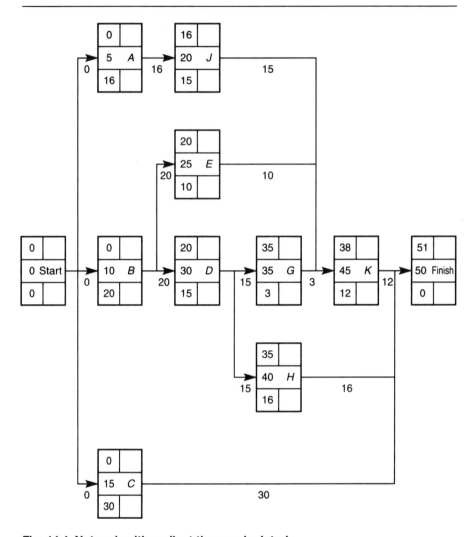

Fig. 14.4 Network with earliest times calculated

7 Start now at the end of the network, that is at the Finish activity.

8 Assign to this activity an LST equal to its EST. This is equivalent to a statement that the project will be completed as quickly as possible.

9 By successively subtracting dependency times from LSTs calculate the LST of each activity. Thus, for activity K:

$$LST(K) = LST(FINISH) - 12 = (51 - 12) \text{ weeks} = 39 \text{ weeks}$$

and for activity G:

$$LST(G) = LST(K) - 3 \qquad = (39 - 3) \text{ weeks} = 36 \text{ weeks}$$

This gives the results as shown in Fig. 14.5.

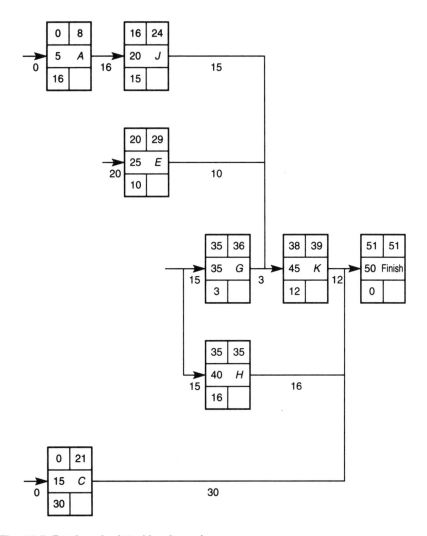

Fig. 14.5 Partly calculated backward pass

10 Two activities, G and H, emerge from activity D. The latest start time (LST) of activity D is therefore given by the smaller of the differences between the LST and the duration times. Thus:

If *only* G is considered, the LST for D is (36 – 15) weeks = 21 weeks.

If *only* H is considered, the LST for D is (35 – 15) weeks = 20 weeks.

Since both G and H must be considered, the LST for D is 20 weeks.
   Similarly for activity B:

If *only* E is considered, the LST for B is (29 – 20) weeks = 9 weeks.

If *only* D is considered, the LST for B is (20 – 20) weeks = 0 weeks.

Since both E and D must be considered, the LST for B is 0 weeks. Finally, for the Start activity:

If *only* A is considered, the LST for Start is (9 – 0) weeks = 9 weeks.

If *only* B is considered, the LST for Start is (20 – 20) weeks = 0 weeks.

If *only* C is considered, the LST for Start is (21 – 0) weeks = 21 weeks.

Since A, B and C must all be considered, the LST for Start = 0 weeks.

Note:
(a) The 'turn-round' time at Finish was equal to the TPT – hence the result of the backward pass must be the same as the EST of the start activity.
(b) The forward and backward passes can be summarised:
   Forward pass – add and choose the latest figure.
   Backward pass – subtract and choose the earliest figure.

The LST is generally placed in the top right-hand box of the node.

11 If required, calculate the latest finish time (LFT) of each activity from:

$$\text{Latest finish time} = \text{Latest start time} + \text{Duration}$$
$$\text{LFT} = \text{LST} + \text{D}$$

Thus, for activity K:

$$\text{LFT} = (39 + 12) \text{ weeks} + 51 \text{ weeks}$$

Since the LFT is such a simple factor to calculate it is recommended that it does not appear on an MoP node.

12 The critical path lies along those activities where there is no 'spare time' and, therefore, in which the EST and LST (or EFT and LFT) are the same. This test only applies if the EST and LST at the finish node are the same – the most usual situation. In the example network, therefore, the critical path is, as can be seen in Fig. 14.6:

Start – activity B – activity D – activity H – Finish

The various times for the network can be tabulated.

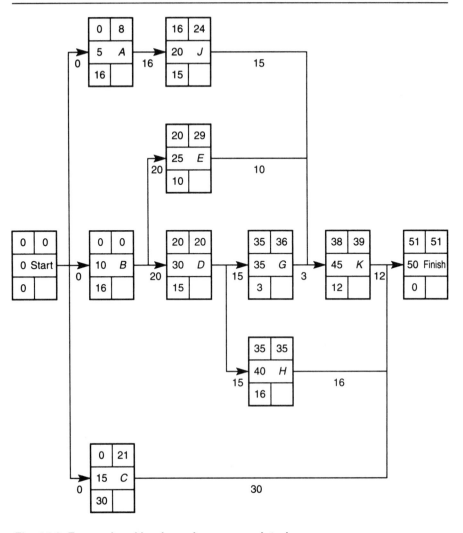

Fig. 14.6 Forward and backward pass completed

Activity description	Duration (weeks)	Start time Earliest	Start time Latest	Finish time Earliest	Finish time Latest
A	16	0	8	16	24
B	20	0	0	20	20
C	30	0	21	30	51
D	15	20	20	35	35
E	10	20	29	30	39
G	3	35	36	38	39
H	16	35	35	51	51
J	15	16	24	31	39
K	12	38	39	50	51

THE AoN NODE IN PRACTICE

The AoN node is undoubtably a very convenient and tidy way of assembling all the information concerning an activity *on the network itself*, something which is virtually impossible in AoA. However, the node itself is tedious to draw. One of the authors, being both a poor draughtsman and always anxious to avoid work, has found that pre-printed nodes on self-adhesive labels simplify the drawing of the network immensely. These labels are easily and cheaply purchased from any of the many jobbing printers who undertake the printing of self-adhesive labels.

In practice, this author fills in the activity description on the label, and disposes the various labels on a large sheet of paper. The activities are moved until the logic is correctly represented, and a tidying up, using a straight edge, achieves a pleasing display. The back of each label is then peeled off and the node located firmly in position. All that is then required is the joining up of the various nodes by the dependency arrows – a relatively easy task.

Other workers record the use of large sheets of paper with a faint grid of nodes printed upon it. Activities are located appropriately, the nodes lined in and dependency arrows drawn in the spaces left between the nodes.

FLOAT

The forward and backward passes on activity-on-node (AoN) networking give the earliest start time (EST) and the latest start time (LST) for each activity. Thus, activity J (Fig. 14.7) may start at the beginning of week 16 or it may be delayed and start at the beginning of week 24 without increasing the total project time (TPT) of 51 weeks (Fig. 14.8).

Knowledge of this ability to 'move' or 'float' is valuable in many ways and the *total* amount an activity may move without affecting the TPT is called the *total float*.

16	24
20 J	
15	

Fig. 14.7

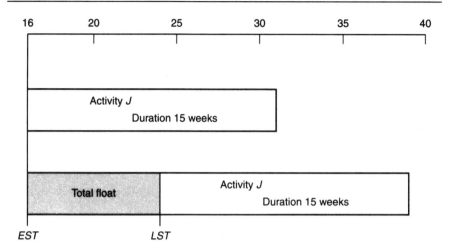

Fig. 14.8

Total float: **the total amount by which an activity can be extended or delayed without affecting the total project time (TPT).**

Total float may be used to delay the start – and hence the finish – of an activity, or it may be used to increase the duration time of the activity, either or both of these being useful in deploying resources.

For activity J the total float is 8 weeks, given by:

Total float = Latest start time – Earliest start time

Since the two finishing times are given by adding a constant (the duration) to the start times:

$$\begin{aligned}
\text{Earliest finish time} &= \text{Earliest start time} + \text{Duration} \\
\text{Latest finish time} &= \text{Latest start time} + \text{Duration} \\
\text{EFT} &= \text{EST} + \text{D} \\
\text{LFT} &= \text{LST} + \text{D}
\end{aligned}$$

Then total float may be equally deduced from the finish times:

Total float = latest finish time – earliest finish time

Total float, therefore, may be found readily by subtracting the first upper figure on the node from the second upper figure on the node.

In the case of Activity J (Fig. 14.7) it is:

Total float = 24 – 16 = 8 weeks

While total float does not affect the TPT it may delay the start of succeeding activities by 'shunting' them. In the AoA formalism it is possible to indicate the ability of an activity to *float* without affecting other activities by calculating its *free* float. This factor is difficult, and in some cases impossible, to calculate in the AoN formalism, so that it will not be discussed here. In practice it is found that adequate control is obtained by frequent reference to the diagram itself and to total float.

Figure 14.9 shows the fully calculated diagram. The detailed analysis will give the following:

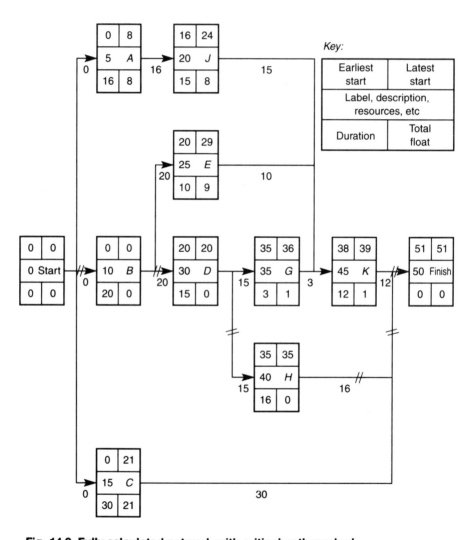

Fig. 14.9 Fully calculated network with critical path marked

No.	Activity description	Duration (weeks)	Start Earliest	Start Latest	Finish Earliest	Finish Latest	Float total
5	A	16	0	8	16	24	8
10	B	20	0	0	20	20	0
15	C	30	0	21	30	51	21
20	J	15	16	24	31	39	8
30	D	15	20	20	35	35	0
25	E	10	20	29	30	39	9
35	G	3	35	36	38	39	1
40	H	16	35	35	51	51	0
45	K	12	38	39	50	51	1

Note: This table is identical with that in Chapter 13 (page 146). This is not surprising since they both derive from the same project: Chapter 13 dealing with the AoA representation; this chapter dealing with the MoP representation.

Negative float

It is sometimes convenient to compare the overall project time with a target or acceptable time, and this can be very conveniently done by 'turning round' at this target time. Thus this target time is inserted in the finish node and the LSTs are calculated using this time. If the target time is greater than the TPT, then *all* activities will have positive float, while if the target time is *less* than the TPT, the critical path and possibly some other activities will have *negative* float. This *negative* float is the time by which the associated activity must be reduced for the project to meet the target time.

Circumstances sometimes require that events other than or as well as the final event should take place at particular times. Should this be so, then the 'scheduled' or 'imposed' time is inserted into the network as noted in Chapter 12. This imposed time is then used in the calculations for that activity and its predecessors in the usual way. This can give rise to zero or negative float on these activities independently of the main critical path, and these are known as secondary, tertiary and so on, critical paths.

CALCULATIONS INVOLVING CONSTRAINTS

Positive constraints in calculations present no difficulty, but negative constraints require care. The situation: 'Activity A of duration 12 is followed immediately by activity B of duration 15, while activity K of duration 36 is an opening activity with activity A and a closing activity with activity B' is represented as shown in Fig. 14.10.

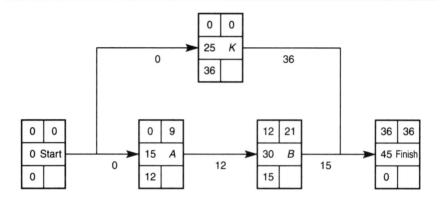

Fig. 14.10

The analyses for A and B are:

No.	Activity description	Duration (weeks)	Start Earliest	Start Latest	Finish Earliest	Finish Latest	Float total
15	A	12	0	9	12	21	9
30	B	15	12	21	27	36	9

so that it would be possible to finish A at time 12 and start B at time 21, an interval of 9 time units between finishing A and starting B. This may not be acceptable: for some reason the interval between finishing A and starting B must be limited to, say, 4 units of time. A negative constraint of $-12 + (-4)$ = -16 pointing backwards from B to A would result in Fig. 14.11.

The forward pass is carried out in the usual way by ignoring the negative constraint. On the backward pass, activity B has two emergent arrows (one the negative constraint arrow). The figure for the latest start of B is determined as follows:

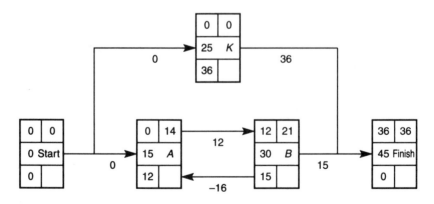

Fig. 14.11

1 Subtract the normal (that is, non-negative) dependency time from the LST of its head activity:

$$36 - 15 = 21$$

2 Subtract the constraint dependency time from the EST of its head activity:

$$0 - (-16) = 16$$

and then choose the smaller (16) of these two. The rest of the backward pass proceeds normally, and the resulting analysis for A and B is:

	Activity	Duration	Start time		Finish time		Float
Number	description	(weeks)	Earliest	Latest	Earliest	Latest	total
15	A	12	0	4	12	16	4
30	B	15	12	16	27	31	4

Thus, even with A finishing as early as possible (12) and B starting as late as possible (16), the 'gap' between A and B cannot exceed 4.

In effect this 'ties' A and B to their earliest possible positions. It may be that a later position is more appropriate. In this case the procedure is to determine the earliest start of A and the latest start of B, *ignoring the negative constraint,* which in this example would give:

EST(A): 0 LST(B): 21

A decision has now to be made as to the most convenient position for the A–B pair, which, for the sake of illustration, is assumed to be such that the LST for B is 18. Using this as the 'fixed point' the EST for A is now calculated using the two 'entering' arrows (one from Start, dependency time 0, one from B, dependency time 16). As these are entering arrows a forward pass is being performed so that the EST of A is the larger of the two:

$$0 + 0 = 0$$

or:

$$18 + (-16) = 2$$

That is, the EST of A is 2. This is used in place of the previously obtained figure of 0, which is struck out and the EST of B (2 + 12 = 14) and the LST of A (18 – 12 = 6) are redetermined (Fig. 14.12).

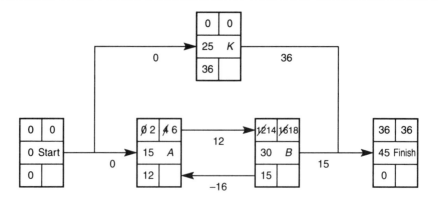

Fig. 14.12

PAIRED JOBS

There are circumstances when one job must start *immediately* after its predecessor has been completed. In MoP this is represented by the diagram in Fig. 14.13.

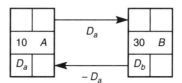

Fig. 14.13

A possibly simpler procedure is to combine the two activities into one activity (A + B) with duration time ($D_A + D_B$) if the logic of the situation will allow this.

Note: All the above calculations apply to simple, start-to-start dependencies. Multiple dependencies follow a very similar pattern.

CHAPTER 15

Precedence networks – multiple dependency Activity-on-Node

The activity-on-node (AoN) system so far described sets out essentially only one relationship between activities: the start of an activity depends on the starts of its predecessors. In the 1960s, IBM developed the 'System 360 Project Control System', which used multiple dependencies and for this the name 'precedence network' or 'precedence diagram' was used. This was an unhappy terminology in the sense that several years earlier the name 'precedence diagram' was given to the diagram setting out the necessary precedence relationships in a production flow line. However, the name is now blessed by BSI and is widely used in AoN literature. Accordingly it is used here.

FOUR DEPENDENCIES

There are four dependencies that can be described. Since many programs exist for processing the data and have differing requirements for coding the dependencies, no single way has been included here. The dependencies are:

1 *Finish-to-start (or normal) – see* Fig. 15.1. Activity B may not start until at least α time units after the finish of A. If activity B may follow immediately upon activity A then α becomes 0 and is either so written or it is ignored.

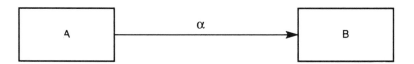

Fig. 15.1 Finish-to-start dependency

2 *Start-to-start* – *see* Fig. 15.2. Here, at least ß time units must elapse between the start of activity A and the start of activity B. The situation where ß > 0 – when the start of activity B lags behind the start of activity A – is sometimes called a 'lag-start' relationship. Again, if ß = 0 it is either so written or ignored.

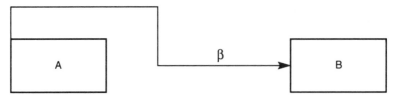

Fig. 15.2 Start-to-start dependency

3 *Finish-to-finish* – *see* Fig. 15.3. Here, at least γ time units must elapse between the finish of activity A and the finish of activity B. Where γ > 0 the relationship is said to be a 'lag-finish' relationship. Again, if γ = 0 it is either written so or ignored.

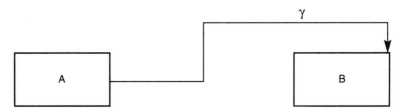

Fig. 15.3 Finish-to-finish dependency

4 *Start-to-finish* – *see* Fig. 15.4. Here, at least δ days must elapse between the start of activity A and the completion of activity B.

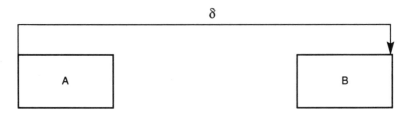

Fig. 15.4 Start-to-finish dependency

It should be noted that in all cases the dependencies can be used in combination. The most commonly used pairing is the start-to-start (lag-start) and finish-to-finish (lag finish) – *see* Fig. 15.5. Here, activity B may not start until ß time units after the start of activity A, and cannot finish until γ time units after the finish of activity A. This lag-start, lag-finish form may be used to represent a parallel dependency by setting γ = 0.

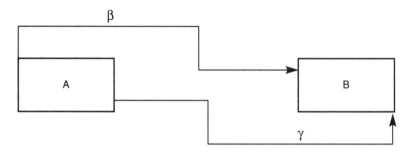

Fig. 15.5 Lag-start, lag-finish dependencies

Note: α, ß, γ and δ must be positive (indicating a delay) or zero in all the current implementations of precedence diagram systems. Some workers write α, ß, γ and δ as percentages of the preceding activity's duration – thus, if the duration of activity A is 10 days and activity B can start 2 days after the start of activity A, then α would be written as 20 per cent.

ACTIVITY TIMES AND PRECEDENCE NETWORKS

Earliest start activity times (ESTs) are calculated by means of a forward pass, where progressive addition gives the EST for the activities and the total project time (TPT) for the network. The TPT is then (generally) used to set the latest finishing time for the network as a whole, and a backward pass, with successive subtraction, gives the latest finish activity times.

A tabular system is often recommended for manual calculation; the authors find that a manual calculation *on the network itself* is simpler and gives a useful insight into the physical meaning of the network and its constituent parts. Although the method of calculation is illustrated here by a series of examples, it should be noted that manual calculations in multiple dependency networks are seldom performed: it is usual to use the computer for even very small projects. The problems in multiple dependency networks, from the manual calculation viewpoint, are the likelihood of error arising from the complex interactions which are possible and, therefore, the amount of checking which must be carried out before the activity time figures can be stated with certainty. The computer is good at such things, people working at speed are less so.

It should also be noted that an AoN network, using multiple dependencies to the full, generally appears as a more complex diagram than either single dependency AoN or AoA networks. It is a very sophisticated tool, and the use of multiple dependencies should be restricted to the short-term planning horizon since *all* projects change and the care required in checking the interactions, when changes are required to the network, is very great with a high probability of error. For this reason alone, if multiple dependencies *must* be used, a simpler approach, using a single dependency, should be used beyond the short-term planning horizon and the level of dependency interaction rolled forward at each update.

In the examples the time units are consistent throughout and have not therefore been specified. To demonstrate most simply the method of calculation, the seven-segment node of Fig. 15.13 (p. 176) is used throughout this chapter.

FINISH-TO-START

Three activities A, B and C with durations of 5, 10 and 15 precede activity X (duration 20). X may not start until at least 13 after the completion of A, until 10 after the completion of B and until 14 after the completion of C. The ESTs of A, B and C are 10, 12 and 14 respectively – derived from some other portion of the network not represented here (Fig. 15.6).

The earliest finishing times (EFTs) of the three activities are:

EFT A = 10 + 5 = 15
EFT B = 12 + 10 = 22
EFT C = 14 + 15 = 29

The EST for activity X is the time when the preceding ESTs and their dependency times are all complete, that is the largest of:

15 + 13 = 28; 22 + 10 = 32; 29 + 14 = 43

That is, 43. Since the duration of activity X is 20, its EFT is 63, and this is filled in on the forward pass for subsequent calculations.

The LFT for activity X derived from some other part of the network is 100, consequently its LST is 80. Since 13 must elapse between the finish of activity X and the start of activity A then its LFT must be 80 – 13 = 67 and its LST 67 – 5 = 62.

Similar calculations give:

For activity B: LFT = 80 – 10 = 70: LST = 70 – 10 = 60
For activity C: LFT = 80 – 14 = 66: LST = 66 – 15 = 51

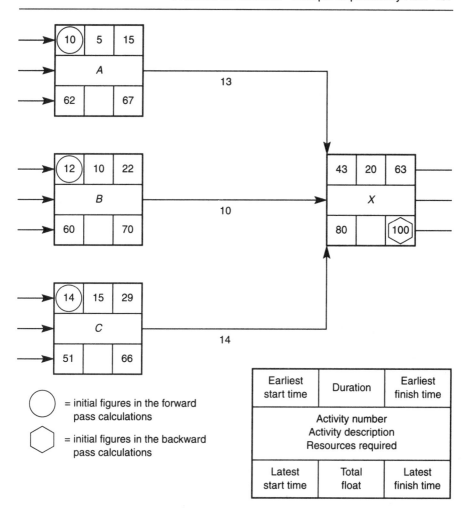

Fig. 15.6 Finish-to-start calculations

START-TO-START

The four activities A, B, C and X have the same durations and (for A, B and C) the same ESTs. The dependencies this time are start-to-start dependencies (Fig. 15.7).

The EST of X is the latest of:

$$10 + 13 = 23; \ 12 + 10 = 22; \ 14 + 14 = 28$$

That is, 28. The EFTs are then:

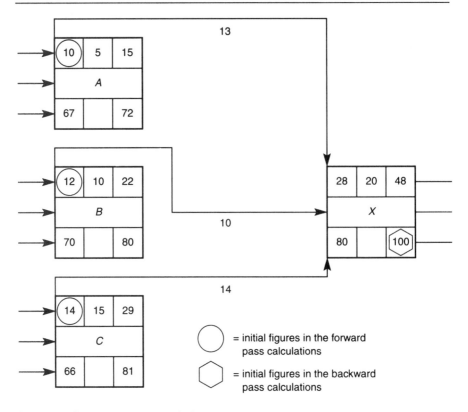

Fig. 15.7 Start-to-start calculations

EFT (A) = 10 + 5 = 15
EFT (B) = 12 + 10 = 22
EFT (C) = 14 + 15 = 29
EFT (X) = 28 + 20 = 48

It is given, from some other part of the network, that the LFT for activity X is 100, hence:

LST (X) = 100 – 20 = 80

Since activity X may not start until 13 units of time have elapsed after the start of A, then:

LST (A) = 80 – 13 = 67
Similarly LST (B) = 80 – 10 = 70
and   LST (C) = 80 – 14 = 66

and hence (Fig. 15.7):

LFT (A) = 67 + 5 = 72
LFT (B) = 70 + 10 = 80
LFT (C) = 66 + 15 = 81

FINISH-TO-FINISH

The same four activities are used in illustration as before with an additional activity Y, duration 25, which has a finish-to-finish relationship of 14 with activity C and an LFT of 90.

The EFTs of activities A, B and C are:

EFT (A) = 10 + 5 = 15
EFT (B) = 12 + 10 = 22
EFT (C) = 14 + 15 = 29

Activity X cannot finish until 13, 10 and 14 time units have elapsed after the finish of its predecessors, hence the EFT of X is the latest of:

15 + 13 = 28; 22 + 10 = 32; 29 + 14 = 43

that is:

$$\begin{aligned} \text{EFT (X)} \quad &= 43 \\ \text{Hence: EST (X)} \quad &= 43 - 20 = 23 \end{aligned}$$

Note: If another dependency between X and a predecessor – say a start-to-start dependency – had 'required' X to have a *later* EST, then this would have been adopted, and the resulting *later* EFT also used.

Since activity X may not finish until 13 time units have elapsed after the completion of activity A, and the LFT of X (determined elsewhere) is 100, then the LFT of A is 100 – 13 = 87. Equally:

LFT (B) = 100 – 10 = 90

Activity C has two finish-to-finish relationships (Fig. 15.8) and consequently its LFT is the earlier of:

100 – 14 = 86 (from activity X)
and   90 – 14 = 76 (from activity Y)

That is: LFT (C) = 76.

EFTs are derived by subtracting duration times from LFTs.

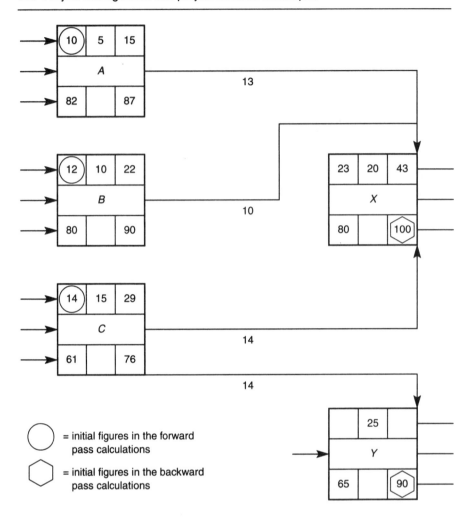

Fig. 15.8 Finish-to-finish calculations

START-TO-FINISH

The four activities A, B, C and X have the same durations and A, B and C have the same ESTs. The dependencies this time are start-to-finish dependencies so that the EFTs of A, B and C are 15, 22 and 29 as before (Fig. 15.9).

The EFT of X is the latest of:

$$10 + 13 = 23; \ 12 + 10 = 22; \ 14 + 14 = 28$$

That is, 28. Hence EST (X) = 28 − 20 = 8.

Since the LFT (X) has been determined from its successor activities the LSTs of A, B and C are determined by:

$$
\begin{aligned}
\text{LST (A)} &= 100 - 13 = 87 \\
\text{LST (B)} &= 100 - 10 = 90 \\
\text{LST (C)} &= 100 - 14 = 86
\end{aligned}
$$

and hence the LFTs are:

$$
\begin{aligned}
\text{LFT (A)} &= 87 + 5 = 92 \\
\text{LFT (B)} &= 90 + 10 = 100 \\
\text{LFT (C)} &= 86 + 15 = 101
\end{aligned}
$$

and the LST (X) = 100 − 20 = 80

It should be noted that in all cases the interactions with other activities and the addition of other dependencies will change the figures and can in some cases cause anomalies. Systems differ in how such anomalies are processed

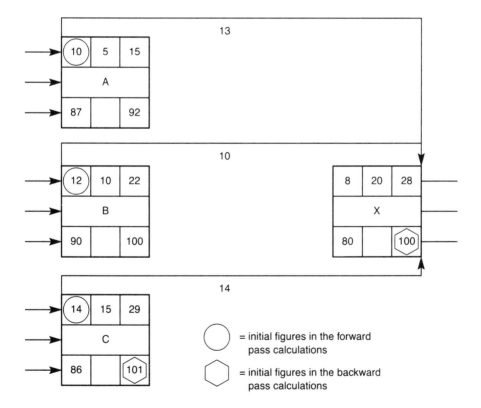

Fig. 15.9 Start-to-finish calculation.

and should always be checked to ensure that the procedure is understood. For example, in the cases of the start-to-finish and finish-to-finish dependencies the EST of the successor activity (activity X) may be set at 'time now' unless the activity is defined as non-splittable, in which case it will be determined from the EFT as shown in the examples.

SEVERAL DEPENDENCIES AT A NODE

The fact that two 'entering' dependencies may have arrow-heads at different ends of a node may cause one or other to be overlooked in manual calculation. For example, activity L (duration 10) has a finish-to-start dependency of 1 with activity J (duration 2, EST 7) and a finish-to-finish relationship of 6 with activity K (duration 12, EST 13) (Fig. 15.10). The activity starting times for L are calculated:

> EST: the earlier of $9 + 1 = 10$ and $25 + 6 = 21$
> that is, 10
> LST: the later of $9 + 1 + 10 = 20$ and $25 + 6 = 31$
> that is, 31

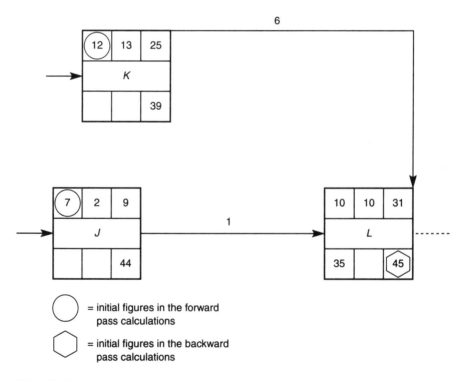

Fig. 15.10

The LFT for L, determined elsewhere, is 45, hence (Fig. 15.10):

EFT(L) = 45 – 10 = 35
LFT(K) = 45 – 6 = 39: EFT(K) = 39 – 13 = 26
LFT(J) = 45 – 1 = 44: EFT(J) = 44 – 2 = 42

LAG-START, LAG-FINISH

Four activities A, B, C and D (durations 6, 18, 10 and 8 respectively) are in parallel, with the following constraints:

1 Activity B may not start until at least 1 time unit after the start of activity A. At least 2 time units are required for the completion of activity B after activity A is finished.

2 Activity C may not start until at least 2 time units after the start of activity B. At least 3 time units are required for the completion of activity C after activity B is finished.

3 Activity D may not start until at least 2 time units after the start of activity C. At least 4 time units are required for the completion of activity D after activity C has finished.

This situation is represented by Fig. 15.11. Assume that the EST for activity A is 0, then the EFT for activity A is 0 + 6 = 6.
 Assume that the EST for activity B is 0 + 1 = 1, then the EFT for activity B is the later of:

6 + 2 = 8 and 1 + 18 = 19, that is, 19

The EST for activity C is 1 + 2 = 3, then the EFT for activity C is the later of:

3 + 10 = 11 and 19 + 3 = 22, that is, 22

The EST for activity D is 3 + 2 = 5, then the EFT for activity D is the later of:

5 + 8 = 13 and 22 + 4 = 26, that is, 26

Assume that activity D is a closing activity, then the LFT for activity D is set at 26.

(*Note:* If other activities are present they may set a larger LFT to be adopted.)

The LST for activity D is 26 – 8 = 18.

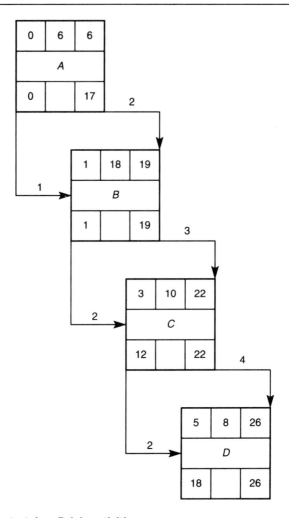

Fig. 15.11 Lag-start, lag-finish activities

The LFT for activity C is 26 – 4 = 22, then the LST for activity C is the earlier of:

22 – 10 = 12 and 18 – 2 = 16, that is, 12

The LFT for activity B is 22 – 3 = 19, then the LST for activity B is the earlier of:

19 – 18 = 1 and 12 – 2 = 10, that is, 1

The LFT for activity A is $19 - 2 = 17$, then the LST for activity A is the earlier of:

$17 - 6 = 11$ and $1 - 1 = 0$, that is, 0

FLOAT

Float is defined as the time available for an activity in addition to its duration. For an activity N, duration d:

Time available $=$ LFT – EST
Float $=$ LFT – EST – d

Thus, for activity L of Fig. 15.10:

Float $= 45 - 10 - 10 = 25$

This calculation assumes that all previous activities start as early as possible and all succeeding activities finish as late as possible (Fig. 15.12), hence this is the *total* amount of float – the *total float*:

Total float = Latest finish time – Earliest start time – Duration

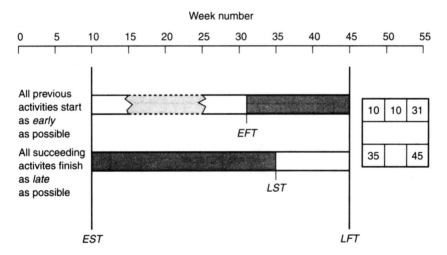

Fig. 15.12 Total float in precedence diagrams

Note: The presence of multiple dependencies at the node may make the calculation used in single dependency AoN of:

Total float $= LST - EST$
or $= LFT - EFT$

invalid since there may be a starting or finishing constraint on an early or late start or finish. Thus, for example, the finish-to-finish relationship between activities K and L means that even though activity L has an EST of 10, it has an EFT of 31. Some workers define:

Early total float $= LFT - EFT$
Late total float $= LST - EST$

but these terms are not in general use.

In AoA two other floats – free float and independent float – are identified, although only free float has been discussed in this text. However, the presence of multiple dependencies of different kinds at a node means these types of float cannot be calculated, and in general in AoN only total float is calculated and used.

Note: In practice, most fieldworkers, whatever type of networking is being used, find that total float provides all the information necessary, hence the loss of the ability to calculate anything but total float is of little significance.

NODE SYMBOLS IN AoN NETWORKING

The latest version of the British Standard BS 4335 makes the recommendations shown in Figs 15.13, 15.14 and 15.15 concerning the symbols to be used for a node in Activity-on-Node networking.

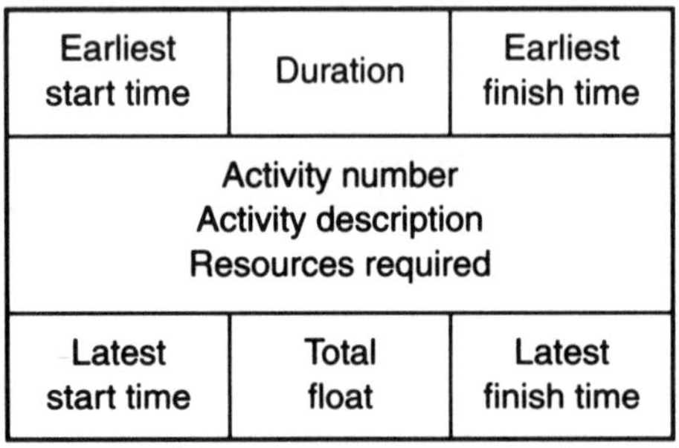

Earliest start time	Duration	Earliest finish time
Activity number Activity description Resources required		
Latest start time	Total float	Latest finish time

Fig. 15.13 Single dependency networking

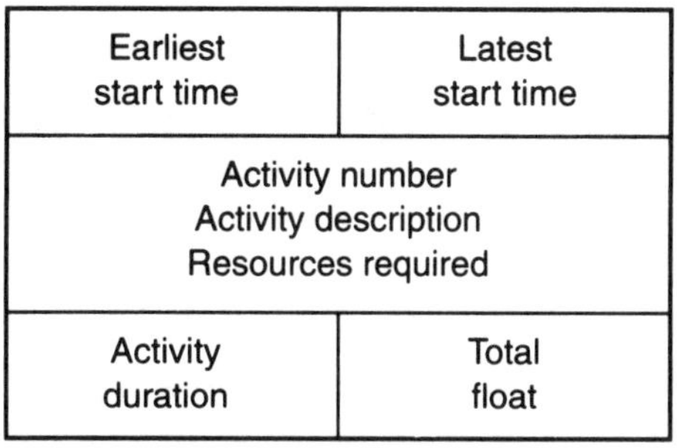

Earliest start time	Latest start time
Activity number Activity description Resources required	
Activity duration	Total float

Fig. 15.14 Method-of-potentials networking

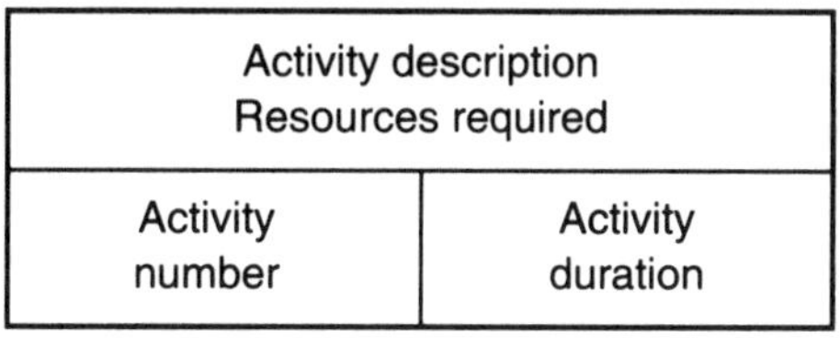

Activity description Resources required	
Activity number	Activity duration

Fig. 15.15 Multiple dependency networking

It will be noted that the first two symbols permit manual calculations to be written in the node box on the network. The likelihood of such manual calculations being carried out in multiple dependency networking is so small that no provision is made in the node box for writing in the results of such calculations.

CHAPTER 16

The network and the bar chart

Despite the difficulties with the Gantt chart discussed in Chapter 4, the authors have found the ability to translate a network into a bar chart valuable for four reasons:

1 It is more readily understood by 'unskilled' persons at all levels than a network diagram. One of the authors knows a company where all plans are made using project network techniques (PNT) but they are presented to top management as bar charts.

2 Progress can be easily displayed on it.

3 The meaning of float and activity times of all kinds can be understood by examining a bar chart. The authors have found the drawing of a bar chart an invaluable aid when teaching.

4 Simple resource allocation can be performed on, and the mechanics of complex resource allocation illuminated by, consideration of a bar chart.

There are, broadly, two ways whereby a bar chart may be derived from a network.

1 By carrying out a forward and backward pass, calculating the various activity times (either manually or by computer) and using these to give the locations of the time-scaled activity bars. This is so simple that it requires no explanation. It is the only way in which part of a network can be drawn as a bar chart.

2 By drawing the activities to a time-scale and by using the node numbers to ensure correct interrelationships. There are a variety of methods of carrying out this transformation. Over the years the authors have come to the conclusion that the *time-scaled network* is the most useful form.

THE TIME-SCALED NETWORK

The network that has been used extensively earlier will be employed again here as an illustration (Figs. 16.1 and 16.9). Any network, particularly if it has been drawn according to the 'activities parallel to the edges of the paper' recommendation, can be readily time-scaled.

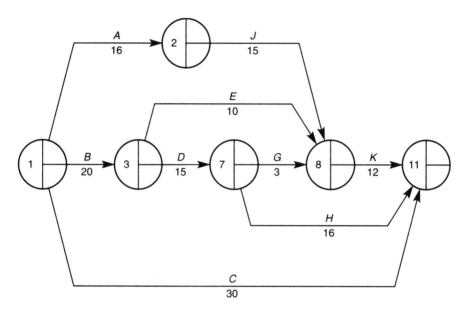

Fig. 16.1

Activity number	Activity description	Duration (weeks)	Start Early	Late	Finish Early	Late	Float Total	Free
1–2	A	16	0	8	16	24	8	0
1–3	B	20	0	0	20	20	0	0
1–11	C	30	0	21	30	51	21	21
2–8	J	15	16	24	31	39	8	7
3–7	D	15	20	20	35	35	0	0
3–8	E	10	20	29	30	39	9	8
7–8	G	3	35	36	38	39	1	0
7–11	H	16	35	35	51	51	0	0
8–11	K	12	38	39	50	51	1	1

Activity-on-arrow (AoA)

Start at the initial event and draw to scale all opening activities, identifying them by their node labels. It is desirable at this stage to space these well out on the page (Fig. 16.2).

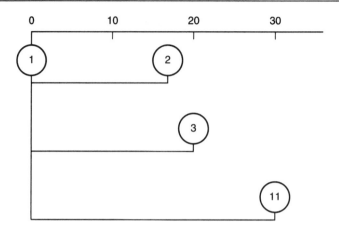

Fig. 16.2

Each activity will then either:

- *continue* as a single activity (1–2 continues as 2–8);
- *burst* into two or more activities (1–3 bursts into 3–7 and 3–8);
- *merge* into a node with one or more other activities (1–11 merges into node 11 with 7–11 and 8–11).

Proceed as follows:

- In the case of 'continue' activities, extend the activity by the length of the next activity (Fig. 16.3).
- In the case of 'burst' activities, draw a single vertical line and from this draw to scale the 'bursting' activities (Fig. 16.4).
- In the case of 'merge' activities, wait until all activities merging into a common node have been drawn – for example, wait until activities 2–8, 3–8 and 7–8 have been drawn, and then draw a vertical line to form a 'barrier' across the end of the activity that extends furthest to the right. Join all the merge activities to that fence by means of dotted lines. These lines represent free float (Fig. 16.5).

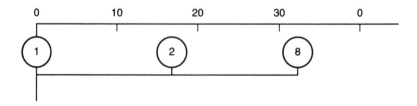

Fig. 16.3

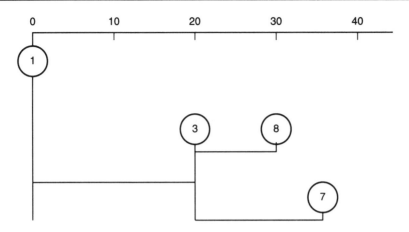

Fig. 16.4

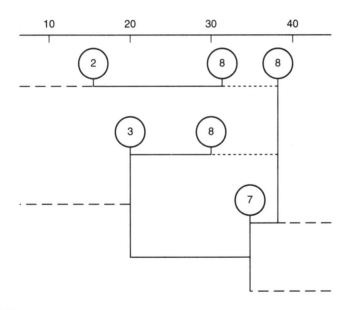

Fig. 16.5

Repeat the above until the last node is reached. Redraw if desired to emphasise special organisational or resource features. Using this procedure, the network of Fig. 16.1 becomes Fig. 16.8.

Note: Any dummy must be drawn in as a vertical line, its head and tail labels being shown. For example, Fig. 16.6 would become Fig. 16.7.

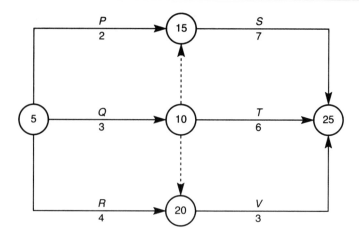

Fig. 16.6

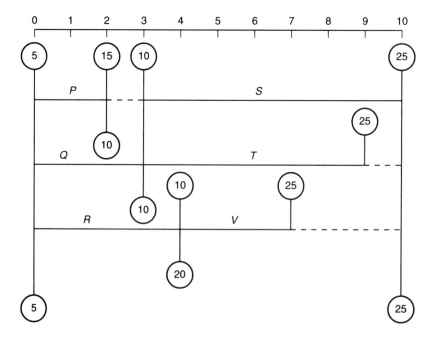

Fig. 16.7 Time-scaled network for Fig. 16.6.

Activity-on-node (AoN), single dependency

The AoN network is shown in Fig. 16.9. Start at the initial activity START and draw this as a vertical line. Draw to scale all activities A, B and C.

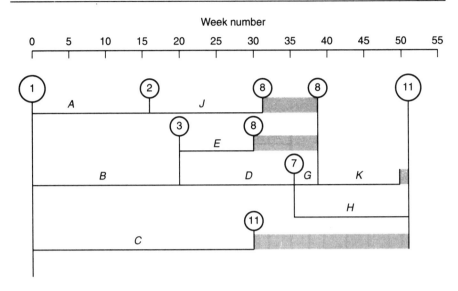

Fig. 16.8 Time-scaled network for Fig. 16.1.

Draw a short vertical line at the end of each of these activities. Place the activity labels at the beginning of each time-scaled activity. To the *right* of the vertical end line inscribe the labels of the appropriate succeeding activities (Fig. 16.10).

From each right-hand number draw the appropriate activity forward to scale (Fig. 16.11). Thus, from '20' draw activity J, duration 15. After activity B there are two labels 25 and 30. Accordingly, two activities need to be drawn (E and D). Activity C precedes activity Finish, but since other activities not yet drawn also precede Finish, no action is taken at this stage.

Again, from each right-hand label the appropriate activity is drawn. Activities J and E each precede activity 45 (K) (Fig. 16.12 on page 186). Examination of the network shows that three activities J, G and E precede this, and as only two have been drawn, no drawing takes place until this third predecessor is in place. However, activities G and H can be drawn; the three activities preceding activity 45 (K) having now been drawn, it can be located. Clearly it cannot start until the latest completion date of all preceding activities, i.e. after G. A 'fence' drawn up from the start of activity K enables the floats of E and J to be drawn. Activity K also precedes activity 50 (Finish) as does activity H. Accordingly, this activity too can be drawn in, completing the diagram (Fig. 16.13 on page 186).

The network of Fig. 16.14 on p. 187 – the AoN representation of the AoA network of Fig. 16.6 – translates very simply into a time-scaled network using the above procedure (Fig. 16.15, p. 187).

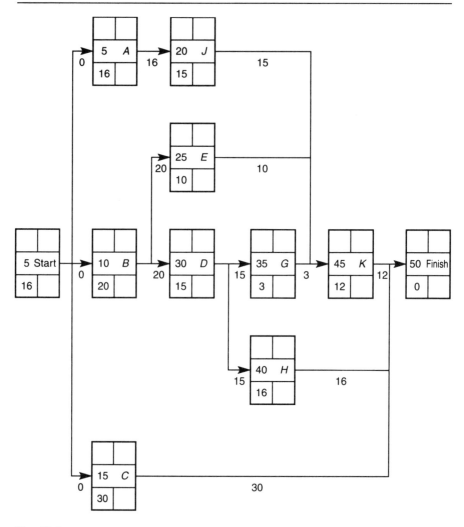

Fig. 16.9

ANALYSIS BY BAR CHART

The diagrams in Figs 16.8 and 16.13, one derived from the AoA network, the other from the AoN representation, give, not surprisingly, the same result. The analyses in Chapters 13 and 14 can be carried out from these diagrams.

Effectively, the bar chart as drawn represents an 'earliest start' situation – thus activity C has an earliest start of 0 and an earliest finish of 30. If it is imagined that Start and Finish are fixed posts between which wires are

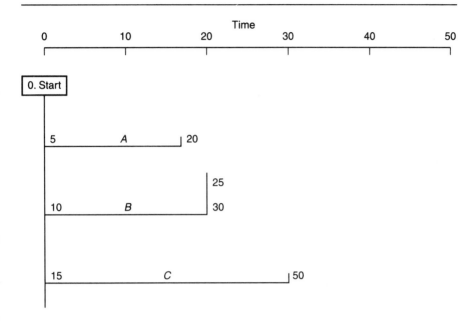

Fig. 16.10

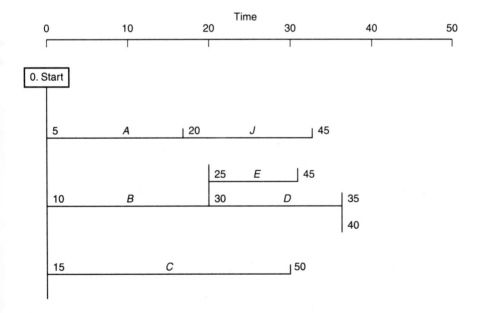

Fig. 16.11

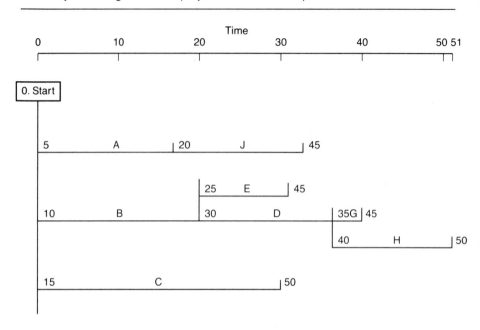

Fig. 16.12

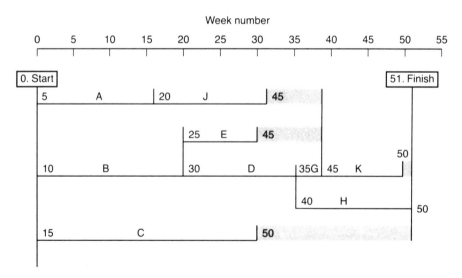

Fig. 16.13 Time-scaled network for Fig. 16.9. Compare with Fig. 16.8.

stretched, then the various activities are sleeves or tubes that can slide along the wires. The 'latest start' situation then is represented by an activity sliding as far to the right as possible – activity C having a latest start of 21 and a latest finish of 51.

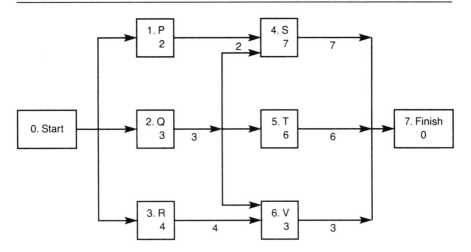

Fig. 16.14 AoN representation of Fig. 16.6.

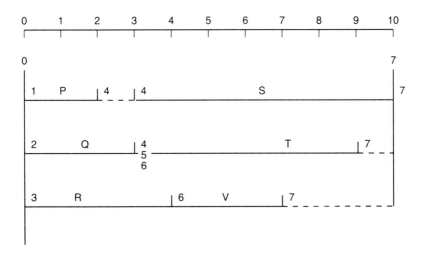

Fig. 16.15 Time-scaled network for Fig. 16.14. Compare with Fig. 16.7.

Activity K can float 1 week – it therefore has a total float of 1. Since it does not 'push' along a *succeeding* activity it also has a free float of 1.

Activity G can 'move' by 1, but only by 'pushing' activity K forward – hence it has a total float of 1 and a free float of 0.

Activity J has a total float of 8 – a movement of 7 before it 'pushes' activity K and a further 1 as it shunts activity K along – hence it has a total float of 8 and a free float of 7.

All the results of the tables on p. 146 and 159 are deducible in the above fashion, and students are strongly advised to work them out for themselves.

In the early days of studying PNT it will often be found that calculation difficulties can be resolved by cross-checking with a bar chart. It is often useful, and it can be very revealing, to draw an overlapping sequence of activities as a set of bar charts. Thus, Figs 11.31 and 12.12 become Fig. 16.16.

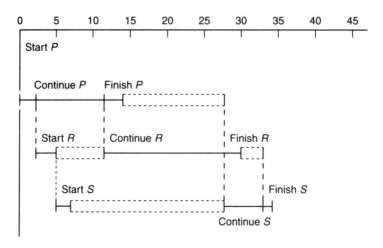

Fig. 16.16 Time-based network (bar chart) at Early Start.

This should be contrasted with the bar chart for the original situation in Figs 11.26 and 12.11 from which Figs 11.30 (AoA) and 12.12 (AoN) were derived, namely Fig. 16.17.

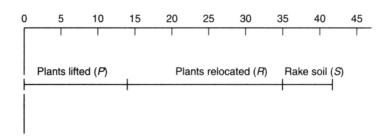

Fig. 16.17

The above procedures describe drawing a chart from an unanalysed network. It is sometimes more convenient to draw the chart from a network which has already been analysed, for example when the chart for only part of the network is needed. As a fuller example of this procedure the drawing of a 'cascade' chart will be illustrated in Figs 16.18 and 16.19. In this form the activity bars fall from 'top-left' to 'bottom-right' in conventional bar chart fashion, but ensuring that dependent activities are always lower in the chart. For anything other than small projects it is usual to use a computer to produce the chart.

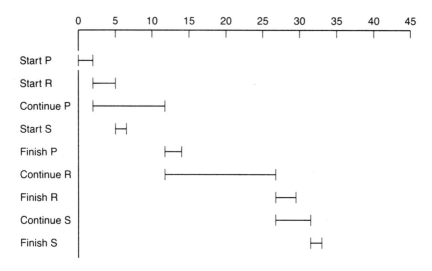

Fig. 16.18 Cascade chart in Early Start order for Fig. 16.16.

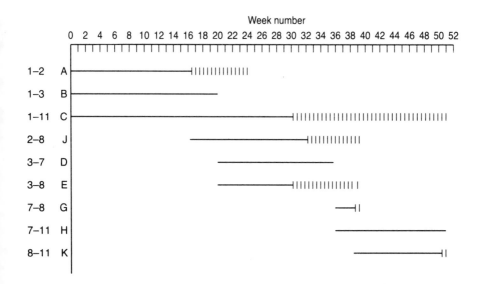

Fig. 16.19 Cascade chart of project in Early Start order with time scale for Fig. 16.6.

Computer-drawn bar charts

Modern computer packages can output the results of the network analysis in a variety of ways, usually defined by the user. With a plotter available any of the forms discussed can be used.

If the the only output device is a printer most systems will produce output in bar chart form, again usually as specified by the user. This will generally be in early start order or float order. If no specific ordering is specified the output bar chart will probably be in input list order, i.e. fairly random, and difficult to use. However many systems do in such cases output the bar chart as a cascade chart in which dependent activities are always lower in the list. A further simple illustration of such an output is shown in Fig. 16.19 for the example network. Unlike a manually drawn chart the node labels are not usually included on the bar, but are listed down the side of the chart with the other activity information.

Although a chart in this form is more useful than most other similar charts, in that the interactions are more obvious, it still leaves much to be desired when compared to the time-scaled network which, as stated earlier, is preferred by the authors.

CHAPTER 17

Resource analysis I

In all the discussions so far, it has been assumed that *time* is the most important factor, and in very many cases this is indeed so. However, it may well be that not only is time important, but the resources employed are equally or more important; for example, the number and skill of the people employed, or the special equipment used may impose severe restrictions.

BASIC CONSIDERATIONS

The problem is one that has been well known to the production control engineer since any form of activity has been undertaken. The name given by production controllers to this aspect of their work is *loading*; regrettably, new names have been devised by some of the earlier project network technique (PNT) workers, among them *manpower smoothing* and *resource allocation*. In the present text resource allocation will be used

Loading is defined as 'the assignment of work to an operator, machine or department', and is the most important feature of producing a timetable. When too much work is required of a work source, the work source is said to be *overloaded* while if too little is needed it is said to be *underloaded*. Ideally, the work required should be exactly equivalent to the work available, when the work source is *fully loaded*. This is an ideal situation which is seldom, if ever, encountered except in large-scale flow production, where it is possible to adjust supply and demand to reach some form of parity. In the type of work for which PNT is most useful, it is frequently impossible to adjust both supply and demand and some form of compromise is essential. This usually takes the form of *underloading* since this, at least, produces an acceptable result with respect to time; that is, the promised delivery date can be met. Deliberate *overloading* is foolhardiness to the point of sheer irresponsibility. Projects whose starting and finishing dates are fixed are said to be 'time-limited', while those where available resources are limited are 'resource-limited'. Many project managers would claim that they are required to achieve both a fixed time and resource limit, and while there *may* be projects in which both can be met they are rare; normally, when there is a conflict of objectives, one limit can be assumed to have priority. Unfortunately, in many situations that priority can change over time leading to confusion in the definition of the objective.

WORK REQUIRED

In BS 4335:1987 a resource is defined as:

Any variable capable of definition that is required for the execution of an activity and may constrain the project.

It may be:

(a) *non-storable:* **a resource whose availability has to be renewed for each time period (it does not remain available for use in the next time period even if it has not been utilised in the current period);**

(b) *storable (pool resource):* **a resource that remains available if not used and is only depleted by usage. Such a resource may also be replenished by activities producing credited/storable resources.**

For (a) labour is a typical example of such a resource, while for (b) cash is an equally typical example.

Resources are not therefore just the four Ms – men, machines, money and material – and normally include some which can be regarded as abstract, such as space, but which none the less present very real constraints in many projects. With modern project management software multiple calendars are available against which activities, with particular time pattern requirements, can be scheduled and there is no longer the need for as many dummy resources as was necessary with early systems. However, as noted, space and other abstract resources may still need to be considered.

In the discussion of resource analysis in this chapter *money* as a resource is specifically excluded and dealt with separately in Chapter 10. In many projects money is not the important element, *time* of completion and the economy of physical resource usage being the criteria for success. In these cases physical resource analysis can be of tremendous benefit. In major capital projects *money* becomes the principal consideration. In principle money is no different from any other resource, yet in practice it is constantly used by management for control purposes even when no other resources are being considered. As a result, special programs have been developed to deal with money as a control device and their bases are also dealt with in Chapter 10.

The control of resources is the most important and, in most cases, the most difficult part of project management. It has been noted by many researchers on project management that only about 10 per cent of organisations using network techniques are using resource control techniques linked to the networks. In most cases, crisis management is still the order of the day with the 'shout loudest' rule governing the allocation of resources.

RESOURCE DEFINITION

Resource allocation and analysis requires, as a point of departure, a statement of the work required. This can only be given in terms of man- (or machine-) hours; it should not be given in other units *unless* those units are readily and acceptably capable of being translated into resource-hours. For example, it may be that to dig a hole 4 ft × 4 ft × 6 ft in a particular location would take one man 12 hours. The work content should then be specified as 12 man-hours of work, *not* as 96 cubic feet of digging, unless it is well established that:

12 man-hours of digging = 96 cubic feet

or:

1 man-hour of digging = 8 cubic feet

The resource information on an activity can be specified in two separate forms:

- The first – known as *rate constant* – is in the form of the number of units of resource required by the activity. In early systems it was necessary to specify a *constant* usage rate for the duration of the activity; in modern systems it can be specified as a *pattern* of usage over the duration.
- The second – known as *total constant* – specifies the work content of the resource for the duration of the activity, as discussed above.

In modern computer-based systems it is not necessary to use only one of the two forms of specification for the resources employed by an activity; they can be mixed. However, great care is necessary to ensure that the effects of so doing are properly understood. In principle *rate constant* defines a duration for the activity which must be maintained, while *total constant* will allow the activity duration to be varied in a manner dependent on the units of resource available at the time the activity is scheduled. If in the example above, two men were available and can carry out the work without interfering with each other, then the activity would take six hours not 12.

It *must* be realised that in most tasks it is unlikely that there is a linear relationship between units of resource employed and activity duration for the full duration of the activity. Since current computer systems assume a linear relationship, the limits for which this assumption can be accepted as true have to be specified as part of the data. For example, a 100 man-day job is not usually a one-day job for 100 men, or a 100-day job for one man. It may be that the *normal* practice for the activity is 10 men for 10 days, and that this can change between five men and 15 men without significant effects on the work rate per man. The activity duration could then vary between 6.7 days and 20 days depending on the number of men available in the scheduling period.

In all cases the work required is specified by reference to the usual way of carrying out the activity, with the *usual* methods and the *usual* resources working at the *usual* rates, although the current circumstances need to be considered in determining what is *usual*. Initially, no cognisance is taken of the need by other activities for the same resources – 'infinite capacity' is assumed, any constraints being considered later.

It is useful, and should be a normal part of the project team's information systems, to record data on activities as part of an organisation's databank. This should include estimated and actual durations, resource levels, costs and notes on any change in circumstances between the planning stage and the actual carrying out of the activity. This data is useful not only to the current project but also to future projects with similar activities.

WORK AVAILABLE – CAPACITY

To complete the task of *loading*, it is necessary to know the amount of work *available* – that is the *capacity* available. This, too, must be specified in the appropriate resource units, but, in order that the completed schedule is not fictional, it is essential that the capacity should be strictly realistic. Thus, if 100 men are employed, it is unwise to assume that the available capacity each week is 100 man-weeks. In calculating available capacity it is necessary to know:

- the usual efficiency of working;
- the usual or anticipated, sickness or absenteeism rate;
- any existing commitments which require resources;
- any ancillary tasks which have to be performed, e.g. routine maintenance;
- holidays – annual, religious and statutory holidays with dates;
- any constraints on normal work methods on this occasion, e.g. confined space or machine capacity limitations;
- the limitations on the possibility of extending capacity by, say, overtime or subcontracting work. These have cost implications which must also be known.

In practice, it may well be that some of these factors can be ignored, but it is probably wise to consider each of them as a matter of routine; the number of projects that have not been completed on time because the summer holidays were forgotten is not on record, but it must be uncomfortably high.

Many organisations, following the assessment of capacity, add manual 'shortcuts' in setting out their network data to try to 'deal with' anticipated constraints on some key resource, and they do not at that stage, or at all, intend to proceed to a full resource analysis procedure. Thus, for example, a series of logically unconnected activities may be connected sequentially because it is known that they all require a particular resource which is in limited supply. Unfortunately, while appearing to be sensible, the decision on the sequence in which the activities are ordered may have serious effects on other logically dependent activities. Also, if at a later stage a decision is made to proceed to a fuller resource analysis all these 'short-cuts' have to be removed so that the system can perform the allocation properly – and some are sure to be forgotten because they are so 'normal'.

The difficulty is that, in the majority of cases and particularly for multi-project situations, there is no easy way of deciding what level of each resource should be made available to the project being considered.

CALCULATION OF LOAD

An approach to determining the extent of the problem is an aggregation routine. The project shown in Fig. 17.1, as both AoA and AoN networks, is used as the example for this and the following allocation procedures. The time analysis is provided in Table 17.1. In this small project, for which the

Table 17.1

Label AoA	AoN	Activity	Duration (days)	Resource (units)		Start Early	Late	Finish Early	Late	Total float
–	01	Start	0	0		0	0	0	0	0
1–2	12	A	4	3	XX	0	0	4	4	0
1–3	13	B	1	3	XX	0	5	1	6	5
1–4	14	C	1	2	XX	0	4	1	5	4
2–5	25	D	3	4	YY	4	4	7	7	0
3–5	35	E	1	3	YY	1	6	2	7	5
3–6	36	G	3	3	YY	1	6	4	9	5
3–7	37	F	5	2	ZZ	1	10	6	15	9
4–6	46	H	4	3	ZZ	1	5	5	9	4
5–7	57	I	8	3	YY	7	7	15	15	0
6–7	67	J	6	5	ZZ	5	9	11	15	4
6–8	68	K	1	3	YY	5	15	6	16	10
7–8	78	L	1	4	ZZ	15	15	16	16	0
–	80	End	0	0		16	16	16	16	0

networks express the logical interactions of the activities involved, three separate resources – XX, YY and ZZ – are involved in a non-trivial interaction as shown.

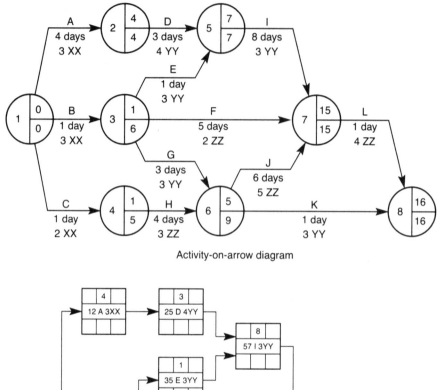

Activity-on-arrow diagram

Activity-on-node diagram

Fig. 17.1 Finish-to-start dependency.

Aggregation

An aggregation is a simple summation of the requirement for each resource, time period by time period, throughout the life of the project(s) with the project activities set at a defined state within their range of possible movement, e.g. all at earliest start or all at latest start. This usually gives a peak requirement for the resource in the project condition specified; an early peak for earliest start or a late peak for latest start. The cumulation of the resource requirements for the two project conditions, of all at earliest start and all at latest start, can then be used to give an indication of a reasonable uniform requirement for each resource. The results of the two basic aggregations for the example network of Fig. 17.1 at earliest start and latest start are shown in Figs 17.2 and 17.3.

Cumulation

A better way of assessing the data having obtained the aggregation results is to generate for each resource being considered the cumulative requirement curve known as the 'S Curve' (the Summation Curve) from each of the aggregations. This is obtained simply by adding each period's aggregation result to the summation of all the preceding periods' usage to give a cumulative requirement to date curve. For large labour-intensive projects the result is a smooth 'S curve' for the costs and manpower cumulations. For other resources and for small projects the cumulations may not generate the smooth S shape. Nevertheless, the curve, of whatever shape, is known as an 'S curve'.

If, for each resource, the earliest start and latest start cumulative curves are plotted on the one graph against time they will normally produce a closed loop. The one exception to this rule is money as a resource, which has a time value. In a long project, with differing rates of spend between the two extreme conditions, this factor can cause the loop to be open ended. In theory all resources can be converted to money and aggregated in this way, but it is not useful to do so when considering the effect of limiting constraints on individual resources.

Having plotted the two cumulative requirement curves for each resource being considered, the minimum slope straight line which will fit inside the loop is drawn as shown in Fig. 17.4. (This figure is illustrative only and is not drawn from the data of Figs 17.2 and 17.3.) The slope of this line gives a measure of the minimum constant level requirement for the resource, and thus is a good indication of the problems likely to be encountered in providing the level set by external or internal circumstances.

This requirement, when considered in its own right for a single project or in conjunction with the requirements from the other projects in a multi-project situation, gives a useful measure of the 'criticality' of each resource

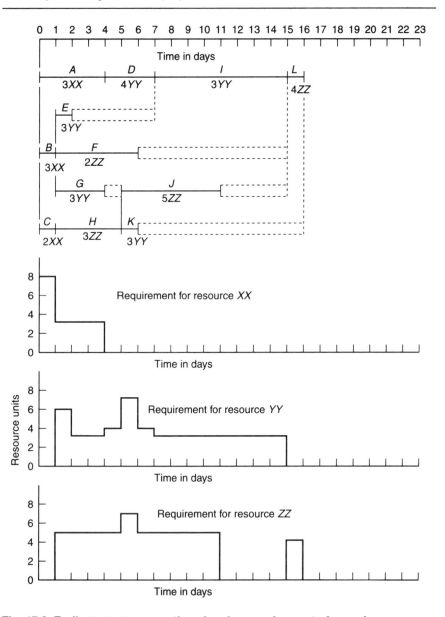

Fig. 17.2 Earliest start aggregation showing requirements for each resource.

by relating the requirement to the availability of the resource – if it is known. It should be realised that the minimum slope level obtained is an *indication* only, not an absolute value, since the interactions between activities and the resources in the project(s) will affect the situation and may not, in practice, allow the minimum slope level to be achieved.

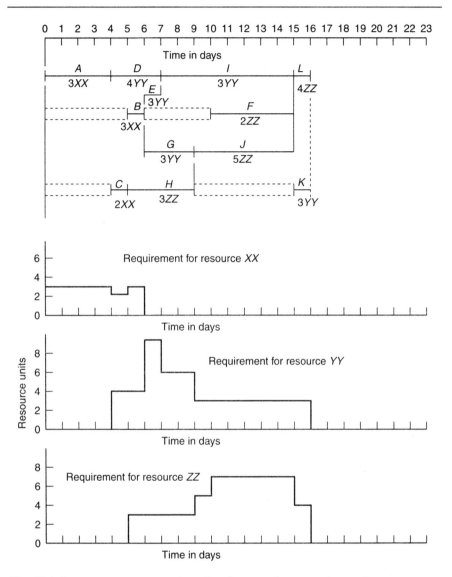

Fig. 17.3 Latest start aggregation showing requirements for each resource.

FURTHER CONSIDERATIONS

Once aggregation and/or cumulation of the resource data has taken place some form of allocation will almost inevitably follow. It is the authors' joint experience that in very few projects is the level of resources obtained from the aggregations acceptable, although usually if some fifteen differing resources are being considered, only six or seven at most will be causing a problem in the majority of projects.

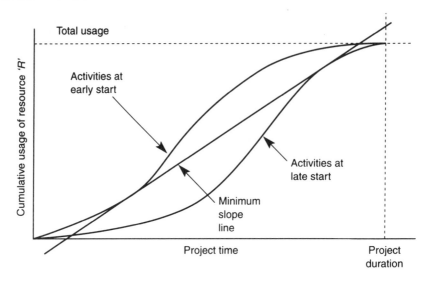

Fig. 17.4 Cumulative resource usage diagram for Figs 17.2 and 17.3.

In carrying out any form of activity scheduling which involves constraints on time and/or resources a number of alternative approaches are
available. These are as follows:

- *Allocation* requires either a time limit or resource limits to have been
  defined. The procedures then schedule activities so that the defined
  resource or time limit is not exceeded. No particular importance in the
  procedure is attached to the shapes of the resulting resource usage profiles.
- *Levelling* has as its starting point a schedule generated by some procedure, an aggregation or possibly an allocation, and attempts to 'level
  out' the peaks and troughs in the resource usage profiles without changing the duration of the project.
- *Smoothing* does not require any prior resource scheduling to have taken
  place. It does require a start time and a project duration to be defined
  and each resource to be assigned a priority for consideration. The procedure then schedules activities to give as smooth a profile of resource
  usage as possible within the project time frame.

Three problems

In dealing with any of these procedures at least three problems arise.

Imperfection of the data

The procedures involved in each case require that at least some, if not all,
of the following are known with a reasonable degree of accuracy:

- activity logic and durations;
- resources required by each activity;
- resources available in each time period for the project;
- priorities of resources, projects and activities.

The problems of alternatives

There are at least three different kinds of alternative which have to be considered:

1 *Alternative resources*. In most projects alternative resources can be used to carry out some activities. These have to be defined, and in many cases a new duration (usually longer) for the activity must also be defined.

2 *Alternative methods*. Any network is a statement about *one* method of achieving an objective. It is certain that in anything other than a very small project there will be other methods which could be used, and it is seldom possible to identify which of these is 'the best'. It can happen that too much time is spent debating the alternatives, the people concerned defending their own ideas. It is worth remembering that *any* method is better than *no* method. Nevertheless, an alternative method may well be desirable and Chapter 8 discusses a systematic approach to the search for that alternative.

3 *Alternative sequences*. In many parts of any project there are alternative ways in which the logical interactions between activities can be arranged, that is, there is more than one way of doing a job. However, in a case where there are no technological constraints between, say, four activities, there are 24 ways in which the ordering of the activities can be arranged. For N activities there are $N!$ ways of ordering the activities, and $N!$ increases very rapidly. For instance, with ten jobs there are $10! = 3\,628\,800$ possible sequences. Of the possible sequences there will be a sub-set which is 'optimal' according to the objectives defined. However, it is not feasible in most practical situations to be able to evaluate all possible sequences in order to identify which are in the sub-set and which are not. In such cases the need is to obtain a 'good' sequence which is feasible within any other known constraints, and to be able to generate it quickly.

The problem of optimality

It is often loosely stated that an 'optimum' allocation is achieved by a procedure. Quite apart from the problem of defining what is meant by 'optimum', there is the virtually insuperable problem of the size of the combinatorial problem which has to be solved for practical projects.

The definition of the objective to be achieved by any 'optimising' algorithm is difficult in the context of projects. For one manager it will mean minimising the peaks in resource usage, for another ensuring constant level use of a resource once it is used on the project, for others minimum cost, etc. These differing objectives are frequently in conflict with each other and since, in most cases, it is extremely difficult to see the interrelationships between the various factors, a decision will be made on purely arbitrary grounds and will probably change over time in the life of the project. The one commonly agreed objective is to minimise the extension to the project duration caused by the resource constraints.

It has been shown by Hastings ('On resource allocation in project networks', *OR Quarterly,* 23(2), pp. 217–221, 1972) and others that using 'minimising the extension to the project duration due to resource constraints' as the objective function, networks of up to about 200 activities and five different resources can be solved optimally. Although computing power has increased considerably in the meanwhile, the problem increases so rapidly in size that there is little to be gained from pursuing this approach. Optimising routines are of interest academically, but of little use industrially where few networks are so small. The main interest in the area has resulted from being able to show that the decision rule procedures used by the commercially available project management software packages produce optimal or near optimal solutions for similar size networks, given the same objective function, and thus should give equally good solutions to much larger problems.

A LIMITED CASE EXAMPLE

The general problem of resource analysis is, as has been seen, an extremely complex one and will be further illustrated here by a very simple example using just one resource.

The load as a histogram

It is convenient to represent the load as a histogram – that is, a vertical bar graph, the length of the bar being proportional to the load. For example, if the weekly load in a department that has a capacity of 10 man-weeks is:

Week no.	Load (man-weeks)
1	6
2	7
3	8
4	10
5	12
6	6

this would be represented by Fig. 17.5, which shows very clearly that the department is underloaded in weeks 1, 2, 3 and 6, fully loaded in week 4 and overloaded in week 5. (*Note:* some workers in this field refer to the available capacity as the manpower ceiling, so that week 5 exceeds the manpower ceiling.) Although this representation gives no more information than the corresponding set of figures, it has the usual virtue of a graphical representation, namely great vividness, and in practice it is found that it is almost invariably easier to work in histograms than in numbers, even though the histograms have been derived from the numbers. With experience, a great facility is obtained in viewing a histogram and assessing whether a 'peak' (i.e., an overload) can be toppled into a 'valley' (i.e. an underload) in order to 'smooth out' the loading.

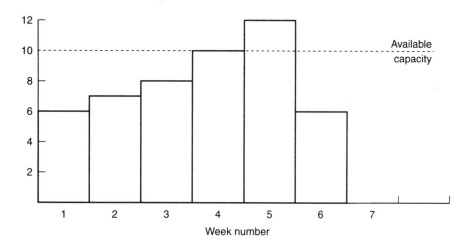

Fig. 17.5

Drawing the histogram by hand

The simplest way of drawing a histogram is probably found by drawing the appropriate bar chart and, by running down each time division, aggregating the usage of the various resources. For example, consider the network that has been so frequently discussed (Fig. 13.5, p. 134 and Fig. 14.2, p. 149) and assume, for the purpose of illustration, that the only resource used is *people*, and that each activity requires manpower as follows:

Activity	Duration	Men
A	16	2
B	20	6
C	30	4
J	15	3

D	15	2
E	10	5
G	3	2
H	16	4
K	12	4

Redraw the bar chart, as described in an earlier chapter, inserting the requirement on each activity bar within a circle. By running down each week, it is possible to add up the manpower requirements very simply. These can then be plotted on a histogram which it is normal to arrange below the bar chart as shown in Fig. 17.6.

In practice, it is possible, by the exercise of a little common sense, to reduce the number of additions; for example, it is clear that the loading for weeks 1 to 16 is the same, so that one addition (2 + 6 + 4) suffices.

If the capacity is also inserted on the histogram, the labour situation is very clearly shown. Assume that the available capacity is 10 man-weeks, and that all people are interchangeable. The dotted line shows this capacity and the over- and underloading. A quick check can show at this stage if the available capacity is adequate. The resource time commitments are calculated and totalled:

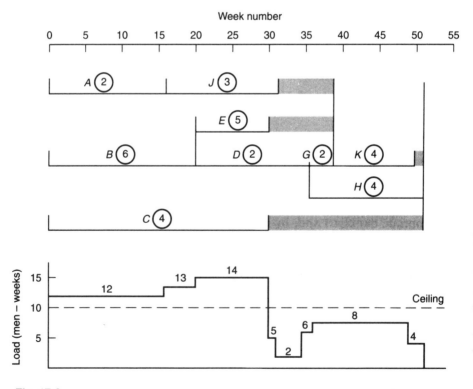

Fig. 17.6

Activity	Resource time
A	32
B	120
C	120
J	45
D	30
E	50
G	6
H	64
K	48
Total	515

The TPT is 51 weeks, hence the minimum possible resource demand is 515 ÷ 51 = 10.1 people. Two choices are now possible: set a new ceiling of, say, 11 people, or use the existing ceiling and then see where an increase of resources is necessary. Since the 'theoretical' demand is so near the ceiling, the second course is followed.

Levelling the load

The situation revealed by the histogram is one that is completely unacceptable. For 30 weeks the load exceeds the capacity, which can have only one result, namely the activities will take longer than planned, and the overall project time will increase. For 21 weeks the capacity exceeds the loading, and this will mean that people are idle. Clearly it is desirable to try to shift some of the earlier overload into the later underload. If this could be completely done, then the load would be 'levelled'.

The problem is an extremely familiar one to all those who have been in charge of the organisation of the disposition of labour. Virtually intractable, PNT does assist by providing guidelines along which to work. Of the various activities some are fixed in time (that is, are critical), while others can move (that is, they possess float), and, if an increase in TPT is to be avoided, levelling must take place in the 'floating' portion of the load. Furthermore, significant changes can only be made where float is substantial. Thus activity G has only one week free float; its overall effect is therefore small.

Activity C possesses the greatest float, and it should therefore be examined first. It will be seen that its duration is so great that, while floating it as much as possible will reduce the load at the beginning of the period, it will not seriously reduce the 'lump' between weeks 20 and 30. The next activity in order of magnitude of float is activity E. If this is moved as much as possible, activity K will advance by one week and activity E will extend from week 29 to week 39. This will then give a bar chart and histogram as shown in Fig. 17.7.

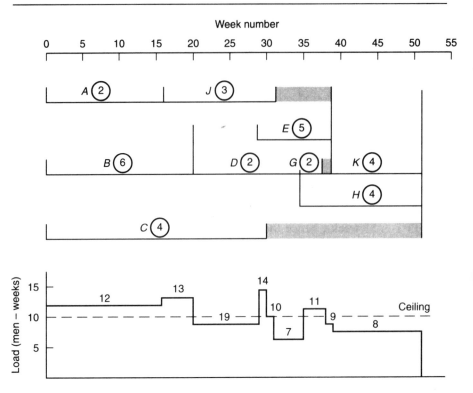

Fig. 17.7

The overload has been completely removed during weeks 20 to 29, and a small overload has been introduced during weeks 35 to 38. All float has been removed from activities E and K. The remaining activity with any substantial float is activity J. Shifting this forward by four weeks would reduce the 'lump' during weeks 16 to 20 and fill the 'trough' during weeks 31 to 35. The chart and histogram would then look as shown in Fig. 17.8.

Moving any other activities – and there are only activities A, C and G that *can* be moved – would produce no significant change in the load. Hence the arrangement in Fig. 17.8 is that which gives least overload and, using this as a criterion, is the 'best' arrangement.

Note: In practice, the virtue of any particular arrangement can only be judged within the context of the local circumstances.

The above discussion is offered as the kind of thinking that lies behind a loading task. The answer arrived at is not ideal, but answers seldom are in practice. The result, however, does give a sound basis for further consideration by which the problem can only be resolved managerially. For example,

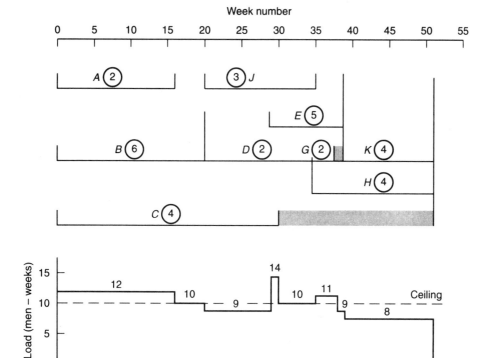

Fig. 17.8

- The 'spike' in week 29 can be removed if activity E is advanced by one week, but this will move the critical path forward by one week and hence the overall project time will increase from 51 to 52 weeks. Is this desirable/acceptable?
- The overload during weeks 1 to 16 can be removed by splitting activity C into two parts, the first 20 weeks long, the second 10 weeks long, and performing the second part during weeks 42 to 51. Is this desirable/ acceptable/possible?

PNT does not solve the resource allocation problem, but it does provide a method for systematically examining the possibilities. If there are more resources than one, then the examination becomes correspondingly more difficult.

The effect of levelling

What is the effect of levelling on the project as a whole? To examine this, assume that the last situation above (Fig. 17.8) is taken to be the acceptable one. This requires that activity E should not start until week 29, and that it must finish in week 39. Thus, the earliest and latest start time (EST and LST) for activity E is 29 and the earliest and latest finish time (EFT and LFT) is week 39 and, since the duration is 10 weeks, all float has disappeared. Effectively, another activity, 'wait for availability of labour for activity' has been inserted, and the relevant part of the arrow diagram has changed to include a new activity, W, 'waiting for labour', duration 9 weeks, which precedes activity E and succeeds activity B to create a second critical path:

B–W–E–K

in parallel with the first. Similarly, fixing the starting time of activity J at not earlier than week 20 has removed the float in the activity. The effect of this sort of action is to reduce the freedom in the network as a whole, while improving the utilisation of labour.

Scheduling

Levelling enables actual dates to be affixed to activities, and this is sometimes known as 'scheduling'. Thus, while initially there were bands of time during which work could start and finish, more starting dates can be fixed as follows:

Activity	Duration	Start time Early	Start time Late	Finish time Early	Finish time Late	Float Total	Float Free	No. of people
A	16	0	4	16	20	4	4	2
B	20	0	0	20	20	0	0	6
C	30	0	21	30	51	21	21	4
J	15	20	20	35	35	0	0	3
D	15	20	20	35	35	0	0	2
E	10	29	29	39	39	0	0	5
G	3	35	36	38	39	1	1	2
H	16	35	35	51	51	0	0	4
K	12	39	39	51	51	0	0	4

On comparing this to the original network analysis it will be seen that the apparent float has changed. It should be realised that the apparent float may not in fact exist since the interactions between activities and resources in the one project, let alone between projects, may prevent the activity or a *successor* activity being moved. It is unusual to find anything other than activity start and finish dates given in the output of a resource analysis program, because delaying an activity can require resources which *must* be available elsewhere at that point in time.

CHAPTER 18

Resource analysis II

It should be noted that for all but quite small projects there is no way of producing optimal results since the problem turns out to be a large and complex combinatorial one.

OPTIMUM-SEEKING PROCEDURES

Dynamic and branch-and-bound linear programming techniques have been successfully used to produce optimal solutions for networks of up to about 200 activities with a few resources. However, such projects are trivial compared to real projects which may have 5000 activities and employ 10–20 differing resources, a number of them being used in complex patterns on the activities. There is, of course, no requirement in modern systems that resources must be used for the entire duration of an activity or that only one can be used on an activity at a time or that activities cannot be split. Finally, it should be remembered that the data is imprecise – being based on estimates – and any error would invalidate the optimum.

Levelling

An early attempt to address the resource/time-limited problem was the technique of levelling. This in its simplest form means taking a schedule produced by some procedure and attempting to level out the peaks and valleys in the resource requirements by rescheduling some activities at alternative times. The starting schedule in many cases is an earliest start aggregation as described in Chapter 17, but it could be a complex schedule produced by a highly sophisticated allocation procedure. As a procedure, levelling sounds simple but in practice it is not. The interaction between the different resources makes for extreme difficulty, a difficulty which is vastly increased if more than one project exists in the organisation. Furthermore, since, as discussed earlier, there is no generally agreed definition of what is meant by 'level' it is extremely difficult to define a stop point for the 'levelling' procedure. In many cases the practice is to set a run time for the system and accept the result obtained at the end of that time.

It should be noted that some of the commercial software houses use the term levelling incorrectly to mean allocation against a *level* of resource availability. Equally there are some which are actually levelling and claim allocation.

Allocation

In the early 1960s two approaches to the allocation problem, known as the serial and parallel resource allocation procedures, were developed. There were hopes that these might prove suitable for the two alternative problems of resource or time limits. In fact they both give good solutions to the resource limited case in different scheduling environments.

The difference concerns the amount of 'splitting' of activities which is planned into the project. Splitting an activity is defined as 'The stopping of an activity, which is currently in progress, by the removal of its resources for use on an activity of higher priority.' Activity splitting is usually implemented in both procedures, it is the expected degree of splitting planned which should govern the choice of procedure. If a significant proportion of activities in the project are expected to be split, a parallel procedure should be used; otherwise use a serial procedure. Construction-type projects tend to contain a high proportion of splittable activities; most others do not, although almost all projects will contain some which could be planned as splittable if required.

The question therefore arises as to why consider the serial approach if all projects have splittable activities and the parallel procedure is better at dealing with them? The answer to that question is indirect in that it involves a number of related factors which add up to a significant case.

The first is the question of speed of processing. A parallel procedure can require up to 10 times the run time for the same 5000-activity project as a serial procedure and for large or multi-project processing it will be much greater – a figure of 30:1 can be expected for 12–15000 activities.

The second major factor, which is reducing in importance with the steadily increasing capacity of each new generation of PCs, is that of the computer working memory space required by the two procedures. That much greater memory is needed for the parallel procedure than for the serial, has been a significant problem for PC systems which have therefore usually offered serial procedures, particularly when this has been linked to a database.

A third factor is that for many projects with little or no splitting of activities a serial procedure will usually produce a 'better' result than a parallel – better, that is, in terms of minimising the extension to the project duration caused by the resource constraints.

A further consideration is the additional data which must be entered into the system in relation to any splittable activity. If an activity is nominated as 'splittable' it is usual to specify the minimum time for which it must be in progress before it becomes eligible for splitting. It is then usual to specify the minimum and/or maximum time for which it must remain stopped before again becoming eligible for scheduling, with a repeating cycle of these two stages if necessary. These data have to be collected, considered and entered for each splittable activity in order to prevent 'fragmentation' of the activity and other nonsense situations.

The procedures used for resource analysis are based on decision rules which produce, in general, good feasible schedules within the constraints which have been set by the user. These constraints will usually be either a limit on the availability of some resources or a limit on the duration of the project, or some mixture of both, depending on the facilities available in the system being used.

THE RESOURCE-LIMITED CASE

The serial and parallel procedures are used in all the currently available project management software in some form or another, and the designation is still a useful way of classifying programs. As noted earlier they both address the problem of the resource-limited case successfully under differing conditions.

The serial allocation procedure

This is a procedure in which all the activities in the project(s) are ranked, using a constant priority rule, before any scheduling takes place. The activities are then scheduled in strict order, from this priority list, at the earliest possible point in time consistent with the availability of resources and the precedence requirements of the network(s).

It is normal in a serial procedure to use ranking rules which automatically take the precedence constraints into account, such as those based on the time analysis of the network. The most commonly used rule is to use the activity latest start dates, in ascending order of those dates, and to resolve any ties which occur by the use of total float, again in ascending order. This rule produces results which have been shown to be as good, on average, as any other and better than most. Table 18.1 gives the ranked list produced from the analysis of Fig. 17.1.

In scheduling the activity being considered, the system first checks for the earliest point in time at which the activity can be allocated, on the basis that all preceding activities must have been completed. The system then determines whether sufficient resources are available at that time to enable the activity to proceed. If there are not it carries out a forward search of the resource availability tables to determine a period when the activity can be scheduled. Having scheduled the activity, the next activity from the ranked list is considered in the same way.

Table 18.1 Serial allocation procedure – ranked list of activities

Activity	Duration (days)	Resource required		Latest start	Total float
A	4	3	XX	0	0
D	3	4	YY	4	0
C	1	2	XX	4	4
H	4	3	ZZ	5	4
B	1	3	XX	5	5
G	3	3	YY	6	5
E	1	3	YY	6	5
I	8	3	YY	7	0
J	6	5	ZZ	9	4
F	5	2	ZZ	10	9
L	1	4	ZZ	15	0
K	1	3	YY	15	10

This constitutes a simple one-pass procedure which is very fast and gives good results. Figure 18.1 shows the results produced for the example network using this procedure with resource availability limits of five XX, six YY and seven ZZ.

The parallel allocation procedure

A procedure in which only those activities which are able to start, by virtue of preceding activities being complete, are ranked in priority order using a constant rule at each scheduling period. Activities are considered sequentially from this list for scheduling, depending on the availability of resources. Unscheduled activities are retained in the list for ranking with new activities at the next scheduling period.

Table 18.2 shows the series of time steps which would be activated and the sub-set of activities which can be considered at that time in each case. The time steps shown assume, of course, no activity splitting. If splitting was included the time step would be one unit of duration, which in this case would be one day.

This is a very different philosophy of scheduling since it gathers together in the one list *all* the activities which can be considered at a particular scheduling period. Since all the information is available it means that the decisions on whether to schedule or delay an activity can be reasonably made. This is particularly important with splittable activities and is the reason why this approach should be used if many activities in the project are to be splittable.

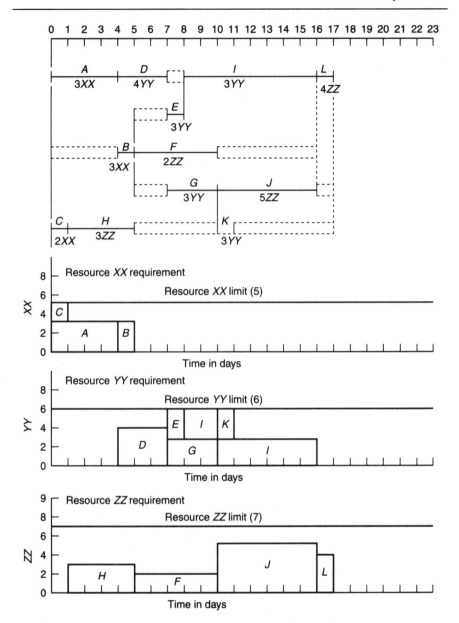

Fig. 18.1 Result of the serial allocation procedure.

This procedure also produces good feasible schedules, but, as noted earlier, takes considerably longer – in computing terms – to do so. The reason for this lies in the live list of activities which need to be sorted into ranked order. This is the slowest operation that a computer carries out on any file

Table 18.2 Parallel allocation procedure – list of time steps with sub-lists

Sub-list number	Time now (start of period shown)	Activity sub-list	Duration (days)	Resource required		Latest start	Total float	Activities scheduled at 'time now'
1	1	A	4	3	XX	0	0	*
		C	1	2	XX	4	4	*
		B	1	3	XX	5	5	
2	2	H	4	3	ZZ	5	4	*
		B	1	3	XX	5	5	
3	5	D	3	4	YY	4	0	*
		B	1	3	XX	5	5	*
4	6	E	1	3	YY	6	5	
		G	3	3	YY	6	5	
		F	5	2	ZZ	10	9	*
5	8	E	1	3	YY	6	5	*
		G	3	3	YY	6	5	*
6	9	I	8	3	YY	7	0	*
7	11	J	6	5	ZZ	9	4	*
		K	1	3	YY	15	10	*
8	17	L	1	4	ZZ	15	0	*

of data and is performed at every time step in the parallel procedure, while only being performed once in the serial procedure. The results of the procedure – with no splitting included for the sake of simplicity – are shown in Fig. 18.2. It will be seen that the resource usage profiles are the same in both cases, with the same limits on the availability of the three resources. If splitting of some activities had been included in both procedures the results could have been different.

THE TIME-LIMITED CASE

Unfortunately, although they are not the best way of addressing the time-limited problem, most commercial programs use the above procedures, with restrictions added, to address this problem also. The main restriction is of course that the search field is now limited to the remaining float on the activity being considered, rather than being open ended as it is in the

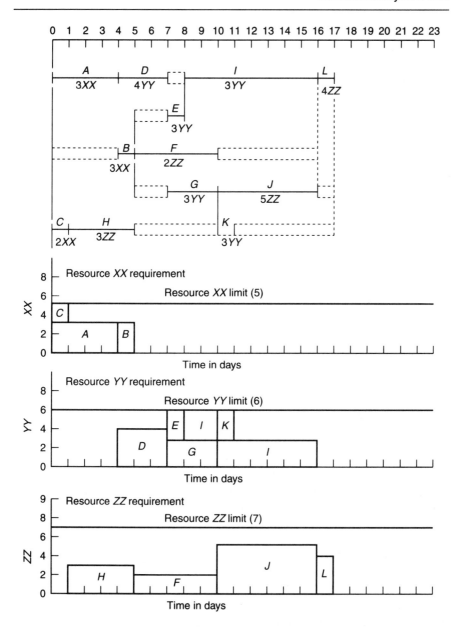

Fig. 18.2 Result of the parallel allocation procedure.

resource-limited case. Systems differ in the action they take if no period with sufficient resources for the activity exists in the field. In all cases the resulting resource requirement profile tends to an 'S-curve' shape with under-utilisation at the start of the project and over-utilisation at the end.

This is inevitable because of the way the procedures work, and the production of more acceptable results relies on the skill and experience of the user in fixing some events – as milestones – in order to reduce the amount of float available at the start of the project and thus force earlier scheduling of some groups of activities.

SMOOTHING

The objective of a smoothing system is to produce a feasible schedule within the time constraint boundaries with as smooth a resource requirement profile as possible. Although several alternative procedures have been devised only one is currently available as a commercial system. The basic principles of its method of operation are therefore described here.

The procedure works with multi-project scheduling as well as with single projects, but only a single project situation is considered in this discussion. The procedure requires two major pieces of information. The first is a start date and time frame for the project (if no finish date is given the system will assign it from the forward pass of the CP calculation), and second that the resources involved are ordered in a priority sequence, since in scheduling it will consider the highest priority resource required by the activity first before considering the next most important, etc. Techniques for assessing the relative importance of the resources are discussed later.

In scheduling any activity the measures which govern the importance of the activity and which need to be considered are:

- the type of resource(s) required by the activity and its importance;
- the total work content of the activity (which is the sum of the units of resource multiplied by duration of use on the activity for all resources required by the activity);
- the available float on the activity.

It is intuitively obvious that, other things being equal, if two activities have the same total work content the one with the smaller amount of float must be more difficult to schedule, and this is the basis for the decision rule which is used to select activities for scheduling.

At any time in the procedure when an activity is required for scheduling from the unscheduled activity list, the one which has the greatest value of the following expression is selected:

$$\frac{\text{Total work content of the activity}}{\text{Float remaining on the activity}}$$

Needless to say if the time required for the project is the calculated TPT (CP time) all the activities on the critical path(s) will be scheduled first since there is no option as to where they must be scheduled, and if at any time in the process the float on any activity becomes zero, that activity is automatically scheduled.

Having selected the next activity with the greatest value of the expression described above, it is necessary to determine the 'best' place to which it should be allocated. Again it is obvious that when presented with a diagram of committed resource usage to date and a span of time within which the selected activity can be scheduled on that diagram, the 'best' position is that which gives the lowest usage increase in that time span.

Since a computer is not able to *look* at the diagram, an alternative quantifiable measure must used to determine the 'best' position. In practice the system sets up, for the effective time span to be considered, a 'sum of squares' of the committed usage profile of the highest priority resource required by the activity. Figure 18.3 shows an example of the position at some stage in the procedure and shows the current committed levels of resource 'R' arising from the activities so far scheduled, and the range of possible positions to be considered for the next activity which maximised the expression and is being considered.

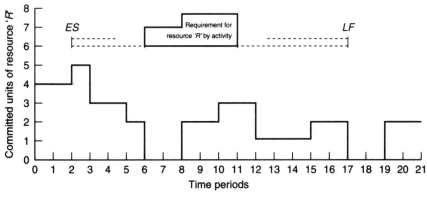

Committed resource units | 5 | 3 | 3 | 2 | 0 | 0 | 2 | 2 | 3 | 3 | 1 | 1 | 1 | 1 | 2 | 2 |

Squares of the profile of committed resource between *ES* and *LF* | 25 | 9 | 9 | 4 | 0 | 0 | 4 | 4 | 9 | 9 | 1 | 1 | 1 | 1 | 4 | 4 |

Sum of squares of committed resource profile = 84

Fig. 18.3

As shown in Fig. 18.4 the system will then position the activity in the first position it can occupy between its earliest start and latest finish, and will then calculate a revised sum of squares for the new profile of requirement. This is carried out for each position which the activity can occupy by moving it up one unit of duration at each step and calculating a sum of squares for that position. The results for this series of calculations is shown in the table below:

Position of activity	ES	ES+1	ES+2	ES+3	ES+4	ES+5	ES+6	ES+7	ES+8	ES+9	ES+10
Total sum of squares	134	118	116	118	126	134	134	128	122	122	122
Sum of squares of committed profile	84	84	84	84	84	84	84	84	84	84	84
Sum of squares difference	50	34	32	34	42	50	50	44	38	38	38

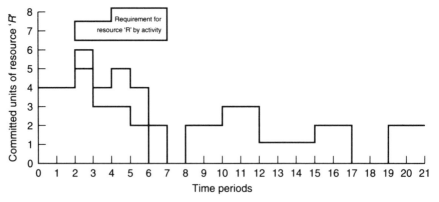

Squares of the | 36 | 16 | 25 | 16 | 4 | 0 | 4 | 4 | 9 | 9 | 1 | 1 | 1 | 1 | 1 | 4 | 4 |
profile of
resource with
activity at *ES*

Sum of squares of committed resource profile = 84
Sum of squares of new profile with activity at *ES* = 134
Difference in sum of squares 134 − 84 = 50

Fig. 18.4

The 'best' position is that which minimises the sum of squares increase from that of the original committed profile, in effect filling in the lowest point possible in the profile in the same way as one would as a project scheduler using a visual model. In this case the 'best' position is earliest start plus two time periods and this results in the profile shown in Fig. 18.5.

Having selected the 'best' position for this resource the system considers the next highest priority resource required by the activity for just those positions which are a minimum for the more important resource – given

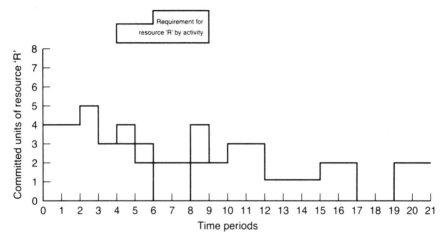

Squares of the profile of resource with activity at 'best' position

| 25 | 9 | 16 | 9 | 4 | 4 | 16 | 4 | 9 | 9 | 1 | 1 | 1 | 1 | 4 | 4 |

Fig. 18.5

that there is more than one such position. This cycle continues until either there is only one position for the activity – which is therefore used – or there are no further resources to be considered. In the latter case, if there is more than one possible position the earliest is selected since that maximises the remaining float on any uncommitted activities.

Having scheduled the selected activity the system updates the remaining float on all the unscheduled activities and selects the next activity to be scheduled as before. This results in a fast one-pass procedure which is extremely effective in producing a broadly 'level' requirement for the use of resources without needing to be able to specify the resource limits in advance.

As noted earlier, the procedure requires the priority ordering of the resources. This can, of course, be on a purely intuitive basis but it is preferable to use a more rational approach based on the information which can be obtained from the two aggregation runs described earlier.

In the discussion on aggregation it was noted that the minimum slope straight line within the resource requirement loop gives a good indication of the constant level requirement for each resource. Since in the time-limited case the availability of the resources is usually unknown, a direct comparison cannot be made. However, some knowledge will certainly be available and this can be compared with the requirements from the aggregations to give a good indication of the relative priority of the resources. Normally, the more projects that are being considered together, the better the subjective assessments on total availability are likely to be, and the better the consideration of the relative priorities.

GENERAL CONSIDERATIONS

In many multi-project situations the real difficulty is that of deciding in advance the level of each resource which can be made available to a project. In all except a project-orientated organisation, projects are an addition to the normal business of the organisation. Usually it is only when the number and frequency of projects becomes a problem that the organisation takes action to set up independent project teams. Again, it is usually then that the resource problem becomes apparent because projects are crossing departmental/functional boundaries and effective control of the resources passes from the department to the project team. In most functional organisations this visibility of the transfer of control is at the heart of the problem of introducing resource analysis, even if network-based project planning techniques are being successfully used.

As noted in Chapter 17 the organisation will have other commitments, the *normal* work, which is unlikely to be networked, and which requires resources. How much of each resource can be made available for projects, and – what is equally important – when they will be available is largely a matter of guesswork since few organisations have planning systems which yield the necessary data. Even if the gross data on resource availability can be obtained there still remains the difficulty of deciding what proportion of the available resources shall be made available to each of the projects in a multi-project situation. There are no easy answers to this problem.

If possible, it is in fact better to sidestep the problem and generate the requirement from a time-limited procedure, preferably a smoothing procedure if available. If the resulting levels are unacceptable then the time frame (total duration) of some, or all, projects must be adjusted and a new run carried out. Usually this situation will only arise when a new project is being introduced to an existing portfolio of projects, so that the amount of freedom for alteration of end dates for current in-progress projects is limited. However, an acceptance of some change is implicit if the new project is to be added to the portfolio, without, that is, causing unacceptable overloads in the resource requirement profiles.

The output of the system is of course a statement of resource requirements for the activities in each project together with a timetable for those requirements in the form of activity start and finish dates in each project and a total requirements profile against time. This is essential information in any situation for the managers who have to provide the necessary resources.

CHAPTER 19

Line of balance

Historically, line of balance (LoB) was developed before project network techniques (PNT), and the two systems are often considered to be separate but related techniques. However, if the original time-scaled stage-time diagram is abandoned, then LoB can be seen to be a quite conventional PNT system applied to a single batch.

WHERE LoB CAN BE USED

Just as PNT can be used to schedule and control a single project, LoB can be used to schedule and control a single batch. The following requirements need to be satisfied:

- There must be identifiable stages in production at which managerial control can be exerted.
- The manufacturing time between these stages must be known.
- A delivery schedule must be available.
- Resources can be varied as required.

While it is possible to use LoB to control a number of separate batches, just as it is possible to use PNT to control a number of separate projects, the computational difficulties become great. It is therefore usual to employ LoB in 'single batch' situations where the batch concerned is of some considerable importance to the organisation. An estate of houses, a batch of guided weapons or a batch of computers are likely to be the type of work appropriate to LoB control.

Again, as with PNT, LoB can be used in a hierarchical manner, considerable detail and a small timespan being displayed at the bottom of the hierarchy, while little detail but a considerable timespan is shown at the top.

LoB IN USE

The LoB technique will be illustrated by reference to the following hypothetical example.

Product Z is assembled from five components: A, B, C, D and E. A is purchased outright and B is made, tested and then joined with A to make subassembly 1 (S/A1). C is also made and tested, and then assembled with S/A1 to give subassembly 2 (S/A2). The material for D has to be purchased, and it can then be made up and tested, and then joined with S/A2 to give subassembly 3 (S/A3). E is a purchased item which is assembled to S/A3 to give the complete product Z. The final assembly stage can be considered to include the act of delivering the product to the customer. The delivery schedule is as follows (first delivery in week ending 1 January):

Week number	Quantity
1	2
2	4
3	8
4	12
5	10
6	10
7	16
8	18
9	20
10	22
11	24
12	26
13	28
14	24
15	10
16	6
17	4
18	2
19	2
20	2
	Total 250

Step 1

Construct an arrow diagram to show the logic and timing of the production (Fig. 19.1). It will usually be found most convenient to start to draw this from the end (in this case 'final assembly'), and work towards the various opening activities. The network need not be closed at the start – multiple starts are quite permissible and useful here – and nodes need not necessarily be identified, although for the purposes of the present text the nodes are identified here by letters. Duration times indicate the time required for unit production: these times are maintained constant during production by the variation of resources. The final chart is now very similar to the 'GOZINTO' diagram discussed by, for example, Vaszonyi.

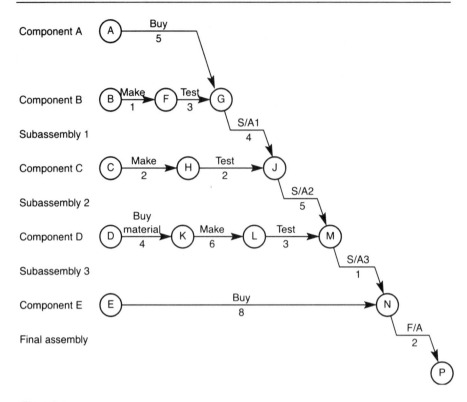

Fig. 19.1

Step 2

Carry out a reverse forward pass from time 0 at the final node, that is assign to the final node a time 0, and then successively add duration times for each activity in order. This will give the set of figures inscribed against each node: 2 at N, 3 at M, 8 at J and so on (Fig. 19.2).

The result of this reverse forward pass can also be represented on a time-scaled diagram, which is the form in which LoB results are often presented (Fig. 19.3)

Node times

While the node times represent the latest possible finishing times for the various activities, it is probably more useful to consider these times in relation to the quantities that would pass through the head nodes at any given time. Consider, for example, the activity 'make component B'. Any single component B having been made will subsequently require 3 weeks for testing, 4 weeks to be assembled into S/A1, 5 weeks to be assembled into S/A2,

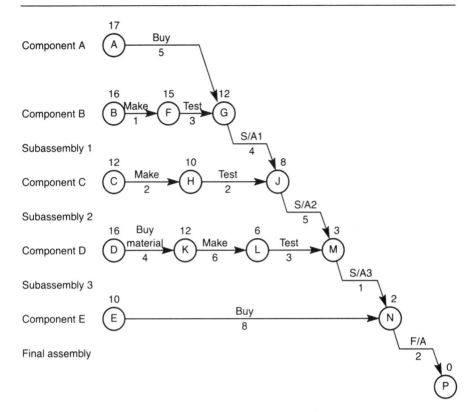

Fig. 19.2

1 week to be assembled into S/A3 and a final 2 weeks to be incorporated into the final assembly. Therefore, the interval of time in weeks that must elapse between a unit being made and its final assembly into product Z is:

$$
\underset{\text{(Test B)}}{3} + \underset{\text{(S/A1)}}{4} + \underset{\text{(S/A2)}}{5} + \underset{\text{(S/A3)}}{1} + \underset{\text{(F/A)}}{2} = 15
$$

If the conclusion of the final assembly is the delivery of the complete product Z to the customer, then the cumulative quantity of Bs that should 'pass through' node F by time t is the cumulative quantity that should 'pass through' node P (i.e., be delivered) by a time $t + 15$. For example, 2 weeks *after the start of delivery of complete 'product Z' to the customer*, the total quantity of B which should have been completed is equal to the cumulative quantity which should be delivered by week $15 + 2 =$ week 17, that is 244. This node time obtained by the reverse forward pass is called elsewhere the 'equivalent week number' for all activities entering the node being considered.

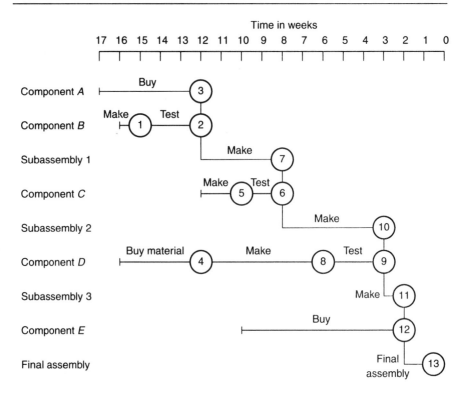

Fig. 19.3

Step 3

Rank all the activities in descending order of 'equivalent week number'. This ranking gives the activity number – sometimes, in LoB, called the stage – and is carried out to produce later a tidy 'cascade' chart.

Activity	Equivalent week number	Activity number
Make component B	15	1
Test component B	12	2
Buy component A	12	3
Buy material component D	12	4
Make component C	10	5
Test component C	8	6
Make subassembly 1	8	7
Make component D	6	8
Test component D	3	9
Make subassembly 2	3	10
Make subassembly 3	2	11
Buy component E	2	12
Carry out final assembly	0	13

Step 4

Prepare a calendar in combination with an accumulated delivery quantity table:

Date	Week number	Quantity	Cumulative quantity
4 September	−17		
11 September	−16		
18 September	−15		
25 September	−14		
2 October	−13		
9 October	−12		
16 October	−11		
23 October	−10		
30 October	−9		
6 November	−8		
13 November	−7		
20 November	−6		
27 November	−5		
4 December	−4		
11 December	−3		
18 December	−2		
25 December	−1		
1 January	1	2	2
8 January	2	4	6
15 January	3	8	14
22 January	4	12	26
29 January	5	10	36
5 February	6	10	46
12 February	7	16	62
19 February	8	18	80
26 February	9	20	100
5 March	10	22	122
12 March	11	24	146
19 March	12	26	172
26 March	13	28	200
2 April	14	24	224
9 April	15	10	234
16 April	16	6	240
23 April	17	4	244
30 April	18	2	246
7 May	19	2	248
14 May	20	2	250

Step 5

From the above two tables deduce the quantity of each activity which should be completed by any particular date. For example,

It is now 22nd January. How many of each component should be completed?
Consider 'make component D'.
The time is now week 4.

The quantity through 'make component D' is equal to the quantity which
can pass through the final stage in 6 weeks time, that is in week 4 + 6 = 10.
From the table in Step 4 this is a total of 122 units.
    Similarly for all activities:

	Volume of work completed is equivalent to volume delivered at week	Total units
Make component B	4 + 15 = 19	248
Test component B	4 + 12 = 16	240
Buy component A	4 + 12 = 16	240
Buy material component D	4 + 12 = 16	240
Make component C	4 + 10 = 14	224
Test component C	4 + 8 = 12	172
Make subassembly 1	4 + 8 = 12	172
Make component D	4 + 6 = 10	122
Test component D	4 + 3 = 7	62
Make subassembly 2	4 + 3 = 7	62
Make subassembly 3	4 + 2 = 6	46
Buy component E	4 + 2 = 6	46
Carry out final assembly	4 + 0 = 4	26

This can be represented on a chart – the traditional LoB chart as in Fig. 19.4.

A complete table for the whole 'life' of the batch can be drawn up if
desired (Fig. 19.5). The 'Ss' in the table indicate the latest dates by which
the various chains of activities should start, this date being derived from
the equivalent week numbers from the opening activities. The 'Cs' in the
table show that work must be continued.

Step 6

Record the actual progress upon either the LoB chart or the 'life' table. For
example, if at 22 January the achieved and planned results are:

	Achieved	Planned
1 Make component B	200	248
2 Test component B	200	240
3 Buy component A	200	240
4 Buy material component D	200	240

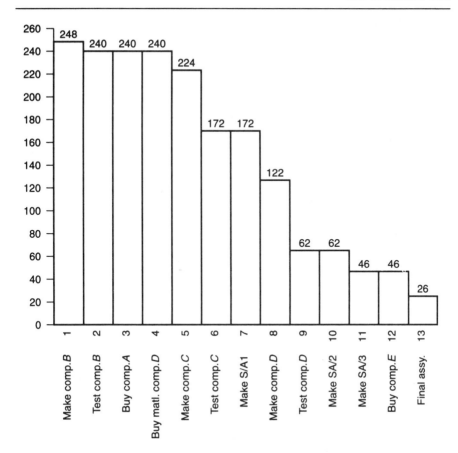

Fig. 19.4

5 Make component C	200	224
6 Test component C	200	172
7 Make subassembly 1	190	172
8 Make component D	200	122
9 Test component D	200	62
10 Make subassembly 2	150	62
11 Make subassembly 3	100	46
12 Buy component E	90	46
13 Final assembly	90	26

the LoB chart will be as in Fig. 19.6 while the life table will be as Fig. 19.7.

Despite the over-fulfilment of the delivery schedule (90 delivered and only 26 required), it can be seen that a 'choking-off' of production will occur in the weeks to come due to under-fulfilment on some activities, and, equally important, there is an over-investment in work-in-progress on other

Week number	Week starting	1 Make comp. B	2 Test comp. B	3 Buy comp. A	4 Buy matl. D	5 Make comp. C	6 Test comp. C	7 Make S/A1	8 Make comp. D	9 Test comp. D	10 Make S/A2	11 Make S/A3	12 Buy comp. E	13 Final assy.
−17	Sept. 4			S										
−16	Sept. 11	S		C	S									
−15	Sept. 18	2	S	C	C									
−14	Sept. 25	6	C	C	C									
−13	Oct. 2	14	C	C	C									
−12	Oct. 9	26	2	2	2	S		S	S					
−11	Oct. 16	36	6	6	6	C		C	C					
−10	Oct. 23	46	14	14	14	2	S	C	C				S	
−9	Oct. 30	62	26	26	26	6	C	C	C				C	
−8	Nov. 6	80	36	36	36	14	2	2	C		S		C	
−7	Nov. 13	100	46	46	46	26	6	6	C		C		C	
−6	Nov. 20	122	62	62	62	36	14	14	2	S	C		C	
−5	Nov. 27	146	80	80	80	46	26	26	6	C	C		C	
−4	Dec. 4	172	100	100	100	62	36	36	14	C	C		C	
−3	Dec. 11	200	122	122	122	80	46	46	26	2	2	S	C	
−2	Dec. 18	224	146	146	146	100	62	62	36	6	6	2	2	S
−1	Dec. 25	234	172	172	172	122	80	80	46	14	14	6	6	C
1	Jan. 1	240	200	200	200	146	100	100	62	26	26	14	14	2
2	Jan. 8	244	224	224	224	172	122	122	80	36	36	26	26	6
3	Jan. 15	246	234	234	234	200	146	146	100	46	46	36	36	14
4	Jan. 22	248	240	240	240	224	172	172	122	62	62	46	46	26
5	Jan. 29	250	244	244	244	234	200	200	146	80	80	62	62	36
6	Feb. 5		246	246	246	240	224	224	172	100	100	80	80	46
7	Feb. 12		248	248	248	244	234	234	200	122	122	100	100	62
8	Feb. 19		250	250	250	246	240	240	224	146	146	122	122	80
9	Feb. 26					248	244	244	234	172	172	146	146	100
10	Mar. 5					250	246	246	240	200	200	172	172	122
11	Mar. 12						248	248	244	224	224	200	200	146
12	Mar. 19						250	250	246	234	234	224	224	172
13	Mar. 26								248	240	240	234	234	200
14	April 2								250	244	244	240	240	224
15	April 9									246	246	244	244	234
16	April 16									248	248	246	246	240
17	April 23									250	250	248	248	244
18	April 30											250	250	246
19	May 7													248
20	May 14													250

Fig. 19.5

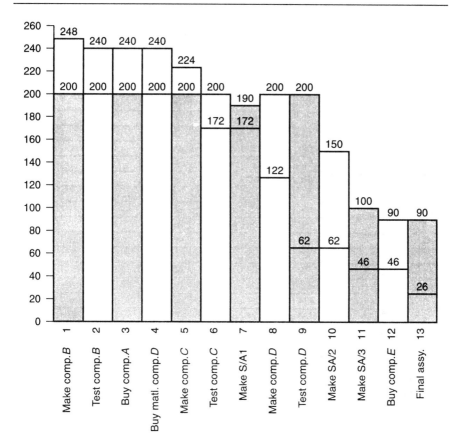

Fig. 19.6

activities. It may, therefore, be possible to transfer resources from the 'rich' activities to the 'poor' ones while preserving the delivery schedule: decisions here can only be taken in the light of local knowledge, and will require reference to both the PNT diagram and the progress results.

DESIGN/MAKE PROJECTS – JOINT PNT, LoB

It is not uncommon to find projects that involve a setting-up stage (design, plan, make jigs and tools) followed by the production of a batch of equipment. Here it is possible to use conventional PNT for all the work up to and including the making of the first complete equipment, and then to employ LoB to control the subsequent batch production.

Week number	Week starting	1 Make comp. A	2 Test comp. B	3 Buy comp. A	4 Buy matl. D	5 Make comp. C	6 Test comp. C	7 Make S/A1	8 Make comp. D	9 Test comp. D	10 Make S/A2	11 Make S/A3	12 Buy comp. E	13 Final assy.
−17	Sept. 4			S										
−16	Sept. 11	S		C	S									
−15	Sept. 18	2	S	C	C									
−14	Sept. 25	6	C	C	C									
−13	Oct. 2	14	C	C	C									
−12	Oct. 9	26	2	2	2	S		S	S					
−11	Oct. 16	36	6	6	6	C		C	C					
−10	Oct. 23	46	14	14	14	2	S	C	C				S	
−9	Oct. 30	62	26	26	26	6	C	C	C				C	
−8	Nov. 6	80	36	36	36	14	2	2	C		S		C	
−7	Nov. 13	100	46	46	46	26	6	6	C		C		C	
−6	Nov. 20	122	62	62	62	36	14	14	2	S	C		C	
−5	Nov. 27	146	80	80	80	46	26	26	6	C	C		C	
−4	Dec. 4	172	100	100	100	62	36	36	14	C	C		C	
−3	Dec. 11	200	122	122	122	80	46	46	26	2	2	S	C	
−2	Dec. 18	224	146	146	146	100	62	62	36	6	6	2	2	S
−1	Dec. 25	234	172	172	172	122	80	80	46	14	14	6	6	C
1	Jan. 1	240	200	200	200	146	100	100	62	26	26	14	14	2
2	Jan 8	244	224	224	224	172	122	122	80	36	36	26	26	6
3	Jan. 15	246	234	234	234	200	146	146	100	46	46	36	36	14
4	Jan. 22	248	240	240	240	224	172	172	122	62	62	46	46	26
5	Jan. 29	250	244	244	244	234	200	200	146	80	80	62	62	36
6	Feb. 5		246	246	246	240	224	224	172	100	100	80	80	46
7	Feb. 12		248	248	248	244	234	234	200	122	122	100	100	62
8	Feb. 19		250	250	250	246	240	240	224	146	146	122	122	80
9	Feb. 26					248	244	244	234	172	172	146	146	100
10	Mar. 5					250	246	246	240	200	200	172	172	122
11	Mar. 12						248	248	244	224	224	200	200	146
12	Mar. 19						250	250	246	234	234	224	224	172
13	Mar. 26								248	240	240	234	234	200
14	April 2								250	244	244	240	240	224
15	April 9									246	246	244	244	234
16	April 16									248	248	246	246	240
17	April 23									250	250	248	248	244
18	April 30											250	250	246
19	May 7													248
20	May 14													250

Fig. 19.7

ELEMENTAL TREND ANALYSIS

In some types of batch project a technique developed at the Building Research Station by Brian Fine and David Hutchings – 'elemental trend analysis' – can be a remarkably useful planning and control tool. This requires that:

- items in the batch are independent of each other;
- the same resources carry out the same activities (elements of work) on each unit of the batch;
- while an activity is being completed by one resource (trade) no other resource can work on that item;
- any constraints of material or subassembly availability must be removed at the planning stage.

Two examples of such projects which are in fact very similar in concept, but from very dissimilar industries, are:

- repetitive building construction – where a number of similar units are to be built on a site by tradesmen who work on each in turn;
- heavy engineering assembly – where units remain static in the assembly shop and are progressed by tradesmen who work on each in turn.

In such cases the conventional bar chart and network presentations are not particularly useful since each unit becomes a simple string of activities with no convergent or divergent branches.

Since two trades (resources) do not work on the same unit at the same time and the constraints of material have been removed, the operating constraints in this type of batch production are those of space and time. For a smooth flow of work, therefore, it is necessary to balance the time spent on each unit by each resource by adjusting the resources available or by modifying the methods. Plotting the progress of the first resource acting on the first activity throughout a batch of units gives a simple straight line as shown in Fig. 19.8.

If the second resource acting on the second activity throughout the batch operates at a *slower* rate than the first resource, its straight line will rise more slowly. The physical effect of this is an increasing delay between the finishing of the first activity on a batch unit and the starting of the second activity on that same unit, and a consequent delay in the completion of the batch. This is illustrated in Fig. 19.9.

On the other hand, if the second resource operates *faster* than the first, there is the possibility that it will require to work on a unit before the first resource is clear, something which is not possible and it will be held up. This is illustrated in Fig. 19.10.

Some allowance can be made for the different progress rates by adjusting the interval between the start of the first activity of a resource and the start

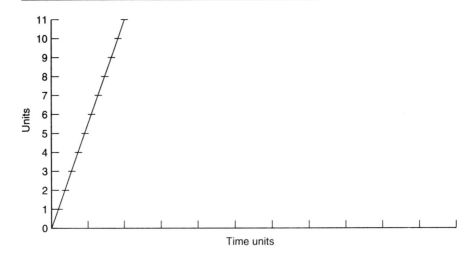

Fig. 19.8

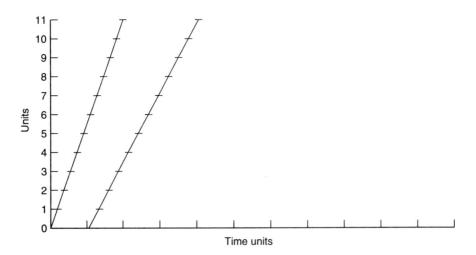

Fig. 19.9

of the next resource on its first activity (the 'heading'). If all progress rates are different throughout the batch, then each heading will need to be specially selected and will give rise to managerial difficulties. Ideally, the resource levels are adjusted to give parallel progress rates throughout the batch, as illustrated in Fig. 19.11.

This will give a smooth flow of work and a continuous steady use of the resources. In practice it may not be possible to balance the resources as pre-

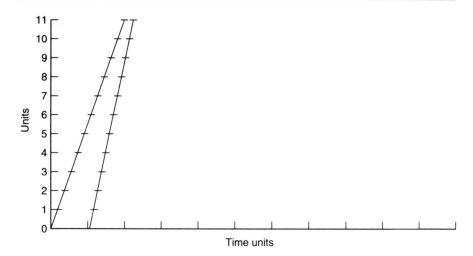

Fig. 19.10

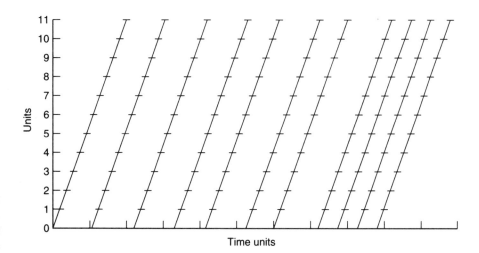

Fig. 19.11

cisely as is ideally desirable, and use must be made of the heading to accommodate the imbalance. For example, Fig. 19.12 shows a situation where resource 5 employed on activity 5 is operating slowly while resource 7 on activity 7 is operating fast.

Clearly, there is little point in speeding up activities after the fifth since subsequent activities will be held up waiting for the output from resource 5. On the other hand, if resource 5 can be increased then the whole batch

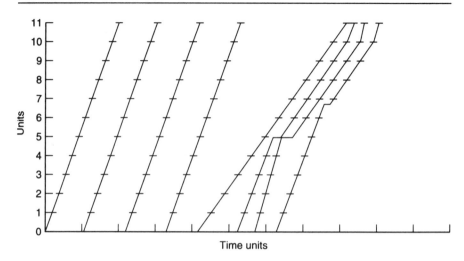

Fig. 19.12

completion will be speeded up. Equally, it may be possible to effect savings by reducing the level of resource 7 – and later resources – so that the progress rate balances that of resource 5.

In use as a control tool, progress is plotted directly on to the graphs and the trend of actual achievement as against the planned achievement gives a dramatic indication of possible problems to come and suggests possible preventive action to avoid them. The simplicity of the technique belies its power.

CHAPTER 20

Some practical considerations

As discussed in Chapter 1, there are four basic phases to any project: conception, development, realisation and termination. These can all be expanded into sub-phases to suit the project or parent organisation's needs. The practical hints given in this chapter, which are based on the authors' experience of many years of industry, teaching and consultancy, have been arranged to fit into the four phases.

CONCEPTION

It is assumed for this discussion that the project has been accepted by the parent organisation.

1 *Establish the project objectives.* Just as it is important to know the destination before setting out on a journey, so it is important to identify and define as precisely as possible the objectives the project is to achieve. The explicit objective – '... to build a new structure, to launch a new product, to install a new system, ...' – will obviously be known at the outset. It is the implicit objectives which need to be carefully thought through before any sensible planning can take place.

2 *Acceptance criteria.* The criteria by which the project will be judged should be set down unambiguously before the project is accepted. It is usually said that the project should be achieved 'on time, within budget and to the right specification'. This requires three interdependent questions to be answered:

(a) What standard (degree of excellence) does the project specification envisage?
(b) What time constraints are imposed?
(c) What cost and resource constraints are imposed?

In each case the acceptable range of variation needs to be discussed and recorded. For example, it may be that achieving the project early is worse than a degree of lateness and that 'on time' means in this case 'on time or not more than X per cent late, but not early'.

Clearly, each of the three depends to some extent on the others (Fig. 20.1), and the primary objective *must* be identified. When, as is inevitable, a problem arises during the project run, this prime objective is the one against which alternative solutions are judged. It must be noted that, as time passes in the project, the changing circumstances may well cause a change in the primacy of objective since there is a trade-off between them.

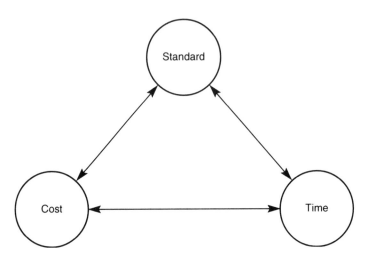

Fig. 20.1

3 *Appointment of the project manager.* It is, of course, desirable that the project manager should be appointed as early in the project as possible. However, good project managers are seldom available on a full-time basis just when needed, so that a part-time involvement with the project will probably be all that can be arranged. This will at least ensure that the project manager is aware of, and can take part in, the major decisions and commitments which affect the course of the project.

4 *The project 'log' (diary).* A project log *must* be started as soon as possible in the conception phase of any project. The lessons learned from it may be vital for future projects – in particular the reasons why a project was closed down!

5 *Appointment of the project team.* As soon as the project manager is appointed, he or she must be involved in the selection of the members of the project team, in particular the co-ordinators, the accountant and the procurement officer, given that the project is big enough to warrant such appointments. They, like the project manager, may be on a part-time

basis in this phase of the project, but will wish to be involved, with the project manager, in the selection and training of their staff, some of whom will be on a full-time basis. Some of the team may already be in post, having been with the project from its earliest inception, and sometimes may have views on the project which are at variance with the new members. This can cause significant problems.

6 *Involvement in design.* Once the project manager and members of the project team are appointed they must be involved, so far as is possible, in the preparation of the specification of the project product and in the design work resulting from that specification. In many cases the specification for the product will have been drawn up elsewhere, so that it is the *interpretation* of that specification and the design of the product to meet it, with which the project manager and the team should be involved.

7 *Establish the planning techniques.* Plans can be produced for at least two purposes: either to determine whether a task is capable of being carried out successfully (a feasibility study), or to assist in the management of a project (a management tool). Since the objectives are different in the two cases, the plans are unlikely to be the same and will certainly differ in detail. To produce a detailed management plan for the feasibility study would in many cases be more costly than is justified; to use a feasibility plan for project control may well be too broad-brush. However, a management plan can well grow out of a feasibility plan.

8 *Investigate the computing facilities.* There are now so many excellent computer-based project management packages available that it would be an act of extreme folly for any project planner to write a new program for a project. That having been said, it is essential to discover precisely the facilities that are being offered by any available software. It does not follow that, because a package has been successfully used in the past, that it will be equally suitable on this occasion. For instance, it may be that extensive graphical output is required in the reports for this project and the package is not capable of providing it.

DEVELOPMENT

1 *Update the specification with the customer.* The conception phase will probably have included a feasibility study. The results of such a study may well result in changes to the detail of the specification of the product. *Any* changes *must* be agreed with the customer and incorporated in the specification *before* the contract is signed. Further changes may result from the development phase; these too *must* be agreed by the customer.

2 *Procurement items.* All procurement items, in particular critical ones, should be separately identified in the plans, not just bulked together as 'procure all materials (items) or services'. Critical items are likely to be goods or services or specially made equipment which are on a long lead time and decisions on these are likely to have to be made on the basis of inadequate knowledge. The procurement officer should be aware of these and be prepared to update the specification with the supplier. The procurement officer should ensure that the project manager is involved in the process of selecting subcontractors and suppliers.

3 *Ensure that all plans are dated.* Always ensure that all plans are dated so that all using one can be sure they are up to date and, in discussion, are talking about the same plan!

4 *Preparing network plans:*
   - Use a large sheet of paper, a *pencil* and a *rubber*. It is extremely unlikely that the first attempt, for even a small project, will be the final version, so that changes must be capable of being made easily. The authors have seen incorrect networks being used just because they had been drawn in ink and were too difficult to change. A good eraser is the planner's most useful tool.
   - When producing the final versions of the network – assuming that they are to be manually drawn – aim to have no more than 200 activities to a drawing sheet and, in a large project, try to ensure that each sheet contains a subproject or linked subprojects if they are small. So far as is possible, try to ensure that the flow of time is from left to right across the drawing sheet. Try to avoid arrows which point backwards in time; these are a potent source of logical errors, particularly between the separate drawing sheets. See also BS 6046: Part 2: Guide to the use of graphical and estimating techniques.
   - Always involve the person responsible for the execution of that part of the project in all discussions on drawing the network logic, particularly where difficulties are likely to arise. Much of the time needed for drawing the network is taken up in discussing the logical interactions of activities where responsibilities change. It is far better if the planner can arrange for discussion to take place between the managers responsible for the interface than for each to talk separately and blame the planner for any problems.
   - Always involve the person responsible for the execution of an activity in all discussions on setting durations and/or dependency times. Failure to do so may well result in the network being discredited as 'impractical'.
   - Duration times for activities *must* be based on the best estimates for this occasion and should be based on *normal* methods of working unless

otherwise specified. In collecting resource information *no account* should be taken of calls on the resources by other activities; it is always assumed that the necessary resources will be available when required.

- It is probable that subsequent analysis may change the assumption on availability for some resources, but that should be left to that analysis if such is to be performed.

- A problem often occurs in assigning a duration to a novel activity. In such cases it may be useful to break the activity down into more detail, when it will probably be found that the 'novelty' applies to a comparatively small part of the whole activity. This part can then be discussed in detail with the person responsible for its execution and, since it forms only a small part of the whole, any error which still remains will be diluted.

- Once the network has been drawn and analysed, it is worth rechecking the durations of critical and near critical activities, particularly in the early part of the project. Activities with substantial amounts of float can absorb considerable inaccuracy in duration estimates without causing problems.

- There is no 'best' point at which to start a network. Pick any activity, locate it approximately on the sheet and work from there by asking:

> What *had* to be done *before* this?
> What *can* be done *after* this?

- When drawing the network do not attempt to use the duration times or any resource information until the network is complete. A belief that such-and-such an activity is *bound* to be critical or that a resource is *bound* to be a constraint is likely to distort thinking.

- Avoid excessive detail. No more detail should be included than is necessary for the level of control which is to be exercised in the project. For example, if progress is to be reviewed weekly, it is pointless to have activities whose durations are measured in hours, with many occurring between reviews. There is always the temptation to include more detail in the belief that it improves the ability to control. In practice, too much detail clogs both thinking and the control system. A simple string of non-branching activities with similar resource requirements as in Fig. 20.2 can often be usefully amalgamated, as in Fig. 20.3.

  Rules concerning such amalgamations have not been defined, but three questions can usefully be posed in each case;

(a) Do separate activities have to be specified because of particular resource usages?

(b) Would an amalgamated activity cover responsibilities assignable to more than one person?

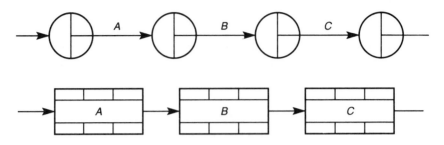

Fig. 20.2

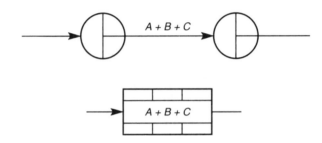

Fig. 20.3

(c) Will the person using the network be able to make sensible decisions in controlling the activity?

– A large network should always be broken down into subprojects. The way the breakdown is structured should reflect the control procedures to be employed and any work breakdown structure.

– Once a first network has been drawn, check the logic, as far as is possible for the planner, by asking the questions above, namely:

What *had* to be done *before* this?
What *can* be done *after* this?

– When using the AoA formalism, always pay special attention to 'crossroad' configurations where numbers of activities enter and leave a node. This is a very rich source of logical errors.

– When using the AoN formalism with multiple dependencies, ensure that the interactions do represent the situation intended and will be correctly interpreted by the system being used.

– Make sure that all leaving activities do in fact depend on all entering activities. These situations are a very common source of *errors*. Make sure that there are no obvious loops or 'dangling' activities unless the program being used will accept multiple start and finish activities, when in such cases the appropriate input data must be supplied.

- When updating *any* network, either as a result of changes to future activities, or as a result of progress data, care must always be taken to ensure that any overlap conditions are correctly dealt with. This is particularly true for multi-dependency AoN where the dependency interactions can be extremely complex. As discussed in Chapter 15, the use of multiple dependencies should be restricted to the short-term planning horizon to avoid too many problems of this nature.

- *Do not* assign labels (numbers) to the nodes (AoA) or activities (AoN) until the logic of the plan has been reasonably determined, then ensure that *all* are in fact labelled. Most current project management software will accept alphanumeric identifiers; however, *all* require uniqueness in the identifiers. Good practice will help in this respect – the label should consist of the *project* number, the *sheet* number on which the activity is drawn and a *unique number* for that sheet. If the recommendation of no more than 200 activities to a sheet is followed, there will be that number as a maximum for an AoN network and about 180 nodes for an AoA network. There should be no problem in keeping that part of the label unique. *Do not* reuse numbers when changes are made. A record of the last used number should be kept.

- It may be necessary to redraw the network to conform to a particular 'house-style' or other required breakdown structure. As far as possible this should be considered in the preparation of the 'first' network.

- Enter the project to the system being used, which will carry out a diagnostic pass to trap any errors such as loops, etc. Then, having corrected any errors, carry out the appropriate analyses required on this occasion – of time, of resources and of costs – and compare the results with the objectives ofthe project. This comparison will always require either modification of the project plan (the network) or modification of the project objectives as being infeasible within the imposed constraints.

- Always start with the simplest possible network since the complexity of the diagram reflects the complexity of the management problem in controlling the project. Keep detail limited to the short-term planning horizon, with less and less detail as the plan extends into the future. It is a fact of life that projects seldom proceed as originally planned and that changes will have to be made – less detail means less changes. The extra detail should be included as required, as activities enter the short-term planning period.

5 *Preparing plans by other techniques.* Bar charts are the only other reasonable way of preparing plans for anything but the smallest project, where it can be 'all in the mind' but would be better on paper. Bar charts have

problems when complex logic is required, since the interactions are not represented, and can cause difficulties, even in simple projects, when changes are required. That apart, the hints given above for networks should be studied and, so far as is possible, applied when using bar charting methods.

REALISATION

Hints on running the project are as follows:

1 *The flow of information.* Ensure that information flows freely to and from the network or other plan. If, for example, something happens which causes a previously critical or near critical activity to acquire float, or which increases the criticality of an hitherto non-critical activity, then let that be known to the person concerned.

2 *Planning flexibility.* No plan should be cast in concrete – it is a tool, and only a model of how the objective is to be achieved, and should be treated as such. Changes in circumstances will occur in the best regulated circles, and the plan must be modified to take cognizance of them. When using networks redrawing them is not a crime, nor is it a problem if the computer system being used can draw the network.

3 *The predictive power of networks.* When a problem occurs, use the predictive power of the network to resolve it by carrying out 'what if' exercises rather than taking time and emotional energy to discover the cause. A later analysis, possibly post-project, can be used to discover the causes of problems with a view to preventing them in future projects, and to build up a database of actual times for future common activities.

   The predictive power of the network should also be used at every stage in the project life-cycle to examine potential problem areas and devise alternative strategies for dealing with such problems should they become real.

4 *Progress reporting.* Progress should always be reported as quickly and accurately as possible, but speed is more important than accuracy. Information *now* with ±10 per cent accuracy is much more useful than the same information with ±2 per cent accuracy next week.

   'Time to complete' is a better statement of progress than percentage of work completed. Never ask 'Are you on schedule?' The answer is always 'Yes'!

5 *Progress meetings.* The schedule for progress meetings should be part of the project plan. The frequency of meetings will probably need to

increase as the project proceeds. Progress meetings should be held on a routine basis, *not* just geared to emergencies.

6 *Maintain the log*. The project log *must* be maintained throughout the life of the project, and must be written up at the time, not later from memory – which is all too often at fault. The information in the log will be invaluable for the final report and for future projects.

TERMINATION CHESTER COLLEGE LIBRARY

At the end of the project there is seldom an opportunity for the project team to carry out all the post mortem activities which *should* be undertaken – they are off to the next project or back to functional jobs. However, it should be part of the wind-down to carry out *some* analysis at least.

In many hardware projects the termination phase will include the handover of the project product to a user. This handover can be a difficult time for the project manager and the team, as responsibility is progressively transferred from them to the users. For their own reasons the users may try – and possibly succeed – to introduce changes and modifications to the product so that it may fail to achieve the specification or performance requirements and result in litigation. The project log will be an essential part of the evidence!

1 *Activity records.* The records of *actual* activity times as against *planned* times should be examined and, where significant differences occur, the reasons should be written up for future reference.

2 *Standard plans.* Any 'standard' networks or bar charts should be stored for future reference, with the logic amended where necessary. A library of 'standard' subproject plans should be built up if possible to save time and effort in future projects with similar subprojects. These plans are 'logic only', since the activity times will need to be reassessed on each new occasion of use.

3 *The project log.* The 'log' of the project should be converted to a report for the benefit of future projects of a similar nature. Any aspects of the project which are likely to form part of any 'claims' must be covered in detail; qually any lessons learned from the project should be properly written up.

APPENDIX 1

Two unanswerable questions

Both authors have been asked on many occasions, in academic and industrial teaching and in consultancy work, two questions to which they have never been able to give satisfactory answers. These questions are:

1 Which is the best form of network diagram: AoA or AoN?

2 Which is the best project management program?

It is hoped that the following brief discussion will indicate why the questions should be difficult to answer in general terms, and will help others to find answers appropriate to their circumstances.

Which is the best form of network diagram?

Both authors have had considerable experience in the use of both forms of network diagram. At the outset it must be said that neither has significant advantage in representing the plan – both are equally flexible – and both are in widespread use. A range of computer programs is available for both, although one author has been informed that much of the recently released software has been for AoN only.

The availability of software for project management may in many cases force the decision, although the more sophisticated packages usually offer both formalisms of AoA and AoN. Modern software is relatively cheap and this should not be a problem.

AoA

This form of diagram displays the logic of the project more clearly than AoN since there is less need to restrict the description of activities due to lack of space, and it is therefore easier to understand. In general, even with single dependency AoN, there will be fewer arrows in an AoA diagram and, when a change of activity duration is required, only one figure has to be changed. However, when changes to the logic are required, more changes may be necessary in AoA. The single greatest drawback to AoA for many is the dummy. This, in the opinion of the authors, is more imagined than real, as with relatively little experience the difficulties disappear.

AoN

This form of diagram will be simpler to draw for the beginner as no dummies are required. However, in any but a simple situation, the diagram will be more complex because of the interacting dependency arrows. Multiple dependencies allow the representation of complex interactions which are very difficult to represent in AoA. Changes to the logic of a plan can be more easily accommodated in AoN, but changes to durations can lead to problems with dependency times which are often forgotten.

Which is the best project management program?

This is a question of the same order as 'How long is a piece of string?'. So much depends on what kind of project it is to be used for both now *and in the future*. A relatively simple internal project will require very different facilities to an external major project, or one with a consortium of partners. Although the majority of modern software is available on PCs, some also have mainframe versions, which may be necessary for some individual projects, but are more likely to be required for multi-project situations in a large organisation.

One of the difficulties in giving advice in this field is the multiplicity of programs available. One author had a student research project in the late 1980s, which found that there were some 100 to 150 different programs on the market in the UK, ranging from the very simple – nothing more than time analysis – to the very sophisticated mainframe systems offering a total integration of the project systems with the company systems. It is, therefore, very much up to the project manager and the project team to make a decision within the context of the project *and* the parent organisation. In any case, any recommendation that could be made at the time of writing would be out of date before publication!

Questions

The first twenty questions are concerned with the management aspects of the discipline of project management, for which there can be no absolute answers, so that none are provided in the *Instructor's manual* which is obtainable by teachers on demand from the publishers. The material presented in the first ten chapters plus an understanding of the remainder of the text is necessary and, in addition, the interpretation put on the material by the teacher (lecturer) will influence the answers.

The remaining questions all follow broadly the same form, namely some text indicates the procedure, followed by a list of activities. In most, but not all, duration times are provided.

It is suggested that after reading the chapters concerned with the drawing of networks the reader should sketch the network implicit in each question, ignoring duration times. The logic of the sketch should then be checked against the model answers provided in the tutor's manual. It is further suggested that the reader should attempt to produce both AoA and AoN networks to ensure a full understanding of the procedures.

When the reader is satisfied that he or she can draw a network, the chapters on analysing a network should be studied, and when understood, duration times applied to the sketches and an analysis carried out. This analysis can then be checked against the model answer. *Note: Use a pencil on large sheets of paper, and keep an eraser handy when drawing networks.*

The authors have found that, whenever a difficulty in analysis arises, it can *invariably* be resolved by drawing a bar (Gantt) chart. Even if the question does not ask for a bar chart it will be found rewarding to draw one.

No general resource allocation problems are provided. This is for two reasons: first, decision rule techniques – the most commonly used methods of resource allocation – do not necessarily provide unique answers unless the rules are specified – and therefore the student's answer may differ from the authors', yet both be equally valid. Second, manual resource allocation is tedious in the extreme and very few students have the persistence to 'follow through' a resource problem. This having been said, students interested in the topic are recommended to apply arbitrarily resources to problems, and draw the resultant histograms in the 'earliest start' and 'latest start' positions.

Questions 39 and 40 are specifically intended to illustrate precedence networking. Question 39 is capable of being solved by any system of networking; Question 40 is a precedence network containing all relationships for analysis.

Question 1

Discuss the problems of introducing project management as a discipline in relation to the main forms of structure which occur in functional, process and service organisations.

Question 2

Discuss the tools and techniques which are available to project management in the context of the environment of projects and the objectives which you see as likely in those environments for a client or contractor.

Question 3

Discuss, giving small examples to illustrate your answer, how and why a work breakdown structure should be constructed for a project and the use that can be made of it in the management of the project.

Question 4

Obtaining resources for individual projects is a problem in manufacturing and service industries. Discuss why this should be so and suggest how you might attempt to resolve the problem from a project viewpoint in a highly functionally structured organisation.

Question 5

Describe from your own experience or from your imagination a project, explaining clearly why you consider it to be a project.

Question 6

What is a matrix organisation, and why is it often appropriate for the governance of a project?

Question 7

Discuss the problems encountered in a project if a dual reporting system is set up.

Question 8

A project may be said to have a semi-autonomous management. What is meant by this?

Question 9

What are the minimum characteristics of a good plan?

Question 10

Why should *strategic* plans be set before *tactical* plans? In your answer make sure that you explain the difference between the two categories of plan.

Question 11

'One man's strategy is another man's tactics.' Discuss.

Question 12

Discuss and explain the five quality concepts of project management.

Question 13

'Procurement is buying. Buying is not procurement.' Discuss.

Question 14

What is meant by a risk? How does it differ from a hazard? Give examples.

Question 15

Suggest areas of a project where risk may be found.

Question 16

'The time for carrying out a project can always be reduced by throwing resources at it.' Discuss.

Question 17

Two tasks A and B require 24 and 36 units of time for their execution. They are initially planned to be carried out in sequence, A preceding B. The total time for these two tasks to be completed in is 60 units of time. Show graphically how these two tasks may be overlapped to reduce the time to 48 units of time, and discuss:

(a) the managerial; and
(b) the resource utilisation consequences.

Question 18

A project manager with a project planned to have a TPT of 1000 days finds that, after running for 250 days, the planned activities which were completed should have taken 220 days. Calculate the current schedule performance index, and, assuming no significant change in performance, the current estimated time slip.

Question 19

Part-way through a project the costs recorded by the project accountant and the parent company accountant differ considerably. Discuss possible reasons for this.

Question 20

Three months into a project the project accountant reports that, while the original budget for that date showed that £75 000 should have been spent, only £60 000 are committed. Discuss possible reasons for this.

Question 21: Four parts from three machines

In the manufacture of a piece of apparatus, the final assembly (which has to be tested by a piece of specially made test gear) is made up from two items:

(1) Component D.
(2) A second assembly of parts.

The second assembly in turn is made up from two items:

(1) Component C.
(2) A first assembly.

and the first assembly is made up from two parts:

(1) Component A.
(2) Component B.

To manufacture these components special machines must be obtained as follows:

First machine   produces component A
Second machine   produces component B
Third machine   produces components C and D

Each component is tested before it is assembled with another component or item, but test gear can be assumed to be available for all testing except final testing where special test gear has to be made. The design of this special test gear is known at the outset of the whole project. The activities involved in the project are:

Activities involved	Duration (days)
Obtain first machine	2
Obtain second machine	3
Obtain third machine	2
Make component A	2
Make component B	2
Make component C	3

Activities involved	Duration (days)
Make final test gear	20
Test component A	3
Test component B	4
Test component C	3
Make first assembly	3
Test final assembly	5
Make component D	8
Test component D	20
Make second assembly	7
Make final assembly	3

Questions

Now answer the following questions.

(21.1) Prepare a schedule showing the times when the various activities must be carried out in order that the total project can be completed in the minimum time.

(21.2) Draw a bar chart for the project.

Question 22: The ATC tower

An air traffic control (ATC) tower utilises an ATC console which, though standard in terms of mechanical design and input/output panels, has to be electrically designed to meet the needs of the particular airfield. The activities involved in building and equipping an ATC tower are:

Activities involved	Duration (weeks)
Design console	3
Order console	2
Make and deliver console	16
Install console	2
Operationally test console	4
Design tower	5
Design foundations	1
Order foundations material	1
Deliver foundations material	1
Construct foundations	1
Order tower constructional material	2
Deliver tower constructional material	3
Erect tower	8

Questions

Now answer the following questions.

(22.1) What is the minimum time that must elapse between the receipt of a 'letter of intent' (i.e. a purchased order) for a fully equipped tower and the 'hand-over' date (i.e. the tower being fully equipped with tested material)?

(22.2) What would be the effect of a delay in the designing of the tower of:
  (a) 1 week?
  (b) 2 weeks?
  (c) 3 weeks?
  (d) 5 weeks?

(22.3) What action, if any, appears desirable if 10 weeks after receipt of the letter of intent the following activities are complete:

> Design console Design tower
> Order console Order tower constructional material

and the following activities are started but not yet complete:

> 'Make and deliver console' requiring 11 weeks more work.
> 'Deliver tower constructional material' requiring 2 weeks more work.

and no other activities are yet started?

(22.4) What saving in time, if any, would have resulted if a completely standard console had been used and the tower designed to match it so that the following times had been obtained:

| Design console | 1 week | Make and deliver console | 8 weeks |
| Order console | 2 weeks | Design tower | 8 weeks |

all other times remaining as in the table above?

Question 23: The telescopic gun-sight

(An exercise suggested by a publication of the Industrial Operations Unit of the Department of Scientific and Industrial Research entitled 'Application of Critical Path Method of Scheduling: A Demonstration'. The modifications to the DSIR report are so great that the exercise can now be considered to be completely fictitious.)

A manufacturer has a telescopic gun-sight assembly that he makes up only upon receipt of a firm order from a customer. The design of this gun-sight is completely stable, and no deviations from the standard product are ever accepted, with the result that all drawings, tools and production aids are always available.

The parts used in the assembly can be considered to be as follows:

(1) Tube.
(2) Eye-piece.
(3) Lens holder.
(4) Locknut.
(5) Lens nut.
(6) Washer.
(7) Spring.
(8) Screw.
(9) Lens.

Parts 1–5 were manufactured internally after purchase of the initial raw material (aluminium) and were sent outside for finishing (anodizing). Parts 6–9 were bought complete, ready for assembly, from outside suppliers.

Upon receipt of a firm order, an internal works order is raised, which initiates all activity. The relevant drawings are then extracted from the drawing library and copies sent to the appropriate departments. Having received the drawings, the material control section scans its records and raises purchase requisitions, which are forwarded to the purchasing department. Purchase orders are then made out and once materials are received they are inspected and passed either to the machine shop (in the case of raw material) or to the final assembly department. Once all parts are available in the final assembly department, they are assembled into the completed gun-sight, which is then inspected, packed and eventually dispatched to the customer. A list of operations follows:

Operation	*Duration (days)*
Raise works order	2
Extract and circulate drawings	4
Raise purchase requisitions	3
Prepare production paperwork	5
Issue production paperwork	2
Place purchase orders	4
Piece part tools withdrawn from store	1
Final assembly tools withdrawn from store	2
Raw material delivered	4
Part 6 delivered	22
Part 7 delivered	24
Part 8 delivered	10
Part 9 delivered	30
Part 1 machined	4
Part 2 machined	8
Part 3 machined	12
Part 4 machined	7
Part 5 machined	3
Inspect part 1 before finishing	2
Inspect part 1 after finishing	1
Inspect part 2 before finishing	2
Inspect part 2 after finishing	1
Inspect part 3 before finishing	3
Inspect part 3 after finishing	1
Inspect part 4 before finishing	4
Inspect part 4 after finishing	2
Inspect part 5 before finishing	2
Inspect part 5 after finishing	1
Inspect part 6	1
Inspect part 7	1
Inspect part 8	1

Operation	Duration (days)
Inspect part 9	1
Anodize part 1	5
Anodize part 2	5
Anodize part 3	5
Anodize part 4	5
Anodize part 5	5
Raw material inspected	1
Final assembly	10
Final inspection	4
Pack	4
Dispatch	2

Questions

Now answer the following questions.

(23.1) A firm order is received on Monday, 30 December, and work is immediately put in train.

(i) What is the earliest date by which delivery can be completed?

(ii) Past experience has shown that the inspection in the machine shop has proved a bottleneck. What could be done to allow one inspector to do all the machine shop inspection without delaying the completion of the job?

(iii) Assume that parts 1 and 2 are made on machine A, parts 4 and 5 on machine B, and that only one machine A and one machine B are available, what could be done to allow one inspector to do all the machine shop inspection without delaying the completion of the job? (Assume no limitation on availability of the machine to make part 3.)

(23.2) Assuming that there are no resource limitations and no changes in duration time and/or logic are made in the manufacture of the gun-sight, examine the situation that would exist if, 20 days after the receipt of the customer's order, the following operations had been completed as early as possible:

> raise works order,
> extract and circulate drawings,
> prepare production paperwork,
> issue production paperwork,
> issue piece part tools,
> issue final assembly tools,
> raise purchase requisitions,
> place purchase orders,

and it was understood that the time for delivery of raw materials would be increased from 4 days to 14 days, and that delivery of part 7 would increase from 24 to 26 days. All other operations were expected to be performed in the times originally estimated.

(3.3) Believing that the overall time from receipt of the customer's order to dispatching the finished goods was too great, the general manager invited suggestions for reducing this time. He specified that the cost was not an important consideration in this case, and that capital expenditure could be tolerated providing that reduction in total time could be demonstrated.

He received the following suggestions:

(i) *From the material control section:* hold bigger stocks of raw material so that machining could start by withdrawing material from stores rather than obtaining it from an outside supplier.

(ii) *From the production manager:* purchase a piece of equipment for £4 000 that would enable part 6 to be made internally in 4 days and another piece of equipment for £3 000 that would enable part 7 to be made internally in 5 days. Inspection time would not be reduced on either part.

(iii) *From the office manager:* purchase a more efficient office duplicator that would enable all the works orders to be raised in 1 day. The cost of this equipment would be of the order of £350.

(iv) *From the chief inspector:* abandon the pre-finishing inspection for the machined parts (parts 1–5) but increase the scope of the post-finishing inspection. This would double the time for the post-finishing inspection and increase the risk that defective parts were finished. The chief inspector stated that this risk was very small.

(v) *From the foreman of machine shop 3:* permit overtime working for machine shop 3 in order to reduce the machining time from 12 working days to 10 working days.

(vi) *From the chief draughtsman:* purchase an electrically operated printing machine to enable the time for the extraction of drawings to be reduced from 4 days to 3 days. Cost estimated to be £450.

(vii) *From the production controller:* purchase a new duplicating machine (cost £100) to reduce the time for raising production paperwork by one half.

(viii) *From the buyer:* part 9 can be obtained from a different source at an increased cost but with a delivery time of 20 days.

Evaluate the above suggestions.

Question 24: Nine phrases

Sketch the following nine 'phrases'. Since they form parts of complete networks, they are not necessarily complete in themselves, that is, they do not start from, nor do they finish on, a single event.

(i) Task K depends on tasks A and B.
(ii) Task K and task L depend on tasks A and B.
(iii) Task K depends on tasks A and B and task L depends only on task B.
(iv) Task K depends only on task A, but task L depends on both tasks A and B.
(v) Task K depends on tasks A and C, and task L depends on tasks B and C.

(vi) Task *K* depends on tasks *A* and *C*, task *L* depends on tasks *B* and *C* and task *M* depends only on task *C*.

(vii) Task *K* depends on task *A*, task *L* depends on task *B*, and task *M* depends on tasks *A*, *B* and *C*.

(viii) Task *K* depends on task *A*, task *L* depends on tasks A and *B*, and task *M* depends on tasks *B* and *C*.

(ix) Task *K* depends on task *A*, task *L* depends on tasks A and *B*, and task *M* depends on tasks *A*, *B* and *C*.

Question 25: Excavate – shutter – pour

Foundations are to be excavated, and shuttering erected to receive poured concrete. The three activities take the following times:

Activities involved	Duration (days)
Excavate foundations	24
Erect shuttering	12
Pour concrete	18

If the three activities are carried out in sequence, each activity being completed before its successor is started, the total time for the project will be 54 days. To reduce this it is decided to start shuttering when only part of the excavating is complete, and pouring when only part of the shuttering is complete. Draw the arrow diagrams for the situations when work on a successor starts:

(i)   after one-half
(ii) after one-third
(iii) after one-quarter

of a predecessor is complete. Assume that only one excavating gang, one shuttering gang and one pouring gang are available, and that these gangs must not be split. Calculate the total times for (i), (ii) and (iii) and then express them as a percentage of the original total time of 54 days.

Questions 26: Draw – trace – print

In the preparation of a set of drawings the following activities occur:

Activities involved	Duration (weeks)
Draw	12
Trace	8
Print	4

The chief draughtsman is prepared to release drawings to the tracers after 2 weeks, and the tracers will release drawings to the print room after 1 week. Sketch the network for this situation.

Question 27: Network V

Draw the network represented by:

	Activity	Precedes	Duration
START	A	D, E	4
	B	F, C	6
	C	G	2
	D	L	3
	E	H	8
	F	H,K	9
	G	L	10
	H	L	6
	K	L	8
FINISH	L	—	1

Analyze this network and draw a bar chart.

Question 28: Overhauling delivery lorries

A fleet of three delivery lorries are overhauled each week. The practice is that Joe, the sole mechanic, overhauls a lorry, and then Fred, the sole garage-hand, cleans and polishes that lorry.

There are three lorries, A, B and C, and they are processed in that order.

Sketch the network for the above situation. Use the following activities:

Overhaul A   Clean and polish A
Overhaul B   Clean and polish B
Overhaul C   Clean and polish C

Question 29: A new machine

Draw the network for the following:

A new machine is needed for which budget approval is required. The use of the new machine necessitates employing a new operator who must be specially trained, using a training manual and some special equipment that is delivered with the machine. The training itself does not depend upon the new machine being installed and working. Once the machine is installed and the operator is trained, production can proceed.

Activities involved

Obtain budget approval
Obtain machine
Install machine
Hire operator
Train operator
Production of goods

Question 30: The machine tool overhaul

Draw the network for the following situation:

Within a factory there are three machine tools that have to be removed from their bases, modified and then reinstalled on the same bases. Assume that there is only one heavy gang to undertake the initial moving, only one fitter capable of carrying out the modifications, and only one gang of millwrights capable of reinstalling the machines.

Activities involved

Remove first machine
Remove second machine
Remove third machine
Modify first machine
Modify second machine
Modify third machine
Install first machine
Install second machine
Install third machine

Question 31: 'The rubble fill ...'

(Courtesy of Building Research Station)

Draw the network for the following situation:

The rubble fill cannot be started until the brickwork below d.p.c., the drainage under the building and the mainlaying under the building are finished. The completion of the drainage will follow after the drainage under the building and the external mainlaying will follow the mainlaying under the building. The external paving must be laid after the external mainlaying and the brickwork below d.p.c. The completion of the drainage and the external mainlaying must be finished before the internal services.

Activities involved
Start internal services
Finish drainage under the building
Finish brickwork below d.p.c.
Finish mainlaying under the building
Complete drains
Complete external mainlaying
Lay external paving
Install internal services
Fill with rubble

Question 32: The stock-taking

Within a small neighbourhood department store there are three sections in the shoe department:

(1) Men's.
(2) Women's.
(3) Children's.

There are three staff:

(1) A junior.
(2) A management trainee.
(3) A manager.

The manager has to have a stock-take and decides to do it as follows:

(1) The junior will remove stock, clean fixtures thoroughly and replace stock conveniently for stock-taking, not being considered experienced enough to do more than this.
(2) The management trainee will then count and record the stock.
(3) The manager will sample check the trainee's stock-take.

It is decided to carry out the work section by section, starting with the men's section, following with the women's and finishing with the children's section.
    Draw the network for the above, considering only the following activities:

Remove and clean men's stock	R_M
Remove and clean women's stock	R_W
Remove and clean children's stock	R_C
Carry out men's stock-check	S_M
Carry out women's stock-check	S_W
Carry out children's stock-check	S_C
Check men's stock-take	C_M
Check women's stock-take	C_W
Check children's stock-take	C_C

Question 33: Network W

The logical relationships, duration times and resource requirements for the activities of a project are:

	Activity	Precedes activity	Duration	Resources X	Resources Y
	A	D, E, F	5	1	2
Opening	B	G	4	5	2
	C	H	6	5	2
	D	G	7	2	2
	E	H	8	2	2
	F	—	10	10	2
Closing	G	—	11	3	2
	H	—	10	3	2

(1) Draw the network for the above and analyse it fully.
(2) Draw the bar charts for the 'earliest start' and 'latest start' situations.
(3) Aggregate the resources for the 'earliest start' and 'latest start' situations.
(4) Draw the two cumulative requirement curves for each resource.
(5) Suggest the likely minimum constant level requirement for each resource.

Question 34: Network X

The logical relationships and duration times for the activities of a project are:

	Activity	Precedes activities	Duration
	A	D, E	4
Opening	B	E	3
	C	G	5
	D	F, G	7
	E	H, J, K	2
	F	N	2
	G	L	6
	H	L	4
	J	M, N	9
	K	M, N	12
	L	—	4
Closing	M	—	8
	N	—	3

Draw the network for the above and analyse it.

Question 35: Network Y

The logical relationships and duration times for the activities of a project are:

	Activity	Precedes	Duration
	A	H, L	43
	B	J, L	40
Opening	C	K, L	16
	D	L, M	37
	E	L, N	30
	X	T, Y	20
Across whole project	Z	—	165
	H	P	30
	J	Q	29
	K	R	40
	L	P, Q, R, S, T	2
	M	S	70
	N	T	62
	P	—	45
	Q	—	60
Close	R	—	70
	S	—	35
	T	—	45
	Y	—	30

Draw and analyse the network.

Question 36: The pre-production models

In the pre-production stages of the manufacturing of a piece of equipment that contains both electrical and mechanical parts, the following procedure is carried out:

The specification is agreed, after which the design department makes a prototype for approval, by the sales department. This prototype is in a form final enough for the later detailed mechanical and electrical design work to proceed independently. Once the detailed design work is complete, further sets of both electrical and mechanical parts are made which are then assembled together to form a series of complete pre-production models (PPMs).

Note: the PPMs require both electrical and mechanical parts.

Enough PPMs are made for electrical and mechanical proving tests to be carried out independently, although both proving tests require special test gear to be made. The manufacture of this test gear can be undertaken once the detailed development is complete. Electrical and mechanical proving tests having been completed, a final approval is given that enables materials to be ordered and production equipment to be made. Once all the material and production equipment is to hand, manufacture can start.

Activities involved	Duration (days)
Agree specification	6
Make prototype	12
Prototype approved	2
Detailed mechanical design	12
Detailed electrical design	10
Make mechanical parts for PPMs	6
Make electrical parts for PPMs	6
Make mechanical test gear	15
Make electrical test gear	10
Make pre-production models (PPMs)	12
Electrical proving test PPMs	10
Mechanical proving test PPMs	8
Final approval given	4
Make production equipment	15
Obtain production material	4
Manufacture	15

Questions

Answer the following questions.

(36.1) Draw the network.
(36.2) Analyse the network.
(36.3) Translate the network into a bar chart.
(36.4) List those activities which, 35 days after work has started must:

(a) have been finished
(b) have been started

if the total project time is not to be increased.

Question 37: The storage heater

A Derbyshire fireclay manufacturer has obtained the manufacturing and selling rights of a new storage heater that will utilise some of his own products. It has been decided that initially the heater will be sold only in the London area, since this represents the largest concentrated market, and transport to London will be by rail since the company has its own railway sidings, but the actual volume of heaters to be offered will only be determined after a market survey. This survey will not require the presence of any sample heaters. In order to obtain the rights to the new heater, the Derbyshire manufacturer undertook to market the heater, but the market price was not fixed by the German company, and had to be determined by local conditions.

Manufacture of first batch

Although the design is complete, a number of models will need to be made for test and approval by both the sales and manufacturing departments. Only after these approvals have been obtained, the market survey has been carried out, and a decision on volume has been made, will the production equipment and material be obtained. The heater itself, though inexpensive, is fragile, and special 'immediate' packing will need to be designed, this packing later forming part of the retailer's point-of-sales display. Within this packing will be an 'operating and installation' leaflet, which can only be prepared after the approval of the samples. The design of the packing itself can start once samples are available, but it need not wait upon the testing and approval by either the sales or the production departments since any modifications to the heater as a result of sales and manufacturing approval are not likely to affect the design of the packing. The cost of packing will be insignificant in relation to the cost of the heater. The production costs can only be extracted for pricing purposes after the first batch has been made.

Transport

Transport from the manufacturer's factory sidings in Derbyshire to the retail shops in London will be provided by British Railways, who will provide special containers into which numbers of the packed heaters can be loaded at the factory. These filled containers will be lifted from the factory sidings on to the trains, and thence taken to British Railways' wharves at a suitable North London depot. From these wharves British Railways' vans will distribute to the London shops. It is expected that both the sidings and the wharves will need to be modified in order that the goods can be handled most effectively.

A substantial part of the cost of modifying the British Railways' wharves will have to be borne by the manufacturer, and thus the *total* transport costs can be assumed to consist of two parts:

(1) The costs of modifying the wharves.
(2) The cost of moving the heaters from the works to the shops (the 'handling' costs).

Any charges incurred in modifying the works sidings will be capitalised by the company and not directly incorporated in the selling price of the heater.

As there are a number of apparently suitable wharves in North London, and a number of alternative routes, a test run will be carried out. This will check:

(1) The rail route from Derbyshire to London.
(2) The suitability of the proposed wharves.
(3) The suitability of the British Railways' container.

Before carrying out the test-run, therefore, British Railways need to survey the wharves and obtain a suitable sample container into which sample heaters can be loaded. For this purpose, only temporary immediate packing, of a type readily available, is necessary, and neither sidings nor wharves need to be modified, the containers being 'man-handled' on and off the train. However, once the wharves have been modified it will be necessary to train the wharf staff in their operation. No such training is needed for the factory staff who will work at the factory sidings.

Marketing

Once the sales department has approved the sample heaters, and the volume has been determined by the market survey, the sales campaign can be prepared. No further sales activity can be undertaken, however, until the campaign and its budget have been approved. This approval will include a statement of the marketing cost, and this, together with the production and transport cost, can be used in the derivation of the final selling price. The final agreement of sales outlets depends upon the setting of the selling price. Sales staff are trained after the sales campaign has been agreed, and their training will involve some of the sample heaters. Once trained they can take orders for heaters from the shops (that is, they can 'sell-in'). Distribution of the heaters from the North London wharves can follow thereafter.

Advertising will take the form of 'photograph + text' advertisements in magazines and the advertising can only be finalised when the selling price, the artwork and the text are available. No advertising will take place until all distribution from wharves to shops has been completed.

Pricing

The final selling price will be determined after:

(1) The total transport costs are agreed.
(2) The cost of producing the first batch is known.
(3) The sales budget is approved.

Activities involved	Duration (days)
Carry out market survey	15
Produce samples sufficient for all tests	15
Arrange and hold first meeting with British Railways	4
Survey wharves	14
Obtain estimate for modification to wharves	7
Agree estimate for modification to wharves	7
Modify wharves	15
British Railways obtain sample container	7
Arrange test run from works to wharves	3
Carry out test run	5
Agree price with British Railways for handling from works to shops (handling costs)	15
Sign contract for modifying wharves	3
Agree total transport costs	5

Activities involved	Duration (days)
Obtain railway containers	15
Modify sidings for easy loading from the works to train	10
Train wharf staff	3
Production departments agree sample heater	7
Sales departments agree sample heater	7
Design packing	15
Obtain quotation for packing	5
Sales department approve packing	7
Production department approve packing	3
Obtain packing	10
Obtain production materials and equipment	14
Produce first batch	14
Agree selling price	5
Pack first batch	3
British Railways collect first batch from works and send to wharves	3
Agree retail outlets	15
Collect from wharves and send to shops	3
Advertise 'In your shops now'	10
Extract production costs	3
Prepare sales campaign	21
Agree sales campaign and budget	3
Train sales staff	15
Take orders from shops ('sell-in')	5
Prepare advertising artwork	10
Prepare advertising text	10
Book advertising space	5
Finalise advertising	3
Send sample heaters to British Railways for test run	12
Prepare operating and installation instructions	14

Questions

Now answer the following questions.

(37.1) What is the shortest possible time that can elapse between the starting of the whole project (that is, the decision to market the heaters in London) and its completion (that is, advertised heaters being available in the shops)?

(37.2) Once started, it is found that the market survey will take at least 21 days to be completed. What effect will this have?

(37.3) The buyer reports that for an increased price he can obtain packing in 5 days rather than the 10 he had previously specified and as time is essential he requests that he be allowed to purchase the more expensive packing. What decision would you recommend the manufacturer to take?

(37.4) The chairman of the committee that is to meet to agree the total transport costs catches influenza and the meeting of the committee is postponed for 5 days. What is the effect of this?

(37.5) By working over two weekends the production manager manages to make the first batch in 10 days. By how much will the total time for the whole project be reduced?

(37.6) Owing to pressure of work, the chief of the railways' supplies department finds it difficult (though not impossible) to obtain the special containers needed for the heaters in the 15 days he had originally quoted. What increase in time, if any, can be permitted?

(37.7) What activities must be completed 40 working days after the start of the whole project?

(37.8) Assuming that it is now 50 days after 'project-start', you learn that the copy writer preparing the operating and installation instructions will not complete his task for another 20 days. What is the effect of this?

(37.9) Draw a bar chart representing the activities of the sales department once the sales budget has been approved, assuming that the advertising 'In your shops now' is completed by the end of Monday, 3rd October.

Activities involved
Agree selling price
Agree sales outlets
'Sell in'
Collection from wharves and send to shops
Advertise 'In your shops now'
Train sales staff
Prepare advertising artwork
Finalise advertising
Prepare advertising text
Book advertising space

Note: The diagram for this question is particularly involved. It is suggested that readers divide the activities into their responsibility areas—*transport* activities, *general and manufacturing* activities and *marketing* activities—and then draw three separate networks corresponding to these three areas, indicating (for example, by means of double nodes or double arrows) which events or activities are common to two or more networks. Once these three networks have been drawn they can be amalgamated into one final network. This is known as *interfacing* and corresponds to the real-life situation where separate departments (in this case the transport, factory and marketing departments) draw diagrams independently and these are then amalgamated by the general manager.

Question 38: The petrol station

A site with appropriate planning permission, has been obtained for a small petrol station. This will consist, essentially, of two islands, one (the sales island) carrying the cash office and the pumps, and the other (the office island) carrying the manager's office, public toilets and an air compressor. Adjacent to the sales island will be a concrete pit which will house the storage tanks for the petrol (Fig. Q38). The pit and the rest of the site (with the exception, of course, of the two islands) is covered with a concrete hardstanding slab and surrounded by a low perimeter wall. Specific planning and design points are detailed below.

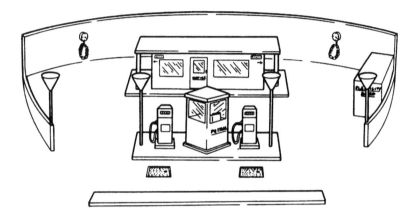

Fig. Q38 The petrol station

Services

Adequate main water and main drainage services are available immediately adjacent to the site so that no special provision must be made for these beyond laying them to such locations on the site as appropriate. There is no electricity on or near the site and the Electricity Board has undertaken to install an electrical supply in the form of a transformer located in a corner of the site.

Petrol pumps

These need to be obtained from the manufacturers, and after being erected on the sales island they are connected to the storage tanks and the power supply. Before use they must be inspected by the local authority to ensure safety and compliance with regulations.

Storage tanks

These are housed in concrete pits and covered by the hard-standing slab. Before they are covered however, the tanks and the associated pipe-work have to be inspected by the local authority.

Manager's office

The manager's office furnishings will include a safe, for the custody of overnight takings. The insurance company insists that the office is efficiently burglar-alarmed; once these alarms are installed the insurance company will inspect them. The alarms are powered by main electricity. All furnishings for the office and toilets must be specially obtained and, when delivered, must be stored under cover to avoid weather damage. Some furnishings are 'built in' and, therefore, require painting when in position.

'Free air' supply

Compressed air for inflating tyres will be supplied by an electrically driven compressor, the receiver of which must be inspected by a competent person before the compressor is put into use. The air lines to the 'free air' points are installed with the general underground services, and the points themselves are mounted on the perimeter wall.

Approach road signs

To advertise the petrol station, signs will be erected on the approach roads. Sites for these signs have not been negotiated in detail, although some surveys work has been done, but actual site negotiation will not start until the project as a whole is started. It is expected that the signs will be in portion by the time that the petrol station is ready for use by the public.

Possession and release of site

Before any work can start on the site, a mobile hut is erected to store tools, furnishings any weatherprone parts, and to act as the site office. The installation of this hut, along with any other preparatory work is known as 'taking possession'. Similarly, when work on the site is complete, the hut, which has been moved as appropriate, is removed, and all scaffolding and plant taken away. This is known as 'cleaning up the site'.

Activities involved	Duration (weeks)
Excavate for sales island base	1
Construct sales island base	1
Construct cash office	2
Obtain pumps	10
Erect pumps	1
Connect pumps	2
Inspector approves pump installation	2

Activities involved	*Duration (weeks)*
Obtain office furnishings	8
Paint and furnish office and toilets	2
Connect office and toilet lighting	1
Excavate for office island	1
Construct office island base	1
Build offices and toilets including all services	2
Install buglar alarm	1
Connect up burglar alarm	1
Insurance company inspects burglar alarm	2
Electricity board installs transformer	10
Connect mains cable to transformer	1
Install area lighting	4
Take possession	1
Set-out and level site	1
Excavate for, and lay, all underground services	1
Excavate for pipe-work and tanks	1
Construct concrete pit	3
Install pipe-work and tanks	2
Obtain pipe-work and tanks	8
Obtain compressor	12
Install compressor	1
Connect power to compressor	1
Competent person tests compressor	2
Backfill and cover tanks	1
Construct concrete hardstanding	2
Construct perimeter wall including air points	2
Connect up air points	1
Clean up site	1
Obtain approach road signs	4
Negotiate sites for approach road signs	12
Erect approach road signs	1
Inspector approves pipe-work and tanks	2

Questions

Now answer the following questions.

(38.1) Draw and analyse the network that represents the construction of the petrol station.

(38.2) Of the activities listed, four involve excavation. Assuming that only one mechanical excavator was available, suggest a possible sequence in which the four excavation activities can be performed.

(38.3) List those activities that must be completed by week 12 after the start of the whole task if the total time for the task is not to exceed 20 weeks.

(38.4) What is the effect of a delay of:

    (a) 1 week
    (b) 2 weeks
    (c) 3 weeks
    in 'taking possession' of the site?

(38.5) The contractor proposes to use one gang to carry out the work of 'construct sales island base,' 'construct office island base' and 'construct concrete hard-standing'. In order that the gang concerned is kept fully employed and on site for the shortest possible time, when should the above activities be started?

Question 39: The new CPU

(Derived from IBM's 'System/360 Project Control System: Application Description' H20–0222–0–modified version of example of precedence diagramming and used with their permission.)

It is decided to develop a new CPU, and in discussion at a preliminary planning meeting it is agreed that the following activities are involved in preparing a firm plan for approval by the CPU manager involved.

Activities involved	Duration (days)
Develop initial plan	8
Prepare initial data	3
Key-punch initial data	1.5
Initial computer run	4.0
Refine plan as a result of initial computer run	4.0
Prepare revised data derived from refined plan	1.0
Key-punch revised data	0.5
Revised computer run	4.0
Derive firm plan as a result of revised computer run	2.0
CPU manager agrees firm plan	2.0

If these activities were carried out strictly 'end-to-end' the time required would be 30 days, and it was felt that this was excessive, and a second preliminary planning meeting was convened. At this it was agreed that the total time for the project could be reduced by starting some activities before their predecessors were complete:

(1) Initial data preparation could start 3 days after the start of the initial plan development, these two activities finishing at substantially the same time.
(2) Key-punching initial data could start after 1 day of initial data preparation, but it would require at least half a day after the finish of data preparation for its completion.
(3) Revised data preparation could start when half the refined plan is complete and the two activities could finish substantially together.
(4) Key-punching revised data could start as soon as the preparation of the revised data started, the two activities finishing simultaneously.

Sketch the network for this situation and analyse it.

(Helpful hint–draw the 'end-to-end' situation *first* and from this draw a modified network.)

Question 40: An exericise in multiple dependencies

Analyse the network shown in Fig. Q.40 and draw the appropriate bar chart.

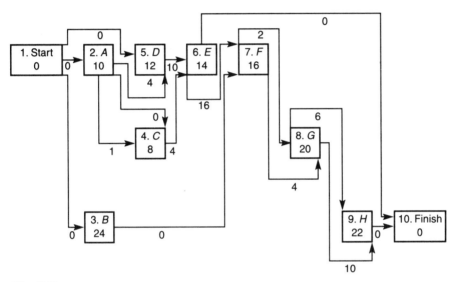

Fig. Q40

Question 41: A costing exercise

Given the project data shown in Table Q41.1 draw a diagram for the project and fully analyse it.

Table Q41.1 Activity data

Activity	Duration (Weeks)	Cost £000s	Precedence
A	8	40	A<B, C, D
B	12	150	B<F, G
C	16	200	C<E, F
D	20	150	D<J
E	8	90	E<J
F	24	300	F<H,J
G	16	160	G<H
H	20	250	H<K
J	12	150	J<K
K	8	100	–

Where *A<B, C, D* means that activity A precedes activities *B, C* and *D*.

Table Q41.2 Reported data

Week	Activities	Duration		Cost £000s	
		Planned	Actual to date	Planned	Actual to date
16	A	8	9	40	43
	C	16	7	200	90
	D	20	7	150	52
24	A	8	9	40	43
	B	12	7	150	91
	C	16	15	200	195
	D	20	15	150	127.5
32	A	8	9	40	43
	B	12	14	150	175
	C	16	17	200	212.5
	D	20	22	150	187
	E	8	6	90	72
	F	24	1	300	13
	G	16	1	160	11
40	A	8	9	40	43
	B	12	14	150	175
	C	16	17	200	212.5
	D	20	22	150	187
	E	8	9	90	108
	F	24	9	300	117
	G	16	9	160	90
56	A	8	9	40	43
	B	12	14	150	175
	C	16	17	200	212.5
	D	20	22	150	187
	E	8	9	90	108
	F	24	24	300	312
	G	16	17	160	170
	H	20	1	250	12
	J	12	1	150	13

If all activities except activity B, the start of which must be delayed until 8 weeks after the completion of activity A, can be scheduled at their earliest start times, obtain a cost curve for the project as planned.

At stages in the life of the project, progress and cost information is reported as shown in Table Q42.2. Given this information prepare predictions at weeks 32 and 56 of the likely final cost and duration of the project.

Question 42: The free-standing garage

A free-standing garage, for which all materials are available, is to be erected on a vacant site which will need to be set out, cleared and fenced. The perimeter is sufficiently level and clear for fencing to be carried out once the site is set out. The only services to be supplied are drainage and water, the main services for both of which are immediately adjacent to the proposed site entrance.

The drive, of concrete on hardcore, opens into a forecourt to be used for car-washing, so the drain rises into the centre, and the standpipe and tap are at the side of this forecourt. The drain and water pipes are to be laid in a trench near enough to the drive to require that the trench be backfilled before the hardcore is laid for the drive.

The garage stands on a concrete on hardcore slab, this slab and the drive being constructed separately. Windows are inserted during building, but the door posts and lintel are fixed after bricklaying is finished. Doors and windows are glazed when in position, and gutters, rain-water pipes, window frames and doors require painting. Painting and glazing may proceed as required without risk of interference, so that, for example, there is no need to delay painting the door until the gutter and rain-water pipes are fixed. The garage is not handed over until the site is cleared up.

Activities involved	Estimated duration (days)
Set out	1
Clear site	3
Fence site	12
Creosote fence	4
Excavate trench for pipes	4
Lay water pipe	2
Erect stand pipe, tap, etc.	3
Lay drain	10
Backfill trench	2
Excavate forecourt and drive	2
Hardcore to forecourt and drive	3
Shutter forecourt and drive	2
Concrete forecourt and drive	1
Strike shuttering	1
Excavate garage slab	3
Hardcore to slab	3
Shutter slab	3
Concrete slab	1
Strike slab shuttering	2
Brickwork to window level	3

Activities involved	Estimated duration (days)
Brickwork to eaves	3
Fix roof structure	5
Fix roof coverings	8
Fix gutters and rain-water pipes	2
Paint gutters and rain-water pipes	1
Fix door posts and lintel	2
Hang door	1
Glaze door	1
Paint door	1
Insert window frames	2
Glaze window frames	1
Paint window frames	1
Clear up site after all work completed	1

Calendar for the project
Time 0 = Midnight, April 30th
Bank holiday—May 29th

Day	Date	Day	Date
1	M 1–5	21	T 30–5
2	T 2–5	22	W 31–5
3	W 3–5	23	Th 1–6
4	Th 4–5	24	F 2–6
5	F 5–5	25	M 5–6
6	M 8–5	26	T 6–6
7	T 9–5	27	W 7–6
8	W 10–5	28	Th 8–6
9	Th 11–5	29	F 9–6
10	F 12–5	30	M 12–6
11	M 15–5	31	T 13–6
12	T 16–5	32	W 14–6
13	W 17–5	33	Th 15–6
14	Th 18–5	34	F 16–6
15	F 19–5	35	M 19–6
16	M 22–5	36	T 20–6
17	T 23–5	37	W 21–6
18	W 24–5	38	Th 22–6
19	Th 25–5	39	F 23–6
20	F 26–5	40	M 26–6

Questions

Now answer the following questions.

(42.1) Assuming that work on the garage can start on the morning of Monday 1 May, when can it be completed? (*Note*: 5–day week, and Bank Holiday on Monday 29 May.)

(42.2) Progress meetings are held every Friday. Assuming that the date found above is to be maintained, what activities should be
(a) Started
(b) Finished

on:

(i) 5 May
(ii) 12 May
(iii) l9 May
(iv) 26 May?

(42.3) Glazing and painting are to be carried out by a sub-contractor who wishes to send one tradesman along to clear the work off in a number of consecutive days, rather than on a number of separate occasions. What dates could be specified for this?

(42.4) Excavation is to be carried out by one gang. Suggest a sequence by which this could be conveniently done.

(42.5) The customer for the garage asks whether the completion date can be brought forward, and made the following suggestions. Which, if any, should be considered further?

(i)   Use a pre-treated fencing material to avoid creosoting.
(ii) Purchase extra shuttering boards to allow the drive shuttering to proceed before the shuttering has been removed from the slab.
(iii) Use plastic guttering and rain-water pipes to avoid painting.
(iv) Use pre-glazed and pre-painted windows.
(v)   Use pre-glazed and pre-painted doors.
(vi) Increase the size of the gang putting down the slab hardcore in order to reduce the time for this activity from 3 days to 2 days.
(vii) Use a pre-fabricated roof structure in order to permit the roof structure to be set up in 3 days rather than the 5 days originally estimated.

(42.6) Connecting the water pipe to the mains involves a substantial initial charge. How may the cost to the contractor be minimised?

(42.7) The activity 'fix roof structure' started on schedule but because of unforeseen labour shortages will now take seven days instead of five. What is the effect of this? What corrective action, if any, appears possible?

(42.8) On Tuesday 23rd of May the foreman finds that the window frames earmarked for this job have been used on another job. How much time is available to obtain another set of frames?

Question 43: Line of balance – the two-chassis job

A product, which requires two weeks in its final assembly stage, is to be made up from four basic components. The delivery schedule to be met is specified in the Table, and the details of the basic components are given below.

Component *A* is a painted chassis. The assembly of the chassis itself requires two weeks and a further week for the painting operation.

Component *B* is a painted chassis. The assembly of the chassis itself requires three weeks and the painting a further week.

Component *C* is a wired-up cable and components board. The assembly of the board requires three weeks and its subsequent testing a further two weeks.

Component *D* is a multiple plug-and-socket assembly. The assembly requires three weeks and the subsequent testing three weeks.

Table of delivery schedule
One hundred units of the final product are to be delivered at the following rate.

Week no.	Quantity	Week no.	Quantity
1	1	11	10
2	1	12	10
3	2	13	9
4	3	14	8
5	4	15	6
6	5	16	5
7	6	17	2
8	7	18	1
9	8	19	1
10	10	20	1
		Total	100

At the end of week 5 it is reported that:

11 final products are complete
22 component *D* are tested
24 component *C* are tested
24 component *B* are painted
22 component *A* are painted
24 component *B* are assembled
32 component *A* are assembled
36 component *C* are assembled
60 component *D* are assembled

Comment on these results.

Question 44: Elemental trend analysis – a new estate

(Based on an original problem by Prof. W. L. Gage)

A construction company has obtained a contract to build a small new estate which consists of 40 identical houses, which have to be completed in 24 weeks of 5 days per week.

Progress meetings are held on the Friday of each week and the management policy is:

(i) To complete at an even rate
(ii) To minimise the investment in inventory.

The activities to be considered in building each house are as follows:

Activity description	Activity duration (days)
Obtain building material	14
Obtain plumbing units and fittings	30
Prepare foundations	6
First-phase brickwork	3
First-phase joinery	2
Second-phase brickwork	6
Second-phase joinery	7
Roof tiling	2
Plumbing	2
Electrical installation	2
Plaster, paint and clean up	6

Notes:

All the building materials must be available before brickwork on a unit can start, although preparation of the foundations can proceed in advance of the material availability. Both the plumbers and electricians can start work four days after the start of the second-phase joinery, all other jobs on site are sequential. The site is isolated and the resources can be built up to full strength as rapidly as you wish but two weeks notice is required for reductions in strength.

The resources required for the durations shown above are as follows:

Foundations	– 1 digger 3 labourers
First-phase brickwork	– 4 bricklayers
First-phase joinery	– 3 carpenters
Second-phase brickwork	– 4 bricklayers
Second-phase joinery	– 5 carpenters
Roof tiling	– 3 tilers
Plumbing	– 2 plumbers
Electrical work	– 3 electricians
Plaster, etc.	– 5 general tradesmen

Questions

Answer the following questions.

(44.1) Plan the first unit and suggest which aspects may need careful control.

(44.2) Plan the complete project. Specify the resources required to fulfil the programme you have prepared.

(44.3) At a meeting on the Friday of week 12 it is reported that:

> 27 foundation preparations have been completed,
> 22 houses have first phase joinery complete,
> 16 houses have all joinery completed,
> 12 houses are tiled, plumbed etc.,
> 10 houses are completed.

Report on this situation with comments.

Glossary of terms

This glossary is not intended to be exhaustive: it contains the basic information necessary for the reader. A much fuller glossary is given in BS 4335:1987, and further information is given in BS 6046, a four part guide to the 'Use of network techniques in project management', and these should be consulted by any serious practitioner. Internationally a number of terms, which apply in wider fields than project management, are contained within ISO 8402 and the latest version of this should be consulted.

Wherever appropriate, the term and its definition as given in BS 4335:1987 are used and appear between inverted commas. In some cases a further brief note has been added.

'**Activity**: an operation or process consuming time and possibly other resources.'

Activity span: the time available for the completion of an activity.

Activity time: *see* 'Duration'.

Arrow: the symbol by which an activity is represented.

Arrow diagram: the statement of the complete task by means of arrows.

'**Backward pass**: the procedure whereby the latest event times or the latest start and finish times for the activities of a network are calculated.'

Circle: the symbol by which an event is represented in activity-on-arrow.

Cost-slope: the cost incurred in reducing the activity time by unit time. (*Note:* a negative cost-slope indicates that the cost of completing an activity decreases as the activity time decreases.)

Critical path: that sequence of activities which determines the total time for the task.

Critical path analysis (CPA): one name for that PNT system wherein an activity is represented by an arrow. Other names which may be used are critical path method (CPM) and program evaluation and review technique (PERT).

'**Dangle (dangling activity):** an activity represented in a network where its start or finish does not connect either with any other activity or to a start or end event or activity.'

Dependency Arrow: (AoN) the logical and timing relationships between a pair of activities which may be any of the four possible in a precedence diagram or will be start-to-start in a MoP diagram. It is always represented by a solid arrow in the diagram.

Dependency rule: (AoA) the basic logical rule governing the drawing of a network. It requires that an activity which depends on another activity is shown to emerge from the head event of the activity upon which it depends, and that only dependent activities are drawn in this way.

Dummy: a logical link, a constraint which represents no specific operation. In calculations it is most usefully regarded as an activity that absorbs neither resources nor time. (*Note:* dummies are usually represented by broken arrows.)

Dummy activity: a dummy.

'Duration: the estimated or actual time required to complete an activity.'

Duration time: *see* 'Duration'.

Earliest event time (EET): the earliest time by which an event can be achieved without affecting either the total project time or the logic of the network.

Earliest finish time of an activity (EFT): the earliest possible time at which an activity can finish without affecting the total project time or the logic of the network.

Earliest independent finish time (EIFT): the earliest time an activity can finish without changing the total project time or changing the float in a previous activity.

Earliest start time of an activity (EST): the earliest possible time at which an activity can start without affecting either the total project time or the logic of the network.

'Event: a state in the progress of a project after the completion of all preceding activities but before the start of any succeeding activity.'

Event time: the time by which an event can (or is to be) achieved.

'Float: a time available for an activity or path in addition to its duration (may be negative)'. It is essentially a property of activities, and is the difference between the time necessary and the time available for an activity.

'Forward Pass: the procedure whereby the earliest event times or the earliest start and finish times for the activities of a network are calculated.'

Free float: the float possessed by an activity which, if used, will not change the float in later activities.

Free float—early: another name for free float.

Free float—late: the float possessed by an activity when its predecessors and successors are achieved as late as possible.

Head event: the event at the finish of an activity.

Head slack: the slack possessed by an event at the head of an activity.

i: the symbol for the event number of a tail event.

'Imposed date: a point in time determined by circumstances outside the network.'

Independent float: the float possessed by an activity which, if used, will not change the float in any other activities in the arrow diagram.

'Interface: an activity or event common to two or more networks.' It will always occur when a network is drawn on two or more drawing sheets.

Interface (to): the act of coalescing two or more networks.

Interference float: a component of float equal to the head slack of an activity.

j: the symbol for the event number of a head event.

Junction: another name for, an event.

Latest event time (LET): the latest time by which an event can be achieved without affecting either the total project time or the logic of the network.

Latest free finishing time (LFFT): the latest time by which an activity can finish without changing the total project time or changing the float in any later activity.

Latest finish time of an activity (LFT): the latest possible time by which an activity can finish without affecting either the total project time or the logic of the network.

Latest start time of an activity (LST): the latest possible time by which an activity can start without affecting either the total project time or the logic of the network.

'Loop: an error in a network which results in a later activity imposing a logical restraint on an earlier activity.'

Method of potentials (MoP): a networking system wherein an activity is represented by a node, and dependency is shown by an arrow. Only one type of dependency is used, the start of a succeeding activity being defined by the start(s) of its pre-decesors(s). The necessary interval between starts is shown as a subscript to the dependency arrow.

'Milestone: (key event): an event selected for its importance in the project.' It will often have an imposed date.

Negative float: the time by which the duration of an activity or chain of activities must be reduced in order to permit a scheduled date to be achieved.

Negative slack: the time by which the difference between the earliest and latest event times for an event must be increased in order to permit a scheduled date to be achieved.

'Network: a diagram representing the activities and events of a project, their sequence and interrelationships.'

Node: another name for event.

PERT: a name for a network analysis technique formed from the words 'program evaluation and review technique'. Originally requiring the use of three estimates of the duration times, the name is now usually accepted as one of the generic names for network techniques.

Precedence Diagramming: a networking system wherein an activity is represented by a node and dependencies are shown by solid arrows. At least four types of dependency can be shown, each having different locations on the associated activity nodes, namely:

Finish-to-start—the *start* of an activity depends on the *finish* of its predecessor.

Finish-to-finish—the *finish* of an activity depends on the *finish* of its predecessor.

Start-to-start—the *start* of an activity depends on the *start* of its predecessor.

Start-to-finish—the *finish* to an activity depends on the *start* of its predecessor

Project network techniques (PNT): the generic term for that group of techniques whereby a project is represented by a set of nodes joined by a set of arrows. It embraces both the system where the activity is represented by an arrow (activity-on-arrow (AoA) technique) and where the activity is represented by a node (the activity on node (AoN) technique).

Resource: anything other than time that is necessary for carrying out an activity. It may be:

Simple (non-storable)—if not used when available it is extinguished.

Pool (storable)—may be used when required.

'Resource aggregation: the summation of the requirements of each resource, and for each time period. (*Note:* where the earliest start time of an activity is used alone, it is often termed an 'early-start' aggregation. Similarly a 'late-start' aggregation uses the latest start times of an activity only.')

'Resource cumulation: the process of accumulating the requirements for each resource to give a total required to date at all times throughout the project.'

'**Resource levelling:** the process of producing a schedule that reduces the variation between maximum and minimum values of resource requirements .'

'**Resource limited scheduling:** the scheduling of activities, so that predetermined resource levels are never exceeded.'

Resource optimisation: the manipulation of the network to try to ensure that the resources required and available are in balance.

'**Resource smoothing:** the scheduling of activities within the limits of their float, so that fluctuations in individual resource requirements are minimised. '

Resource totalling: equivalent to 'resource aggregation'.

Scheduled date } equivalent to 'imposed date'.
Scheduled time }

Secondary float: when a scheduled date is imposed upon an activity which is not a final activity, a secondary critical path can appear which is the time-controlling sequence between the start and the scheduled event, or between two scheduled events. Activities not on this critical path but which contribute to the achievement of the event possess float with respect to this secondary critical path, and this is said to be secondary float.

Semi-critical path: that path which is next to the critical path when all paths are arranged in order of float.

'**Slack:** latest date of event minus earliest date of event (may be negative). The term slack is used as referring only to an event.'

Stage: another name of an event.

Sub-critical path: a path which is not critical.

Tail-event: the event at the beginning of an activity.

Tail slack: the slack possessed by an event at the tail of an activity.

Time available: another name for 'activity span'.

'**Time limited scheduling:** the scheduling of activities so that the specified project duration, or any imposed dates, are not exceeded.'

Total float: the total float possessed by an activity.

'**Trading off:** the transferring of resources from one activity to another. This is usually accompanied by changes in duration times, and is carried out to affect the resource distribution. '

INDEX